THE PSYCHOLOGY OF SUCCESSFUL TRADING

This book is the first to demonstrate the practical implications of an important, yet under-considered area of psychology in helping traders and investors understand the biases and attribution errors that drive unpredictable behaviour on the trading floor. Readers will improve their chances of trading successfully by learning where cognitive biases lead to errors in stock analysis and how these biases can be used to predict behaviour in market participants.

Focussing on the three major types of bias – Belief-Formation, Quasi-Economic, and Social – the book provides a rigorous discussion of the literature before explaining how each of these biases plays out in financial markets. The author brings together the fields of philosophical psychology and behavioural finance to introduce 'Theory of Mind,' providing readers with tools to predict biases in others as well as using these predictions to form optimal trading strategies for themselves. Readers will also learn to understand their own behaviours, counteracting biases such as overconfidence and conformity – and the 'curse' of their own knowledge – to strengthen trade performance. Pairing his skill and experience with an extensive research bibliography, Short positions the foundational sources of cognitive biases alongside concrete examples, experimental designs, and traders' anecdotes, helping readers to apply theoretical guidelines to real-life scenarios.

Shrewd professionals and MBA students will benefit from *The Psychology of Successful Trading*'s intuitive structure and practical focus.

Tim Short spent almost a decade on the trading floor of several investment banks. He is the author of *Simulation Theory*, published by Routledge in 2015.

"Although artificial intelligence is playing a major role in accelerating our understanding of investing and trading, through the analysis of increasingly available data, the ultimate drivers of investment decisions are still based on psychology. From a wealth of practical experience in both fields, Tim explores how our psychology affects our trading decisions."

Christos Danias, StormHarbour Securities LLP, UK

"In a readable and insightful fashion, *The Psychology of Successful Trading* offers a unique account of cognitive biases in financial trading. Tim Short delivers a remarkable synthesis of the topic, integrating philosophical psychology and financial trade practice. A discussion of biases such as the 'Confirmation Bias' or the 'Dunning-Kruger Effect' could not be more timely. Are we as smart as we think we are? This book is a substantial contribution to behavioural finance that would prove useful to academics in the field and to professional traders, as well as to those more generally interested in correcting their own cognitive biases. *The Psychology of Successful Trading* is bound to become a key reference in the behavioural finance and economics scholarship."

Alexandre Gajevic Sayegh, Yale University, USA

"In the last decade, psychologists have uncovered an abundance of new facts about how biases spoil the predictions we make of human behaviour and decisions. Our errors turn out to be remarkably systematic, even in contexts as complex as the financial markets. Working from an extensive survey of scientific findings, Tim Short's lucid and engaging book has done a real service to anyone interested in the effects of biases on trading decisions. Whether you want to study the market or beat it, *The Psychology of Successful Trading* is essential reading."

Dr. Maarten Steenhagen, University of Cambridge, UK

THE PSYCHOLOGY OF SUCCESSFUL TRADING

Behavioural Strategies for Profitability

Tim Short

NEW YORK AND LONDON

First published 2018
by Routledge
711 Third Avenue, New York, NY 10017

and by Routledge
2 Park Square, Milton Park, Abingdon, Oxon OX14 4RN

Routledge is an imprint of the Taylor & Francis Group, an informa business

© 2018 Taylor & Francis

The right of Tim Short to be identified as author of this work has been asserted by him in accordance with sections 77 and 78 of the Copyright, Designs and Patents Act 1988.

All rights reserved. No part of this book may be reprinted or reproduced or utilised in any form or by any electronic, mechanical, or other means, now known or hereafter invented, including photocopying and recording, or in any information storage or retrieval system, without permission in writing from the publishers.

Trademark notice: Product or corporate names may be trademarks or registered trademarks, and are used only for identification and explanation without intent to infringe.

Library of Congress Cataloging in Publication Data
A catalog record for this book has been requested

ISBN: 978-1-138-09627-1 (hbk)
ISBN: 978-1-138-09628-8 (pbk)
ISBN: 978-1-315-10540-6 (ebk)

Typeset in Bembo
by Taylor & Francis Books

BRIEF CONTENTS

Acknowledgements *viii*

1 Introduction 1
2 Beating the Market 11
3 Theory of Mind 24
4 Belief-Formation Biases I 37
5 Belief-Formation Biases II 74
6 Quasi-Economic Biases 107
7 Social Biases I 122
8 Social Biases II 149

Bibliography *176*
Index *186*

CONTENTS

Acknowledgements   *viii*

1 **Introduction**   1
   1.1 Outline Of Book 8

2 **Beating the Market**   11

3 **Theory of Mind**   24
   3.1 Better Traders Have Better Theory Of Mind 24
   3.2 How Theory Of Mind Works 28

4 **Belief-Formation Biases I**   37
   4.1 Belief Perseverance Bias And Correlation 37
   4.2 Representativeness Heuristic 40
   4.3 Rhyme As Reason Effect 49
   4.4 Availability Heuristic 53
   4.5 The Gambler's Fallacy 68

5 **Belief-Formation Biases II**   74
   5.1 Confirmation Bias 74
   5.2 Clustering Illusion 83
   5.3 Position Effect 85
   5.4 Conjunction Fallacy 89
   5.5 Hindsight Bias And The Antifragile 91
      5.5.1 The Antifragile And Options 101

6   Quasi-Economic Biases   107
6.1 Certainty Effect 107
6.2 Reflection Effect 111
6.3 Isolation Effect 114
6.4 Endowment Effect 116
6.5 Conclusions 118

7   Social Biases I   122
7.1 The 'Curse Of Knowledge' 122
   7.1.1 The Advantages Of Disadvantages 125
7.2 Dunning-Kruger Effect And Expertise 130
7.3 False Consensus Effect 140
7.4 Conformity Bias 142

8   Social Biases II   149
8.1 Fundamental Attribution Error 149
8.2 Halo Effect 156
8.3 Self-Presentation Bias And Over-Confidence 159
   8.3.1 Over-Confidence, Or Why Females Are Better Traders 166

Bibliography   *176*
Index   *186*

ACKNOWLEDGEMENTS

Thanks to Stefan Joubert, who lent me the book that gave me the idea for this one. And who is also a terrific piano teacher. I am also grateful to Prof. Grahame Blair, who was crucial in getting me out of one incident which I describe in the book. As ever, thanks for interesting and stimulating times are due to the Gordon Square Dining Club (Mog Hampson, Jerome Pedro, Tom Williams, Karine Sawan, Alex Sayegh, Laura Silva and Lea-Cecile Salje) and the UCL Professors Dining Club (Treasurer Lancaster, Prof. M.A.) of which I am an elected member. I am grateful to Dr James Monk for a useful trading anecdote I have used. Kev Riggs is real and first prodded me to move into philosophy.

1

INTRODUCTION

The central idea of this book is that you can improve your chances of trading successfully by understanding where cognitive biases cause you to make mistakes in stock analysis and, more importantly, in predicting the behaviour of others.

Predicting the behaviour of others successfully is the only way to outperform in financial markets. This is what has been called "second-level thinking" (Marks 2011, Ch. 1). First level thinking is selecting stocks that you think will perform well based on characteristics of the stock-issuing company. To do this, you will engage in an array of standard analysis such as considering P/E ratios, yields, the macro-economic environment, geopolitics and a myriad of other factors including the likely future development of all of the aforementioned factors. This, of course, is what the whole market is doing all the time. This is why it is difficult to make money doing it; others have already got there before you. The key point is that you have to find stocks to buy or sell which are undervalued or overvalued by the market, which is primarily a psychological question and not a financial or economic one. As Marks (2011, p. 1) puts it, practically at the start of his important book, "[p]sychology plays a major role in markets." With even more emphasis, he also writes that the "discipline that is most important is not accounting or economics, but psychology" (Marks 2011, p. 27). This is underlined by Hirshleifer (2001, p. 1533) who writes that in the newer, less purely rational approach to investor psychology, "security expected returns are determined by both *risk* and *mis-valuation*" with mis-valuation being primarily psychological in origin. In this book, I will give you the psychology you need.

This second level psychological thinking will be the major focus of this book. It is called second level thinking because it involves thinking *about* the first level thinking, or more precisely establishing what the first level thinking of others will be and whether it is correct. I will outline the first level thinking I use so it can be understood sufficiently to underpin the second level thinking that I aim to discuss, but the discussion here of first level thinking will be instrumental. The main aim will be finding examples to illustrate how the psychological points will play out in the market rather than exhaustively setting out the financial questions alone. In sum, the first level thinking will be described only to illuminate the second level thinking. The motivation for this approach is described well by Nofsinger (2016, p. 8) who notes that those who learn about biases "may find opportunities to benefit from the biased decisions of other investors."[1]

I am not saying that you can avoid doing the first level thinking. You can get it done for you or learn how to do it yourself by reading the financial and investment press, or by reading some of the many books which do focus on the first level – but the second level thinking is where the action is. Understanding of the markets is rare enough; understanding of psychology is rarer still. Both are needed for success, which is yet rarer still. This is why you need to gain expertise in aspects of psychology, as well as being able to understand investment cases. If you only have time to do one of these tasks, the psychological one is more important because as said, you can outsource the first level thinking. It is much harder to buy in the second level thinking, because few people are doing it well. In this book, I will not be doing the second level thinking for you. I will be showing you how to do it for yourself.

Shull (2011, p. 24) has a useful poker analogy, which can serve to illustrate this distinction between levels. She notes that many people think of poker as a probability game. Now clearly, having the right cards is a very significant part of winning a poker game, but it is not everything. Shull notes that uncertainty arises whenever wagering begins. Her key observation is that winners "in poker rely on the human perception games of the betting." What she means here is, of course, that the key difference between winning players and losing ones is less to do with the cards they are dealt and more to do with their ability to predict the behaviour of others. This is what is known as a Theory of Mind[2] task. Theory of Mind is the psychological term for the way we predict and explain the behaviour of others. Analysing stock-market assets is a useful discipline; it is like counting cards to optimise the underlying numerical probabilities. However, outperforming at the Theory of Mind task, in either poker or the markets, is what makes winners.

Shull (2011, p. 54) has also noticed the importance of first and second level thinking, and the fact that they have already been observed in the literature. She notes that Keynes had already gone to the third level. Third level thinking is thinking about the second level thinking; or predicting how others will predict further others will think. He points out, in his famous beauty contest example (2016, Ch. 12), that the task is really to attempt to anticipate what average opinion expects average opinion to be. This is again a Theory of Mind task. It is an example particularly conducive to the simulation account thereof, which I defend. There are two major accounts of Theory of Mind in the literature. One is called Simulation Theory and is based on the idea that we predict others by putting ourselves in their place. The other account is called Theory Theory and is based on the idea that we have a theory of others which we use to predict their behaviour. I argue in Short (2015) that Simulation Theory is the correct account. Simulation Theory has no difficulty explaining Keynes's multiple levels. Theory Theory, by contrast, would need to postulate that there are rules about what people think about what people think. On a simulation account, the level almost drops away. There is no difference between simulating what someone will think and simulating what someone will think someone else will think. In any case, both authors are correct to emphasise the importance of Theory of Mind to market performance.

This book is partly aimed at retail investors who are investing their own money and need to investigate how psychology and market forces interact in ways which are not necessarily helpful. I will not be explaining any standard financial terminology, but it will mostly be familiar to the fairly experienced individual or at least, capable of investigation in public sources. Professional traders can also gain a lot from specialised psychology, which they will not have come across before unless they have a university level background in psychology and, more specifically, with a focus on bias psychology.

All of the psychology I cover will be explained in depth, with my remarks aimed at an educated individual who has no previous knowledge of academic psychology. I will be citing all of the relevant psychological and financial literature I use thoroughly, so you will be able to pursue the ideas further, if you wish. The point here, though, is that I have read 600 relevant academic journal articles and books – and synthesised here what it means for understanding market participants – so you do not have to. Again, it is worth underlining that understanding psychology is crucial to understanding markets and, in particular, difficult times in markets which can cause enormous damage to investors. Barberis (2013, p. 25), discussing the 2007–2008 financial crisis which continues to have malign effects today in 2016, suggests that "it is very possible that psychological factors were also central to the crisis" as well as institutional failures, which are themselves not immune to psychological causation.

I will not of course attempt to explain the whole of psychology, or even the whole of the psychology of cognitive biases. That would not be possible in a single book. It is also not necessary for the project here. Large parts of psychology, such as, for example, the psychophysics of perception, are not relevant. We will be tightly focussed on cognitive biases because, as I have previously argued (Short 2015; Short and Riggs 2016), they are the dominant causes of Theory of Mind errors. These, then, are the elements of psychology which are the dominant cause of error in predicting the behaviour of others and thus the key to better second level thinking. To the extent we can assume that the bulk of market participants have not read this book, then it will suffice to provide an edge or market advantage.[3] If it becomes widely read, we may need to go to third level thinking, or thinking about the second level thinking, but we can cross that bridge when we come to it. I will restrict myself to those cognitive biases which are important in predicting the behaviour of financial market participants. Large parts of the subject deal with abnormal psychology. While it will occasionally be useful to examine some abnormal conditions for what we can learn from them about neuro-typical subjects, in this book we are interested only in how we can expect the majority of people to behave.

All of us are constantly subject to a wide array of biases in our thinking; for example Confirmation Bias (§5.1) where we tend only to seek information which accords with what we already think. The idea throughout will be to alert you to these biases so that you can make trading decisions which are: a) more optimal initially because you have reduced the impact of bias on your own thinking, and b) more optimal again because you have incorporated the possibility of biases into your analysis of the thinking of other market participants. We are especially likely to resort to heuristics and biases in the context of markets. As Dale, Johnson, and Tang (2005, p. 261) note in the context of a discussion of the South Sea Bubble, "individuals increasingly rely on heuristics, non-rational strategies, and biases when faced by a complex information environment." There is no more complex information environment than a financial market, and so the explanation of Dale, Johnson, and Tang (2005) that investors failed to recognise the South Sea Bubble when it was occurring is plausible. In this case, obviously, the biases of investors did them a great deal of harm. So we can agree with Barber and Odean (2002, p. 456) that "cognitive biases [...] for the most part, do not improve investors' welfare."

Shiller argues that "mass psychology may well be the dominant cause of movements in the price of the aggregate stock market" (Shiller, Fischer, and Friedman 1984). The way this works, as is succinctly explained in the appended commentary by Fischer, is that "smart-money investors [look] ahead to try to predict both dividends and the value of shares the blockheads will be holding in the future" (Shiller, Fischer, and Friedman 1984, p. 502). What this means, simply enough, is that "[c]hanges in expectations of the holdings of blockheads, as well as changes in expected dividends, will change the price" now (Shiller, Fischer, and B. M. Friedman 1984, p. 502). Forecasting future changes in dividends, if it can be done, will be an excellent way to predict future stock price movements. More significantly for our purposes, changes in the value of future holdings by blockheads – which here simply means any change not explicable rationally on the basis of rational reasons to expect future dividend changes – are more important. These changes, I will propose, are driven by cognitive biases on the part of the blockheads. In final comments by Fischer and Friedman, it is complained that while Shiller explains that investing in 'fads' or fashions explain excess stock volatility, he does "not explain how fads are formed and why they subsequently disappear" (Shiller, Fischer, and Friedman 1984, p. 510). I will be adding that missing piece by suggesting that cognitive biases can also be explanatory of that point.[4] For example, Conformity Bias (§7.4), which is just the tendency to copy others, can lead to herding behaviour (Nofsinger 2016, pp. 104–105).

A further underlining of the importance of the idea may be derived from Soros' (1994) subtitle, 'Reading The Mind Of The Market.' Certainly this is the key task, and informally within psychology, 'mind-reading' is often used as a synonym for Theory of Mind. Soros (1994) even mentions biases, but he is mostly concerned with a simple prevailing bias – by which he just means the weight of market participants at a given time on the bullish/bearish spectrum. So while the task identified is the correct one, there is a lot more work to do on elucidating how biases play out in markets. That will be my task in this book.

You may be thinking that bias psychology does not apply to you. Everyone else may be making biased decisions all the time, but you do not. Unfortunately you are wrong about this (I obviously do not claim any immunity for myself either). Pronin, Gilovich, and Ross (2004, p. 781) find that we tend "to see others as more susceptible to a host of cognitive and motivational biases" than ourselves. They ascribe this to what we might describe as introspective asymmetry. The underlying claim involved in introspection is that I know what is going on in my mind directly and unmediatedly while I have no such access to what is going on in your mind. Introspection is the method by which I know what is going on in my mind; you can think of it as a contraction of 'internal' and 'perception' if you like. At least the second part is true, because otherwise there would be no need for Theory of Mind abilities. The first part appears to be true to everyone except some philosophers and psychologists, though it has found some defenders even within those disciplines (Rey 2013).

It has been shown that well-documented psychological biases play a major role in mis-pricing. An analysis by Daniel, Hirshleifer, and Subrahmanyam (1998) simulated the effects of the tendency to ascribe success to one's own abilities, and failure to bad luck or unknowable external factors. I see this tendency as a species of Self-Presentation Bias; it is known in the literature as Self-Attribution Bias. Daniel, Hirshleifer, and Subrahmanyam (1998, p. 1866) state that their "key contribution" is to show that this bias can "induce several of the anomalous price patterns documented in the empirical literature." This is good evidence in relation to a single bias; in this book I will aim to cover all of the most important ones.

One sort of objection here suggests that what I am proposing is a kind of Error Theory. In the view of the objector, I am proposing an account whereby many people are wrong much of the time. This is seen as implausible on the grounds that widespread error does not seem to be the sort of occurrence which could remain widespread and uncorrected. My response to that, as will be discussed more below, is to suggest that cognitive biases are not exactly errors. They may result in sub-optimal decision making but we have them because often they are fast and good enough. One of my aims in the book will be to explain some of the key cognitive biases so you can see when your thinking and that of others may have been influenced by them. That is an essential precursor to the subsequent decision as to whether the output of the cognitive bias is actually the optimal decision in the current instance.

A variant of this objection is based on evolution. Since, the objection runs, we are evolved creatures, our methods of reasoning will not be as imperfect as is suggested by the widespread presence of biases. We would have evolved them away since they are sub-optimal. There are a number of responses to this objection, of which I will only briefly canvass a few.

The first response is to note that although it is true we are evolved, we are still sub-optimal. 'Sub-optimal' means merely that and not maximally so: evolution produced many innovative and intricate solutions to the problem of how reproductive fitness can be enhanced (Pinker 2015, p. 167). However, we do not have bones made of titanium alloy or some super material, despite the fact that this would result in superior engineering properties. This is because evolution does not have any ability to plan. It can become trapped in 'local minima,' meaning that even if it would be better to have titanium bones, if there is no path from here to there in which most intermediate stages are improvements over their predecessor, there is no way for evolution to get there. Our bones are also not made from string. Evolution has done a pretty decent job under the circumstances. But we should not expect perfection either here or psychologically.

The second sort of response is decisive, I think. It suggests that we have these biases not because they are imperfections but because they are, on average, an improvement. It is simply impracticable and inefficient to expend vast cognitive resources on all questions that arise, even if sometimes such expenditure would result in a more optimal solution. Pinker (2015, p. 138) notes the telling example of a hiker wanting to return before sunset who spends 20 minutes planning how to make the route back 10 minutes shorter. Quickly finding a route that is imperfect but good enough is a much better practical solution. Similarly, many cognitive biases are 'good enough' for general purposes. My aim in this book is not to eliminate them, were that possible, but to enable people to notice their operation and decide when to let them make the call and when further work is called for.

It is also worth bearing in mind evidence as noted by Kramer (2008, p. 128) to the effect that "risk tolerance depends on age, income and wealth, gender, and marital status [and also] ethnicity, birth order, education, and personality traits such as self-esteem [and even] levels of hormones and neuro-chemicals." Now, risk tolerance feeds into all financial decisions. Since the factors mentioned are features of psychology or brain chemistry and not based on characteristics of the financial question under consideration, not all of the decisions made can be correct. There is an optimal level of risk tolerance under various market conditions and it does not depend on any of the factors listed. This means that anyone strongly influenced by any of these factors is likely to be some distance away from the correct level of risk tolerance. Sometimes this may be appropriate. Someone with a spouse who is a high earner and relaxed about losses can probably take more risk than otherwise. But there is no way that a rush of testosterone can improve your trading.

I will be suggesting that the influence of cognitive biases is one way that these various factors make themselves felt in our trading and other behaviour. I will also be suggesting, as I have in Short (2015), that failure to take account of the emotional state of others and then, as a result, failing to simulate what they will do accurately is a major cause of making bad predictions of what others will do. As Korniotis and Kumar (2011, p. 1513) point out, "aggregate forces generated by investors' systematic behavioural biases have the ability to influence stock prices and trading volume," so there are wider implications beyond the individual. Understanding how these biases play out more widely is essential to delivering good market performance. Note also the emphasis on *systematic* biases. It is the systematic nature of the biases – meaning that they can be expected to occur every time similar circumstances reoccur – that makes understanding biases in ourselves and others a regular source of value. These effects are not small. Korniotis and Kumar (2011, p. 1550) conclude that individual biases harm the economies of US states: "people's sub-optimal investment decisions aggregate up and the adverse effects of their biases can be detected even in the aggregate, state-level macroeconomic data."

One astute commentator has asked why it is that we do not correct our cognitive biases in economic questions when failing to do so costs us money. Besharov (2004, pp. 13–14) gives three reasons: "individuals have limited knowledge of the system of interacting biases; [...] there may be a set of biases that result in the efficient level of action" and "even an individual with full information about the nature of the biases may rationally choose to correct them only partially when correction is costly." All three, I think, are correct. The first reason asserts that it will be difficult for people to correct for biases if they do not know what they are. This seems unarguably true, and one task I conduct in this book is to describe the key biases and situate them in the trading context, so that first reason is addressed. The second reason is interesting: it points to the fact that since we are influenced by so many biases, more than one of them may be operating at a given time. In reality, I think this is quite probable. This might mean that two biases can counteract each other, such that correcting one of them would result in a less efficient outcome. This is possible but, again, knowing what the biases are is still very valuable – I will return to this below. Finally, it is of course entirely reasonable to consider the costs of correction, which are here likely to take the form of time spent thinking about a problem. It is consequentially of little benefit to work hard to remove the effects of say Conformity Bias in a minor everyday context such as choosing a breakfast option. However, in this book I will only be considering the effects of biases on trading decisions. It is very likely, then, that all such decisions will both be affected by several biases and that it will be of the utmost importance to be aware of that and work against them.

As an example of how biases can offset each other, Besharov (2004, p. 17) notes that hyperbolic discounting can offset over-confidence. Hyperbolic discounting is the tendency we have to behave as if the present is much more important than the future: we heavily undervalue future positive outcomes and are consequently less likely to put the effort in now to achieve them. Overconfidence (§8.3.1) is self-explanatory: we tend to assess a higher probability than is strictly justified to the probability that we are right and that we will be successful. It can be seen that it is indeed possible that the former could offset the latter. Hyperbolic discounting could mean that we are less likely to go to the gym today because we do not attach sufficient value today to the prospect of being healthy in two years from now. Countervailingly, overconfidence may cause us to overstate the chances we have of obtaining good results in the gym, which would make us more likely to go. However: it seems quite unlikely and, indeed, would be the result of a freak confluence of mathematical factors were these two biases precisely to match each other, and there may be other biases at play as well. Therefore, once again, it is very clear that the essential point is to have as high an awareness as possible of biases. That allows one to optimise one's own behaviour and is a prerequisite to making the attempt to predict the behaviour of others, who are naively in the grip of multiple biases.

It has also been argued plausibly that simulation is an important part of how experienced investors outperform. Mauboussin (2008, p. 106) notes that what he terms "naturalistic decision makers" "rely heavily on mental imagery and simulation in order to assess a situation and possible alternatives." A naturalistic decision maker is one who will be 'satisficing' rather than spending time looking for the perfect solution. This means that they act on the first option they see that is 'good enough' rather than working hard to find the best one – there just is not time for that. This is how the marines and firefighters that Mauboussin (2008) discusses act: like traders, they also need to perform in a high-stakes, complex information environment, which changes rapidly. Simulation of the behaviour of other people – as is called for by the Simulation Theory account of Theory of Mind – will naturally be a major element of any simulation of markets, because those markets are made up of other people, or computers programmed by them. So I suggest that adding the right biases to your simulation is what is going to give you the optimal forecasting of markets.

Finally, Korniotis and Kumar (2011, p. 1530) note that "investors' cognitive abilities are negatively associated with their behavioural biases" and that investors with higher cognitive abilities are wealthier. While we cannot be totally certain of the directions of causation here, this clearly means that wealthier investors are the ones who exhibit fewer behavioural biases. I will be suggesting in this book that it is the reduction in influence of behavioural biases which causes the increased wealth, which is a reason, first and foremost, to start by understanding what the biases are.

1.1 Outline Of Book

The programme I will pursue will be as follows.

In Chapter 2, I will handle an immediately obvious objection to this entire project. The objection states that it is not possible to beat the market. If that is true, there is no point in trying and we would all be best advised to buy index funds and forget about them. I will deny this objection.

Having dispensed with that objection, I will turn, in Chapter 3, to the central underlying topic of interest in this book: the area of psychology termed Theory of Mind. That is the term for how we predict and explain the behaviour of others. While the whole book sets out an argument that better Theory of Mind performance is what distinguishes good traders from poor ones, I will add weight to that in the first section of this chapter by describing data showing that better traders have better Theory of Mind. I have outlined an account (Short 2015; Short and Riggs 2016) of Theory of Mind together with an explanation of how we often make errors in such predictions in specific circumstances. Since reducing the frequency of those errors will assist us in making more accurate predictions, it is essential that I set out how Theory of Mind works when it does work, before applying that approach in the markets. We can then see the starting framework of Theory of Mind against which the various biases are deviations which, I suggest, often result in prediction errors. Expecting those biases to be active in the thinking of other market participants is the key to predicting them more accurately and thus more profitably.

In the following chapters, I will apply this framework to a market setting. This is where we will use the psychology I have outlined to make money. In each section, I will discuss a bias and then sketch what it will mean in a market setting. You will be able to examine your own thinking for the traces of biases and seek to counteract them if need be. Sometimes they will not need to be counteracted, but it will still be useful to know that they are there. Most importantly, you can expect that most market participants will not have read this book and will know little about psychology. What they do know could well be gained from journalism of variable quality rather than being empirically supported in the academic psychological literature. Their biases will run riot in their investment thinking. You will find out what to look for and what to do when you see it.

The biases are divided up into three broad types with a chapter or two covering each. I will in each case describe the bias of interest and then outline what I think it means for market participants who operate subject to those biases. The division into types is for convenience as much as anything else and we should not become excessively concerned about whether other classifications would be optimal. The key point is that most of the biases of importance for markets are covered in one chapter or another.

In Chapters 4 and 5 I will look at Belief-Formation Biases. We might also term these 'indirect' biases since they occur at a level back from actual market behaviour. They distort people's beliefs and cause them to be sub-optimally formed, which just means less tailored to the available evidence than they could be and so less likely to be true. The sort of bias I will cover here will include Confirmation Bias (§5.1) which we have already seen briefly.

After that, in Chapter 6 I will look at what I call Quasi-Economic Biases. I use the qualifier 'quasi' here because I do not mean to suggest that these biases are central to mainstream economics as an academic subject. They continue to be psychological biases. It is just that they are operative in ways which have a direct effect on the economic or value-seeking decisions that individuals make. This directness means they are more immediately active in the types of decisions which are of interest to us in seeking to predict the behaviour of market participants. It also means that they are likely to be more insidious in their effects on us as market participants, and so we should be on the lookout for evidence of their influences on our own thinking. At the very least, we should know when we have been subject to a bias and consider very carefully whether the deviation from optimally rational behaviour is really the correct move. Often it will be quite difficult to resist the bias, because doing so will come with negative affect – in other words, it will make us feel bad. Knowing that it is in fact a bias will help in dealing with that affect or emotional impact. The sort of bias I discuss here is illustrated by the Endowment Effect (§6.4), where we value items we own more than identical items we do not own.

Finally, in Chapters 7 and 8 I will look at what I call Social Biases. People are social creatures and this affects how they see each other and themselves. These are also indirect, to some extent, in that they do not un-mediatedly impact on economic decisions. They will also be indirect in that they can result in distortions in belief formation mechanisms, like those discussed in Chapters 4 and 5. An example of this sort of bias would be Conformity Bias (§7.4), which again we have already touched on briefly.

As an additional bonus, you will know much more about what makes people tick after reading this book, whether it is in markets or elsewhere. You will know why they do some of the strange things they do, and sometimes you may even be able to predict it.

Notes

1 Nofsinger (2016) gives an excellent overview of psychological biases in investors. I will be cross-citing it where it also explains a bias I cover. I will be going somewhat further though, since Nofsinger (2016) is aimed primarily at economics undergraduates; I will also be focussing on the prediction of other aspects and providing actual market experience, which is relevant.
2 Shull (2011, p. 63) explicitly mentions Theory of Mind and its crucial importance; this is a rare example of a trader using the term.
3 Glaeser (2004) is an interesting brief sketch outlining the inverse of my project: viz. what can economics tell us about bias psychology?
4 To be fair to the author, Shiller does refer to Asch (1952) at Shiller, Fischer, and Friedman (1984, p. 466), so he does have Conformity Bias in mind as a source of fads. I will explain this later in §7.4.

2

BEATING THE MARKET

One objection to the project I outline in this book is the view that it is not possible to 'beat the market.' There is much truth in this, but there are some caveats. Those caveats are, I will argue, large enough to allow an investor armed with the perspectives I outline here to outperform the market. I will discuss the elements of truth in the objection, bringing in empirical data and further providing background to the project of this book.

What is generally meant by 'beating the market' is investing in a particular asset class and outperforming the relevant index for a given year. For example, the asset class could be US equities and the relevant index could be the S&P 500. As I write at the beginning of 2016, the S&P 500 has in fact had a mildly down year, losing 0.7%. So anyone who made more than that or just maintained the value of their portfolio beat the market in 2015. Now, anyone can get lucky and outperform in a single year. But can it be done for many years?

The idea that it is difficult to beat the market relies to a great extent on Efficient Markets Theory (Fama 1970) which dates from around the late '60s (Marks 2011, p. 7). It claims, put simply, that 'prices are right' because they move to reflect new data. In fact, they move to reflect *all* new data, in the view of the hypothesis. Shiller (2003a, p. 83) captures this well when he defines Efficient Markets Theory as claiming that "speculative asset prices such as stock prices always incorporate the best information about fundamental values and that prices change only because of good, sensible information." If that is so, then you can only beat the market if you have better data than everyone else, which looks very difficult to do consistently. But, as Marks (2011, p. 7) observes, for the market to be that efficient requires that market participants are "intelligent, objective, highly motivated and hardworking" at all times which seems highly implausible. Shiller (2003a, p. 83) observes that in more recent times, "[b]ehavioural finance – that is, finance from a broader social science perspective including psychology and sociology – is now one of the most vital research programmes, and it stands in sharp contradiction to much of efficient markets theory." This again underlines the importance of adding the psychology of real economic individuals to the mix of considerations, which of course is what I will be doing in this book.

If Efficient Markets Theory were exactly correct, then there should be a tight link between stock prices and the NPV (Net Present Value) of the dividends. This is subject to some variation since, for example, companies will not tend to pay out all of their earnings in the form of dividends because they need to use some for investment and building reserves etc. But overall, since there are 500 companies in the S&P 500 index, there should be averaging effects such that the index and expected dividends are linked. However, Shiller (2003a, p. 85) finds over the period since 1870 that while the discounted value of dividends shows a fairly stable trend, the S&P 500 index "gyrates wildly up and down around this trend." This excess volatility needs to be explained. Shiller (2003a, p. 84) notes that "mass psychology" is one candidate explanation; it is the one I will be using.

Shiller (2003a, p. 87) notes that you can make the Efficient Markets Theory a good reflection of the data if you differentiate dividends twice, thus assuming that not just dividend rates but also dividend growth rates are unstable. In my experience in physics (Short 1992), everything you differentiate twice will appear correlated with anything else, especially when you plot it on a log scale as in Shiller's figure 1 (2003a, p. 86). So I think that Efficient Markets Theory is some way short of being a good fit to the data.

Hirshleifer (2001, p. 1562) observed in 2001 that "the thrust of much experimental market research in the late 1980s and 1990s is that in only a slightly more complicated environment, information is not aggregated efficiently." Earlier work had shown that very simple experimental markets were fairly efficient. Later work had added to the complexity studied, and efficiency was seriously impaired. The reason he suggests for this is that there are confounding effects which mean that investors can see other trades but do not know which of several plausible explanations for the trade is correct. We know that actual markets are vastly more complex than any laboratory study, and so this raises a serious question mark about the information efficiency of markets in real life.

Equations that specify the influence of 'near-rational agents' on market efficiency have been proposed. Near-rational agents are actually highly rational; they still approach the rather overly idealised and implausible idea of the perfectly rational agent. Near-rational agents depart from this ideal in that they fail to fully optimise their position or maximise their expected utility to the extent that the costs of so doing exceed the benefits. This is already far too unrealistic to describe real people, but nevertheless Wang (1993, p. 1475) finds that in the presence of such "near-rational agents, asset prices become excessively volatile and deviate significantly from their rational equilibrium levels." The deviations take the form of over-shooting and under-shooting theoretically correct levels. These effects are strengthened by perfectly rational agents acting on the understanding that the market contains near-rational agents and that these deviations will occur.

However, while Efficient Markets Theory is questionable in detail, it remains a good rough first approximation to the truth. In its strong form, it claims that the market is completely efficient, i.e. that all factors relevant to the pricing of a stock are already priced in or will be very quickly because someone somewhere knows every factor and has traded accordingly. Any new data which is price relevant will likewise be priced in very quickly. This is, as I say, roughly correct. If there is a major incident which is price-relevant to a stock, then the stock price will react accordingly and immediately. If there is a dramatic piece of news which is highly likely to affect a company's revenues, then most of the time this becomes widely known quickly and the share price moves accordingly. Shiller (2003a, p. 89) notes evidence suggesting that Efficient Markets Theory performs better on individual stocks than for markets more widely.

One obvious example of this would be the Deepwater Horizon incident, when there was a severe oil spill at a BP-owned rig which was widely televised. There was an immediate and severe negative impact on the BP share price. The fact that it would have been amazing if this had not happened suggests that we see frequent examples of negative incremental news flow causing a share price decline. Likewise, if a drug company announces successful trials or an FDA approval, it would be extraordinary if the share price failed to move. Similarly, there can be broad based moves where almost every company in the S&P 500 moves up because the Fed announces a new stimulus package or there are encouraging developments in data from China. Sometimes it is mysterious why a stock or an index has moved up, but – crucially – the fact that one as an individual has not been able to determine why the move has happened is not sufficient to disprove Efficient Markets Theory completely. It may be that some individuals who do have the information which has caused the price to move have acted on it and caused the move.

Slightly surprisingly in relation to BP, the decline continued over the two or three days after the Deepwater Horizon incident. By continuation here, I mean that the stock price continued to decline more than it had done on the first day. One might think that that type of event should be fully priced in immediately because it was clear that what had happened was going to be very expensive for BP to clear up. The ongoing decline after the first day must be explained if one is a complete devotee to the Efficient Markets Theory by suggesting that new information became available. This could be for example not so much information relating to the accident itself, but to informed estimates becoming available of exactly how the US legal system was likely to function in the aftermath and what the likely costs to BP might be. On this occasion, I did not see any such new developments being publicly discussed. It seemed as though the BP stock was continuing to decline even though absent of new adverse data, and doing so even though it had declined a very large amount immediately. I think this means that a bias was creeping into trading decisions. Traders could not get past the horror that was unfolding on the screen, and so even though the stock had already declined 25%, representing a discount which was likely to be much larger than any reasonable cost outcome, they continued to mark the stock down. I will be suggesting in this book that what might be driving that behaviour is a form of bias, and knowing that and counteracting it in oneself can be a way to beat the market. That is just a hint of what is to come later. I will continue for now meeting the objection that one cannot beat the market.

Another form of this objection is that it is not possible to outperform Wall Street. Again, there is much truth in this. If you try to take on investment banks directly at their own game, you are likely to come off worst on average. High Frequency Trading (HFT) (Lewis 2014) involves writing software that can execute trades incredibly quickly – on the scale of microseconds – and exploit very short-lived price fluctuations. This involves some very expensive hardware, hard-to-find programming expertise and having a physical location close to the exchange so as to minimise cable delays in price signals. All of this is available to the investment banks and none of it is available to the individual investor.

At one trading floor on which I was employed, a single seat started the year in a negative position of $300,000. What this reflects is the enormous infrastructure behind each trader. There are seven 'back-office' support staff to every individual front office – meaning directly client facing, the sharp end if you will – banker or trader. The $300,000 represented the costs of that support, much of which would be in IT and provision of real-time news-flow. So you should not attempt to be a successful in the HFT arena unless you are sitting in an investment bank trading floor, or are prepared to run that sort of cost. Many other individual approaches to the market are similar; none of them are affordable to the non-bank.

Even if one can avoid this type of drawback, surely it is reasonable to be worried about the professionals. After all, they do nothing else all day and have presumably been selected specifically for their aptitude and prior performance. Here it is useful to note the remarks of Abbink and Rockenbach (2006, p. 500) who discuss studies comparing untrained students and professional traders in simulations of trading environments. The results are that the "majority of studies do not detect a substantial difference in the behaviour of students and practitioners. [...] The phenomenon named the 'curse of experience' describes [the way] that practitioners apply certain patterns of behaviour, which are adequate for the real life situation but not optimal for the model, to the experimental situation. This leads to lower performance rates of the professionals, compared to the student subjects." Indeed, Abbink and Rockenbach (2006) find that sometimes the students *outperform* the professionals.

This is a very interesting finding which makes several important points. It appears as though the students outperform the professionals because the students have no alternative but to apply the correct mathematics to the situation at hand. Since the experimental situation is more closely modelled on that mathematics, the students outperform. Abbink and Rockenbach (2006) suggest that the professionals carry over into the experimental situation behaviours which are adequate for real life but not optimal for the model. Note that they do not say that these behaviours are optimal for real-life either. I suggest that they are not, in fact.

Abbink and Rockenbach (2006, p. 503) obtain their professional subjects from an "influential German Bank in Frankfurt/Main;" all were "decision makers." We do not know exactly what "decision makers" means here, but I suspect that if they were senior or even mid-level traders, they would not have actually made a calculation themselves of an option price for a decade or more. There will be analysts or junior non-trading staff on each desk who maintain a spreadsheet of 'nominal' pricing which the traders may or may not consult. They are then supposed to use their skill and judgment to conduct trades at what they believe will be a profitable price; they are not bound to follow the spreadsheet. I suggest that if they did so, they would perform better, because what they believe is their skill and judgment is actually a mix of various biases and errors as well as actually valuable experience. Why do they not themselves observe this? One reason is that we are all blind to our own biases; I will be aiming in this book to open your eyes to your own biases so that you have an opportunity to do better. A second reason may be deduced from asking the question as to what these traders' role actually is, if optimal option pricing is the price given by the relevant mathematics? Bear in mind that the junior analysts on the desk maintain the pricing spreadsheet. If that is all that is needed for an optimal book of trades, then you can get one much more cheaply and you would not need to pay all of these expensive traders.

Abbink and Rockenbach (2006, p. 500) also note an earlier study which showed that "subjects frequently violate no-arbitrage conditions, especially when they are very risk-averse." A no-arbitrage condition is a very strong constraint on pricing accuracy, since its violation means that another market participant can extract risk-free profit from the violator. The other participant is in effect getting a 'free lunch' which should never happen. An example might be someone who is prepared to sell asset A for $10 and asset B for $10 and buy asset C, which is composed only of asset A and asset B, for $22. One could constantly buy A and B and then sell them back as C to this individual and make a $2 profit with no risk as many times as one can get away with it. Clearly one would not expect this to happen where it is obvious that C is composed of A and B; for example if A and B are stocks in two companies and C is a basket of those two stocks.[1] But it might happen when it is less obvious that one asset actually behaves like a pair of other assets even if it is not formally made up of those other assets.

The note that it is risk-averse traders who make this error suggests that it might be more prevalent in markets like China where individual private investors own the majority of stock, unlike in Western markets where institutional investors own most of the stock. However, even some institutional investors will also exhibit risk-aversion to some extent; sometimes they are required to do so by their mandates. So it is always worth looking out for trades in which risk-averse traders are present or assets which are cheap because risk-averse players have avoided them. Remember that risk-aversion simpliciter is always a mistake: one should seek not to minimise risk but to minimise *unrewarded* risk. Looked at from that perspective, risk is your friend because it comes with the opportunity to make profits.

Remarkably, Abbink and Rockenbach (2006, p. 508) also check whether the major of the students makes a difference. Their initial student group was made up of economics majors on a course where option pricing was an available elective. So they also tested social science majors who naturally had not studied option pricing. Abbink and Rockenbach (2006, p. 508) found that the professionals closed the gap somewhat, but with "respect to expected payoff exploitation, the [social science] students have a significant advantage over the professionals."

If you think this looks implausible as an account, ask yourself whether you think that most trading desks are profitable most of the time, or even all of the time. That is implied by the opposite view to the one I am arguing for here. I have personal experience of spending several years working on a profitable structuring desk; I understand that after I left, the desk lost more in a single year than the full much larger team had made during the previous five years. How many desks have a record of good profitability with low risk taken for a couple of decades? And how many of them did that not through blind luck? Bear in mind that many trading desks operate in a field which is a zero-sum game, so they can only make a profit if another equally skilled desk makes a loss. I nevertheless concede that there will be some profitable desks, perhaps if we are very generous half. But the point I am arguing for can succeed anyway: if you can trade without bias, or with less bias than the professionals, as I suggest the students were doing when they stuck to the mathematics – there is no bias in an equation – you can beat the market.

As Hirshleifer (2001, p. 1537) notes, it "is often suggested that the expertise of hedge funds or investment banks will improve arbitrage enough to eliminate any significant mis-pricing" which would make it impossible to beat the market. However, if hedge funds are so smart, they will inevitably make a lot of money. But, the *Economist* [2] reports that hedge funds significantly underperformed the S&P 500 over the period from 2012 to 2016 returning about 20% as opposed to about 60% from the S&P. Hedge funds also underperformed a standard mix (60/40) US equity/bond portfolio during basically the entire post-crisis period to 2016, just about matching that pedestrian portfolio over the first three or four post-crisis years and then falling well short. Much of this underperformance may be due to the high '2 and 20' fees charged, but if one is paying fees like that, one is entitled to expect exceptional performance. Hirshleifer (2001, p. 1537) concludes that in addition, agency problems will support the persistence of mis-pricing. That is not just sufficient for outperformance; it is necessary. After all, one does not want mis-pricing to persist indefinitely, one wants it to persist long enough to trade on it and then disappear so that one can collect the profits. Hirshleifer

(2001, p. 1549) also points out that Confirmation Bias "may cause some investors to stick to unsuccessful trading strategies, causing mis-pricing to persist;" which underlines again the importance of spotting it in others and avoiding it in ourselves.

Investment banks and fund managers are constant battlegrounds of crippling office politics. There is a 'silo mentality' driven by the bonus culture which means that people do not cooperate across teams because they are not paid on the basis of what other teams earn. This can be quite extreme; I was once in a situation where it appeared as though I would be involved in litigation with my own swaps desk. Myriad fragile political truces hold a sufficient peace to keep total dysfunction at bay. In a remarkable example of public-spiritedness, I once passed a promising opportunity on to the real-estate team in the investment bank in which I worked that looked like it fitted their mandate slightly better than mine. (Normally one would adopt the finders-keepers rule, but I think we had recently been subjected to another management 'we are all in this together' talk.) I found out three years later that the email was deleted without being read. It is clear that all of this politics brings costs: Jonsson (2009, p. 174) points out that information about a new practice or innovative product "is not likely to be objectively evaluated, but that it can be subjected to a 'deviance discount,' when the practice [...] is perceived [as] a threat to an existing political truce." Individuals may lack analytical power, but they are at least more likely to be a unified entity of self-interest.

There used to be basically two methods of forecasting future stock movements. These are termed technical analysis and fundamental analysis. The first approach, also known as charting, seeks to predict what a stock will do next by looking at what it has just done. This is clearly not a terrible idea since sometimes a stock will have momentum, as a factor which has propelled it up or down continues to take effect over a number of days or longer. But, generally, I do not believe it will work well enough to be useful. One problem is that, as Shiller (2003a, p. 96) notes, "there is a tendency for stock prices to continue in the same direction over intervals of six months to a year, but to reverse themselves over longer intervals." This means that momentum trading might seem to work well enough to lure people in over shortish periods, but then the reversal will be difficult to deal with and difficult to predict as well. I am particularly suspicious of the analysts who claim that they have identified a particular shape in the curve or have noted some ominous sign, portentously named the 'death cross' or such like which means the stock is doomed. This sort of line looks a bit too much like witchcraft to me. So I agree with the critique of technical analysis given by Marks (2011, ch. 3).

I will just pause for a second to point out an error in Marks (2011, ch. 3). This is the only error I have found in the book, which will go some way to making it clear that I fully recommend that you read it. I think it is useful to discuss it because it shows that experts can make mistakes, which represents another reason to think that you can beat the market. It will also show you some of my thinking and make the point that you should read everything hyper-critically. That applies to this book as well, of course! Take nothing on trust and set all the arguments against each other. In particular, adopt the philosophical techniques of: a) give the opposing arguments their best case, thus avoiding the straw man mistake whereby you show that your argument is stronger than a weak caricature of the opposing position, and b) whenever you see an assertion, think of what the three major objections are to it and what the responses on behalf of the position that affirms the assertion can say in response to the objection. If your argument can overcome even the strongest possible formulation of the opposing argument, then your argument must be right. Similarly, if your argument maps on to the best position available, it must have good responses to all of the most important objections. If all this sounds like a lot of hard work, you can rely on me to do it for you in this book.

The error comes when Marks (2011, p. 18) observes critically that "day traders considered themselves successful if they bought a stock at $10 and sold it at $11, bought it back the next week at $24 and sold at $25, and bought it back a week later at $39 and sold it at $40." Now, Marks (2011) is certainly correct to criticise day traders. Reportedly, the French stock market regulator found that 85% of them lost money.[3] I think that much of my lack of belief in the approach is because they often use technical analysis to make their trading decisions, because fundamental analysis is never going to tell you to buy GM at 10:17 and sell it at 10:20 or even the same day you bought it, unless there are very strange circumstances occurring whereby new data greatly shifts the fundamental value of GM. And even then the fundamentals will probably tell you to buy it and hold it for a long time. We can also see what Marks (2011) means by saying that there is something wrong with this day trader declaring victory when he made $3 in a stock that appreciated $30. However, the error is to forget about risk. The day trader has indeed missed out on a lot of upside, but has been absent from this stock for all but three days of the weeks during which the stock appreciated. While that now looks like a mistake, that is just a reflection of what actually happened as opposed to what could have happened. And risk is more related to what could have happened. What could have happened is that the stock could have plummeted. The day trader was not exposed to that risk.

I will be making arguments like this quite a lot. They can be confusing, because it may look as though I am disagreeing with someone when in fact I support their main conclusion. Here, I think Marks (2011, ch. 3) is completely correct in his general criticism of day traders and for all but one of the right reasons. I even think that he has half a point with his observation that the day trader has not fully participated in the excellent performance of the stock. But that particular element of his argument is not successful.

Fundamental analysis is the alternative approach to technical analysis. This involves – just as an example and much simplified – trying to determine the correct value of a stock by considering such factors as how much cashflow it is generating and how long you would have to wait to get your money back at the current stock price. This is the first level thinking and, as I have already said, what you need to do to make money is not so much that, but to find opportunities where the market has got the first level thinking wrong. That is where you need to use the psychology we will be examining. So if you see an asset price where you believe technical analysis has set the price in contradistinction to what the fundamentals would say, consider trading against the technical view.

I will now illustrate my problems with the technical approach by offering some criticisms of a book length treatment: Williams (1998). This purports to describe chart-based methods of profiting from chaos in stocks, bonds and commodities. The book begins with an intermittently plausible description of chaos and fractal mathematics. I am not a specialist in these areas, but I do have some relevant experience. For example, the first computer program I ever wrote, in 1987, illustrated the behaviour of a strange attractor arising from the repeated application of a parabolic equation. Williams (1998, p. 47) discusses such strange attractors in the context of his discussion of chaos theory.

The main part of the book describes ways of interpreting short-term chart movements in such a way as to predict the future course of the assets in question. Naturally, this will be extremely profitable if it can be done consistently. While, as I mentioned above, the discussion of chaos theory is rather superficial, the more severe criticism is that absolutely no attempt is made in Williams (1998) to link chaos theory and the charting techniques which make up the bulk of the material of the book. It is not sufficient to name certain chart patterns "fractal buy signals" to make out a link between the two areas. One rather suspects that exotic jargon and mathematical terminology has been added to lend a spurious air of gravitas.

This, however, is not my main objection. Trading systems are to be measured by how they perform in real markets. This will generally be done by what is known as back testing. One simulates how a particular system would have performed in previous market situations. Williams (1998) does this at several points throughout the book. He shows the results of trading his system over about a three-month period. The results are extremely positive, with very large profits being made.

Scientifically, there are three major problems with this as an argument. Firstly, there is the lack of what one might term a control group. Whenever we want to claim that a particular effect has a particular cause, we need such a control group which is comparable to the experimental group, but in which the cause was not present. For example, to show that orange juice cures a cold, it is not sufficient to drink some orange juice and observe that one recovers. This is because we do not have the counterfactual. Perhaps you would have recovered anyway. What we need to do is run a large trial of say 200 people with colds. We give 100 of them orange juice. The other hundred are the control group. We give them nothing, or if we are being especially careful about the placebo effect, we give them something that looks and tastes like orange juice but that is not. We then wish to see the orange juice group recover at a higher rate than the control group. This must also be a robust and replicable finding, so other groups in different universities and research institutions must see the same effect. Then we can begin to imagine that the hypothesis has found some confirmation. Transferring this objection back to the trading system outlined, we have been shown that it was successful, but it has not been compared with anything else. For a start, we would like to know how much money would have been made in these markets simply by going long of the assets involved.

The second problem is related to this first problem. The system was very powerful and profitable over a particular three-month period. We actually need to know how it performed over *all* three-month periods. Otherwise we do not know how robust the system is in different market environments. I believe, in fact, that there is almost no system that cannot be made to look highly profitable by selection of the range of dates for back testing. As an illustration of this, I will sketch an extreme case, which cannot succeed. For example, imagine I want to show that June 23 is a very good day each year to short the S&P 500. That, if you like, is a very simple system. If I back test this using 2016 data, I will show that this system is very successful because in 2016, June 23 was the last trading day before the shock result of the Brexit referendum affected markets. Since this is a ludicrous conclusion, we can see that cherry picking the date range for back testing can cause significant problems.

Moreover, what is so special about the three-month period? A wide range of other possible periods should also be reported. A system which yields a 10% profit over three months would be very valuable, but if it also includes some 10% down weeks, it would psychologically be very difficult to persist with it. There are no down weeks shown in the reports but, of course, that may just be a feature of the particular three-month period selected. This problem leads onto another one: Either the system will work for ever, or it has a finite period of applicability. In the former case, someone should have made an extremely large amount of money from using the system. Where are these billionaires? Indeed, there seem to be no known examples of someone making significant sums from a trading system. If, on the other hand, the system is of a limited duration of applicability, then it ought to also include within itself some mechanism to signal that the applicability period is now over. This is not provided in Williams (1998). What this means, of course, is that someone could be using the system successfully and then incur extremely large losses, because even if the system ever worked, it no longer does.

The third problem is an extension of the second problem. It is in spirit closely akin to a criticism frequently and justifiably brought by Taleb (2012), who states that no amount of past historical data will tell us anything about the future. While I think this is too strong a claim, a weaker version is definitely true, and suffices to render all back testing claims dubious. The weaker claim is that previous worst cases that have occurred do not constitute any kind of limit on future worst cases. So while the second problem means that our confidence in the upside of the system is reduced, the third problem reminds us that we have no guarantees on the downside. In my view, this latter is the more serious problem, because the upside will look after itself if one is in the market. At a minimum, we want to see how this system would have performed in its worst three-month period in the past 40 years because, as I have stated, future worst cases could easily be much worse than previous worst cases.

The point of all this is that there are plenty of people in the market who are using such dubious systems to trade, or who are devoted to technical analysis, or both. The market, then, has many such people in it. These are some of the people you need to beat if you are to beat the market. So it looks like it can be done.

Another way in which you can beat the market is to switch markets or change the asset classes in which one is invested. There are cycles[4] in all economies as they swing from boom to bust. Different assets perform differently at different stages. As I write in early 2016, we have just started a Fed tightening cycle, which in normal circumstances signals a late stage in a recovery. Since the 2007–2008 crisis was of such an enormous magnitude in comparison to the previous downturns and there is, for example, still a large amount of QE in the system which will presumably be unwound at some stage, it is possible that the 'new normal' does not look anything like what previous experience would lead us to expect. If that is so, then almost all bets are off, though I would still maintain that trying to trade without making decisions under the influence of cognitive biases will be more optimal even under unusual circumstances. If the future does, in fact, look like the past, then what will happen next is that there will be an outbreak of 'irrational exuberance' in equity markets. This is the point at which your cab driver is giving you stock tips. The S&P 500 is either at a record high or at a high since the last cycle. At this point, USTs (United States Treasury Bonds) are very much out of favour, and so they might be yielding 5% or more when the Consumer Prices Index (CPI) is 2.5%. If the CPI is lower in the future, maybe Treasuries pay slightly less. This is the point at which you sell all of your equities and put your entire portfolio into Treasuries. You then wait for equity markets to crash. This might be a long wait, perhaps two years or more. After the crash, your Treasuries have appreciated and at some point you switch back into equities which are now depressed. Then you wait another seven years. In this way, you can 'beat all the markets' even if it is true that you cannot outperform the S&P 500 by investing in US equities unless you are very lucky. (Note that I am not even accepting that it is impossible; I am merely showing that my argument succeeds whether it is possible or not.) The decision as to when exactly to switch markets is a difficult one, and it is one of such importance that knowledge of biases will be of critical importance.

Where are the inefficient markets which it is possible to beat? You might think that you have to go very far afield to find them. Finding such inefficient markets will involve a lot of hard work. I knew one student who funded his studies by gambling. I do not recommend this approach, and I will merely outline the market in which he chose to gamble in order to outline my point here. This student knew a lot about football. In England, and indeed worldwide, the Premier League is very widely followed and very many people have as much expertise as it is possible to have on a game which remains to an extent unpredictable. My student friend did not choose to use his expertise here because he knew that the bookmakers would be very well informed on the topic and, if they were not, other gamblers who were would soon put them right. So he chose to bet instead on women's college netball in the Midwest. I am sure this is an excellent sport with admirable competitors, but the fact is that it is today followed by fewer people than the English Premier League. There is more of a chance to find an information edge. If you are prepared to invest the time into becoming an expert on stocks in Kazakhstan, go to it. But becoming an expert in anything requires a very significant amount of work.

The equivalent of the English Premier League in mainstream investment arenas is probably the US equity market, personified as it were by the S&P 500 index. So does my argument above mean you should avoid US equities? Marks (2011, p. 13) suggests that "mainstream securities markets can be so efficient that it is largely a waste of time to work at finding winners there." I think this is too strong. After all, Marks (2011) goes on to describe ways of investing successfully and does not exclude mainstream securities markets as a candidate. Marks (2011, p. 8) also notes the very small percentage of investors who ever sell short. I have also noticed this. Whenever anyone tells me that a positive investment idea I have had is catastrophically wrong, I also tell them to put their money where their mouth is and short the stock. They never do. So perhaps you can beat the market by engaging in transactions that are engaged in by very few people. As Marks (2011, p. 13) concludes, I think correctly, efficiency is not universal. It is a good first approximation but there are still opportunities to be found.

Marks (2011, p. 8) suggests plausibly that it is "not easy for any one person – working with the same information as everyone else and subject to the same psychological influences" to beat the market. I think he is correct that obtaining different information to others and using different psychological influences may allow a person to beat the market. However, there is almost no possibility that you can consistently obtain information that no-one else in the market has and which is price sensitive, unless you have inside information. Trading on that would of course be illegal. So that leaves "psychological influences." This book will not eliminate psychological influences. But if you think like I do, then you will agree that knowing what they are is an important first step. And Baddeley (2010, p. 283) notes evidence that "any individual can be a good trader if they have the appropriate training and experience" so there is nothing to stop you. As Hirshleifer (2001, p. 1536) points out, market "equilibrium prices reflect a weighted average of the beliefs of the rational and irrational traders" which means that there are ways to outperform if one moves into the first group from the second.

Much of this book is about biases and how to avoid them oneself and profit by forecasting them in others. As a quick example, consider the day-of-the-week effect. People are generally sad on Mondays and happy on Fridays because the weekend has either just gone or is about to begin. Rystrom and Benson (1989, p. 77) report that this tracks through to trading days, with the mean return being -0.17%

on Mondays and +0.09% on Fridays. This is not large enough to arbitrage in itself, but it does mean that you may as well make your purchases late on a Monday and your sales late on a Friday. It is also worth considering the effects in other markets, notably in the Middle East, that have different weekends.

As a final point, I might observe that actually it is possible to make excellent returns *without* beating the market. For example, on 1 Feb 2009, the S&P 500 closed at 735. Today, on 16 May 2016 it is trading at 2055, so an investor picking the bottom would have made an excellent return of 179% in around seven years. Now, of course, market timing of that quality is basically impossible, but very good returns would have been made by an investor getting in at any point in 2009, as I did. Very few investors did this; most US retail investors did not get back in to the S&P 500 until 2013 which was far too late, and then only gingerly. This is because it is psychologically extremely hard to take a risk like that, even though rational analysis might suggest doing so. I will be arguing in this book that gaining insight into one's own cognitive biases and how they can throw off our predictions of how other investors will behave can allow one to seize opportunities such as this.

Notes

1 Absurdities such as this did occur during the dot.com boom: company X would spin out tech arm Y and the market priced Y above X, i.e. held that all the other assets of X had negative value.
2 *The Economist*, vol. 419, no. 8988, 07 May 2016, p. 64
3 Asking yourself the question 'why do they not stop?' will go a long way to pointing to the need for the psychology in this book.
4 Cf. Marks (2011, ch. 15)

3
THEORY OF MIND

In this chapter I will briefly outline the state of the art thinking in terms of how we predict and explain the behaviour of others, which is known as 'Theory of Mind,' or 'ToM.' As the very first order of business, I will once again briefly underline how important this topic is in financial markets. The central point is made by many commentators, including for example Baddeley (2010, p. 282), who notes an argument from Keynes which I think is correct to the effect that "people will purchase a tulip bulb, house or a dot-com share at a seemingly exorbitant price not because they independently believe that the object is worth the cost but because they believe that other people think that it is." My argument for the importance of Theory of Mind to trading will emerge with more depth and weight on more-or-less every page in this book. But I will add some crucial data at this point before continuing to outline how psychologists see Theory of Mind.

3.1 Better Traders Have Better Theory Of Mind

The central finding of Bruguier, Quartz, and Bossaerts (2010, p. 1703) is that "skill in predicting price changes in markets with insiders correlates with scores on two ToM tasks." This is already quite convincing in my view, but it is such a crucial finding for this project, that it merits unpacking and scrutiny. It is immediately apparent from the above quotation that we want to know more about two points. Firstly, does the caveat in relation to insiders reduce the applicability of the finding. Secondly, there is the perennial question about the link between correlation and causation. In this section, I will show that neither of these potential problems need concern us, as well as explaining how the data was compiled.

The first potential difficulty about insiders can be dispensed with relatively quickly. In the experimenters' paradigm, the market is divided into traders who have key information, and others who do not. The key information in question relates to the dividend stream of a company going forward. As in real markets, a few investors will have a good picture of how the dividends are likely to develop. They might be senior employees of the company in question; indeed, that is often how the term insider is used in relation to stock trading. Naturally enough, if you are such an insider, you should use the information you have to trade successfully, so far as is consistent with the law. In general however, you will not be in such a fortunate position. We are then interested in how uninformed traders can intuit the hidden information held by insiders. This is one aspect of the Theory of Mind task involved. We can therefore be confident that the findings of this paper have wide applicability, since we are all mostly in the position of uninformed traders, according to the definition used by the authors. Dealing with the second question is more complex; I will return to it after I have explained the experimental method and results.

Bruguier, Quartz, and Bossaerts (2010) begin their discussion with the crucial observation that while it is clear that some traders are better than others, and that there does seem to be such a thing as 'trader intuition,' no one has been able to explain why. Various bizarre differences involving finger length and testosterone have been noted, but these do not amount to an explanation, nor is it obvious how they could. In particular, the idea that high testosterone traders are more successful because they are more aggressive seems problematic. As I will discuss later (§8.3.1), aggression seems to go hand-in-hand with overconfidence, which is an indicator of poor trading performance. Moreover, females have less testosterone and so the account would predict that females are worse traders, but this is empirically false, as I will also discuss later. By contrast, showing that good traders differ from bad traders in Theory of Mind capabilities would have an immediate and compelling explanatory force. The aim of the authors was, therefore, to demonstrate this.

It is worth observing that Bruguier, Quartz, and Bossaerts (2010, p. 1705) believe that the operation of Theory of Mind in markets proceeds by tracking changes in the environment rather than by logical deduction. The changes are tracked with the aim of divining the intentions of the human actors behind them. Note, incidentally, how much more easily this sits with a simulationist account of Theory of Mind than with a theoretical one. The former can have people asking themselves questions like: 'what am I thinking if I have acted in such a way as to produce that order flow?' The latter needs to postulate, implausibly, that we have rules linking shapes in stock price evolution over time and mental states.

The first part of the experiment involved running a fairly standard laboratory trading market simulation. This was recorded. In the second part of the experiment, a new group of subjects was shown the recording. This new group of subjects was placed in brain scanners while they were watching. This second group is the important one from our perspective. They were told whether or not there were insiders in the market simulation that they were watching. None of them were themselves insiders. Since their financial rewards depended on it, it was very important to them to decide whether there were any insiders, and if so, what the inside information was. So the successful application of Theory of Mind in a market context is what produces results for the second group.

The first important result reported by Bruguier, Quartz, and Bossaerts (2010, p. 1709) is that there was "increased activation in specific brain regions when insiders were present relative to when insiders were absent" and that "regions that activated could immediately be recognised as those involved in ToM." This suggests that the second group of subjects only activated their Theory of Mind when there was a useful and profitable target to use it on. They also add that there was no activation of mathematical or logical areas; this underlines the special importance of Theory of Mind to the task at hand.

The authors then describe the third part of their experiment. They aimed to build on the hypothesis suggested by the brain imaging study. They wished to confirm that Theory of Mind, and not mathematical or logical analysis, was the key differentiator. A third group of subjects was recruited. All of these new subjects then completed four tasks. Task one involved predicting which direction the stock would move next, when considering the recording of the simulated market. The second two tasks were standard Theory of Mind tasks. These involved predicting what some moving geometric shapes would do next; our Theory of Mind is automated and even triggered by shapes. The other Theory of Mind task involved assessing the emotional state of another person from looking at a picture of their eyes. The final task assessed mathematical and logical ability in the same way as might be done in a job interview on Wall Street.

Bruguier, Quartz, and Bossaerts (2010, p. 1714) make the important observation that their subjects performed quite well on the trading task. Since the subjects were students or graduate students who lacked formal financial experience or training, this suggests that the subjects were using another ability. Naturally, since everyone who is neuro-typical has a serviceable Theory of Mind from the age of five, the implication is that the subjects were using their Theory of Mind to perform well in the trading task.

As to the other four tasks, Bruguier, Quartz, and Bossaerts (2010, p. 1714) report that the "ability to predict price changes in the presence of insiders is correlated with ToM skill," confirming their hypothesis. They find no correlation between the ability to predict price changes and mathematical or logical ability.

Interestingly, Bruguier, Quartz, and Bossaerts (2010, p. 1714) fail to find any outperformance among female subjects. This is in contrast to a substantial amount of evidence, which I will discuss later (§8.3.1), that female traders perform better. That would be consistent with the general view that females have better Theory of Mind. This view is intuitively plausible, but is also suggested by the low proportion of autistic diagnoses applied to female subjects. There could be various reasons for this, but one explanation relies on Theory of Mind. Autistic subjects exhibit severe deficits in Theory of Mind. One candidate explanation for the infrequency of autism diagnoses for female subjects is that they have either a stronger Theory of Mind capacity to begin with, or ways of working around their Theory of Mind deficits, both of which would make them less likely to receive a diagnosis of autism. Perhaps then this particular study should be replicated with a larger number of subjects, in order to see whether a sex difference emerges. This study only had 16 female subjects, which could easily be too low.

I now return to the second potential problem mentioned at the start of this section, regarding the extent to which correlation implies causation. There are two possible directions of causation here. Either having strong Theory of Mind capacity makes one a better trader, or being a good trader improves one's Theory of Mind capabilities. It is not obvious what story can be constructed to support the second line. By contrast, a very straightforward story explains why good Theory of Mind capabilities would lead to improved trading performance. This is simply the claim that using Theory of Mind enables traders to forecast the behaviour of other market participants, and position themselves accordingly. So I think we can conclude that it is good Theory of Mind capabilities that makes one a good trader, rather than vice versa.

This leads on to a final objection. It would not be helpful to show that improving Theory of Mind is a way to improve trading performance if it is not possible to improve Theory of Mind. I think it is possible. We know that children around the age of five dramatically improve their Theory of Mind capabilities, so it is at least possible for them. Many clinical populations exhibit Theory of Mind deficits which are addressable. Savina and Beninger (2007) found that clozapine improved Theory of Mind performance in schizophrenic subjects; Pedersen et al. (2011) found the same with oxytocin and Hasson-Ohayon et al. (2009) report results showing that metacognitive training results in improvement. Significantly, they found that reducing the effects of cognitive biases was one way of doing that.

None of this shows that adult neuro-typical subjects can improve their Theory of Mind, but renders it plausible at least. Further, on the account of Theory of Mind which I have proposed (Short 2015), bias mismatch is the main reason for Theory of Mind errors. It seems quite convincing then that reducing such bias mismatch would result in improved Theory of Mind performance.

One implication of this is that trading with dummy accounts will not be as useful as trading with live money accounts. This is because, as I have also argued in Short (2015), bias mismatch can be caused by affect mismatch. In particular, Theory of Mind is thrown off if a dispassionate observer simulates someone who is deeply interested in the outcome. Someone trading dummy money will not be that engaged in the results. They may therefore have a bias mismatch with actual market participants, who are very interested in whether or not they lose money. But as a general point, I am confident that bias mismatches can be at least partly reduced. In the greater part of this book, I will be describing the main biases of relevance to market contexts, with this exact aim in mind.

3.2 How Theory Of Mind Works

I return now to the bubble buying I mentioned at the start of this chapter, when prices of assets seem to become completely detached from fundamentals or reality and are driven merely by the expectation that others will also bid up the asset further. This type of behaviour is often seen in markets at different points in their cycle, and what is going on is essentially a Theory of Mind task. Investors have become completely detached from the intrinsic value of the assets they are purchasing since they are doing so at not just an exorbitant price, but a price that they would themselves likely agree is 'exorbitant' in at least one sense. They make the purchase anyway because they think that other people will believe that the asset really is worth the exorbitant price. There remain two potential explanations of this. The investor could believe that everyone else genuinely believes the asset is worth the exorbitant price, or he could believe that every other investor is like him, and is cynically bidding up the asset.

This latter explanation looks more plausible to me, partly because it sits more easily with Simulation Theory – because it seems to me that a cynical investor will expect cynicism in others – but also because I think that many investors participate in bubbles even though they know they are in a bubble, which is unsustainable since they think they will be able to get out in time. Others I am sure just get caught up in general enthusiasm and are just engaging in herding behaviour. More technically, they are exhibiting Conformity Bias, of which more below in §7.4.

Note that Theory of Mind is key in all of these variations and is therefore crucial in obtaining success in markets which contain participants of the various different sorts. The cynical investors I mentioned are to some extent exploiting Theory of Mind skills. But we will need to stand above all market participants and make informed judgments about what their Theory of Mind will be telling them and where it will be in error. Only this knowledge can produce an optimal strategy in a market consisting otherwise entirely of people who use their Theory of Mind without understanding anything about it, especially the biases which can throw it off. In this book, I will be supplying the toolkit to do just that.

The operation of our Theory of Mind is fast, mandatory (Samson *et al.* 2010) and without phenomenology. Phenomenology is the term in philosophy for what it is like to experience something. You have a certain phenomenology when you see red and a different one when you see yellow, or hear a piano. It is hard to put into words exactly what it is like to see red and to see yellow, but it is certainly different in each case. There is no particular feeling you have when run your Theory of Mind, you are simply presented with the results in terms of some predictions of behaviour being made available to you.

Of course, the term 'you' is doing quite a lot of work here. Arguably, 'you' are not running your Theory of Mind at all. Your subconscious mind is doing it for you, if we take as a definition of 'you' the conscious active decision-making element of your mind. If, alternatively, we were to stipulate that everything that happens inside your skull is done by you, then for sure you are running your Theory of Mind because it definitely happens inside your skull and it is not being conducted by anyone else. Either way, you do not have phenomenology in relation to the process; you might have some in relation to the result. You might be able to identify an experience or a feeling you have as a result of using your Theory of Mind. You might see someone going in to a coffee shop and decide that they are doing that because they desire coffee. That could prompt you to have a desire for coffee as well. This phenomenology is distinct from the putative phenomenology associated with running Theory of Mind, while I have denied that there is any phenomenology associated with running Theory of Mind.

Note also how you get the results of Theory of Mind quickly, and that you do not have much choice in whether those results become apparent. I suggest that if I tell you that someone is going into a coffee shop, you are going to have to work quite hard to avoid the immediate conclusion that this is because they desire coffee. I think that the only way you could avoid having that conclusion presented to you is by using your Theory of Mind again to come up with an alternative story. The person does not want coffee; they are a famous coffee-hater and they merely desire to meet a friend whom they believe is in the coffee shop. Such a response just illustrates my points about how the process of using our Theory of Mind is fast, mandatory and lacks phenomenology.

These characteristics of Theory of Mind are often what lie behind our responses to literature. This further illustrates how mandatory its use is. For example, we are horrified when Mitchell (2003, p. 351) describes a girl being thrown from a cliff who "mewled in terror and tried to wriggle free." We automatically place ourselves partially in the position of the girl and partly experience her terror. It does not matter that she is a fabricant doll, in the jargon of the book; it does not even matter that this is fiction and nothing happened to any such girl. The affective import is strong and this is what makes the literature powerful. Observe again how all you get is the result of Theory of Mind here: there is no apparent time taken, there is no choice about whether or not you run your Theory of Mind, and all of the phenomenology is driven by the results and not the process. I will be suggesting in this book that these characteristics of Theory of Mind make it a powerful driver of our own behaviour and that of others, and that therefore understanding it is essential to performing well in markets or anywhere else.

Accounts of how we run our Theory of Mind differ. As I have argued at length (Short 2015), the best account of Theory of Mind is Simulation Theory, which holds that our Theory of Mind works by putting ourselves in others' shoes, or simulating them, in other words. This is really just an extension of the sort of idea mentioned by Gladwell (2000, p. 84), to the effect that if "you show people pictures of a frowning face or a smiling face, they will smile or frown back" although possibly only subliminally. We can add to this the well-supported idea that such physical micro-movements also carry affective import so that producing a subtle smile will make someone feel slightly happier. Thus the emotions of others are a little contagious; we then have a basis for a simulationist account of Theory of Mind. When you see someone smile, you feel slightly happier which is somewhat like what they are probably feeling: you can now go on to put yourself in their place and assess why that might be. In the ancestral environment, accurate assessment of the emotions of others, especially hostile ones, would have had obvious importance so it is unsurprising that we are good at it.

The other main competitor to Simulation Theory is called 'Theory Theory' (Gopnik and Wellman 1992). This argues that we predict and explain the behaviour of others by actually having a theory of other people which we learn as young children. It is, if you like, the theory that our Theory of Mind really is a theory. One of the prime arguments I canvass in Short (2015) for Simulation Theory, as opposed to Theory Theory, is that I think it is implausible that children of five or even much younger could have acquired such a theory.

There is no need to be concerned that this book will not be valuable if I am wrong about Simulation Theory being the correct account of Theory of Mind. You can take that side of the argument or, more realistically for our purposes in this book, remain neutral on it and still accept my claims that cognitive biases are widespread, cause sub-optimal decision making and, crucially, cause us to make systematic Theory of Mind errors. While I will be assuming the account I give in Short (2015), you can just take my word for it for the purposes of this book. You just need to agree that we do not adequately adjust for bias in ourselves or others when we predict and explain the behaviour of others. It is fine for now to proceed with that as an assumption; the case for it will emerge later.

The canonical test of Theory of Mind abilities is called the False Belief Task. This test does what it says on the tin: it tests whether someone, often a child under five, can ascribe false beliefs. Children younger than that age tend to think that everyone has the same beliefs about the world and they are the right ones. The idea for the test was first proposed by some philosophers including Dennett (1978), in response to a question about chimps posed by Premack and Woodruff (1978).

The False Belief Task is famous in the psychological literature, with literally hundreds of papers that discuss it. The first of these was Wimmer and Perner (1983). In the test, children around five are told a short story and asked questions about it. In the story, Maxi puts some chocolate in a cupboard and then goes out. While he is gone, his mother moves the chocolate into a different cupboard. The children are then asked the key question as to where Maxi will look for the chocolate when he returns. Adults and neuro-typical children over or around five respond correctly that Maxi will look in the cupboard where he left the chocolate. Children under five, somewhat surprisingly, report that Maxi will look where the chocolate is now located even though in the terms of the story, he was not present when the chocolate was moved and so has no way to know that it was moved. The children who answer wrongly thus have failed the False Belief Task in that they have failed to ascribe a false belief to Maxi. For reasons which are somewhat unclear, children pass through a rapid development stage between the ages of around three and five. At three, very few of them can pass the False Belief Task while at five, most of them can. One possible explanation for this is that children are independently known to be developing their language abilities and Inhibitory Control (Bernstein et al. 2007) on around the same timescale. Having Inhibitory Control means being able to inhibit automatic responses or ignore them; this is necessary in passing the False Belief Task because one has to ignore the highly salient fact that the chocolate has moved. There is also some much disputed but, to my mind, fairly convincing evidence that even children as young as fifteen months (Onishi and Baillargeon 2005) can pass non-verbal versions of the False Belief Task.

You can run your own version of the False Belief Task on any four or five-year-old children nearby. Interestingly, you can ask them what answer they gave and they will give a false response to that as well, even if what they actually said took place only seconds before. Thus, you can show them an egg carton in which you have secretly placed crayons and ask them what is in it. They will say 'eggs.' Then you show them the crayons and ask them what they just said was in it. They claim that they said 'crayons' because they now lack the ability to ascribe a false belief to themselves in the very recent past. Note that there is nothing wrong with your child if they fail the False Belief Task up to the age of five or a bit older: this is entirely normal. This version here is the 'unexpected contents' version of the False Belief Task; the previously described version involving Maxi and the chocolate is known as the 'change in location' version.

Theory of Mind seems to be part of the basic toolkit which neuro-typical adults have. Bernstein et al. (2007, p. 1375) note that "performance on false belief tasks is robust across different procedures and cultures." This means that various different sorts of experiments looking at the False Belief Task show similar results. Also, children in many cultures across the world show a similar pattern of development, beginning to pass the task in large numbers by at most the age of five. This has led some observers to propose that our Theory of Mind is an innate, modular system (Leslie, German, and Happe 1993; Leslie, Friedman, and German 2004). I am myself sceptical of modular views since I think access to potentially one's full belief set may be needed to simulate the relevant parts of someone else's belief set in order to perform a Theory of Mind task; including such a vast amount of data within Theory of Mind is inconsistent with an encapsulated modular account.

If I am right about Simulation Theory being the basis of our Theory of Mind abilities, one consequence is that our starting point for predicting the behaviour of others is a tacit assumption that they are like us in terms of beliefs and desires.

This can be modified, sometimes dramatically so, but it is fair to say that we can generally work on the basis that someone else thinks the way we do unless we have reason to think otherwise. This seems to me to have a plethora of real life examples which I cannot list here. I will just give one market-relevant example now. Lewis (2010, p. 64) discusses a trader who was "transparently self-interested and self-promotional [and also] excessively alert to the self-interest and self-promotion of others." This it seems to me is a natural consequence of Simulation Theory. By contrast, it is hard to explain in Theory Theory because the theory would have to include a generalisation like 'he believes/desires what I believe/desire' and that might need to cover an infinite number of beliefs/desires.

Our Theory of Mind works fairly well; we are often right when we use it. We are also often wrong, in systematic ways. By 'systematic' here, I mean that we will all tend to make the same mistakes multiple times if we are presented with the same scenario to analyse. As I argue, again in Short (2015), one of the main shortcomings of our Theory of Mind is that it does not handle biases well. By biases, I mean such effects as Confirmation Bias, where people tend to look for evidence that supports what they already believe. Falling prey to Confirmation Bias could be very dangerous when trading in financial markets (and indeed making important decisions generally). The existence of these biases is very widely replicated in the literature following some seminal pioneering work (Tversky and Kahneman 1973; Tversky and Kahneman 1974; Tversky and Kahneman 1983).

There can be a sort of bias mismatch between S and O. S and O are my terms for the person doing the simulation, S, and the person S wishes to predict or explain, O. You can think of them as Subject and Object if you like. You can also think of them as Self and Other, though not when S is using his own Theory of Mind to predict his own behaviour in counterfactual circumstances. The problem is that a bias mismatch can arise between S and O. If S simulates O but O is influenced by a bias by which S is not influenced, then S can get O's thinking wrong. S will then make a systematic error about what O will do next. This idea of mine that biases can impair Theory of Mind performance is backed up by a large amount of experimental data. For example, Bernstein *et al.* (2007, p. 1382) found that "the worse one performed on Theory of Mind tasks, the more hindsight bias one showed."

A bias mismatch such as this one described above can arise in several ways. Two of the most prominent are that S can apply in his simulation of O a bias that O does not currently exhibit. Alternatively, O can be operating under a bias such as Confirmation Bias which S does not include in his simulation. Either way, S will have made a systematic error in predicting O's behaviour. This will work for behaviour in financial markets just as much as elsewhere. So now you can see one example of how understanding the relevant psychology here will be helpful in markets. For example, you might work out that O is not buying a particular stock X because he has applied Confirmation Bias in his analysis of it. Since O is here in market terms more than one person – in fact, O can stand for practically all market participants – then that might mean that stock X is underpriced. It is then irrelevant whether X is a financially strong company or a weak one. You should buy the stock either way because it is too cheap.

I suggest two causes of bias mismatch in Short (2015). These are affect mismatch and system mismatch. Affect mismatch means that S and O are in different emotional states, and that this has been enough of a difference to cause one of S or O to exhibit a bias which the other does not exhibit, thus resulting in a bias mismatch between S and O. One type of example of this can be seen in situations where S simply does not care as much as O does about O's situation for the simple reason that O is in the situation and S is not. For example, imagining what it would be like to be hanging off a cliff by one's fingertips has some negative affect associated with it, but nothing like the amount associated with actually being in that situation. Less dramatically, the affect involved in owning a mug may cause the Endowment Effect (§6.4) (Nofsinger 2016, pp. 39–40) to arise, in which Os who are given a mug value it more highly than the value they assessed it at when they did not own it. This means that S has committed a systematic error in Theory of Mind about O, because no-one who has not studied the experiments ever predicts that O will say the mug is worth more when they own it.

The second cause of bias mismatch is system mismatch. It is widely agreed that we have two systems of reasoning (Sloman 1996). System one is fast and dirty, and employs a variety of heuristics and biases to get answers that are roughly right for many circumstances quickly enough to be useful. Many people have had the experience of walking to the gym 'on autopilot' and realising half way there that actually they were going to the shops and they need to turn around. System one is implicit: it delivers its pronouncements and we act on them without noticing that anything has happened. System two, by contrast, is explicit, deliberate and slow. It is the system you use when you are working on something difficult or unfamiliar. We switch between the two depending on what the question is, how important the matter under consideration is, and whether we have time to use the slower system two.

Theory of Mind is also one of the activities which can take place in a fast, approximate way or in a slow, deliberate way (Butterfill and Apperly 2013). If S and O are using different systems, it is likely that S will make systematic errors in Theory of Mind about O. In other words, if a calm S simulates O using explicit reasoning while an agitated O is using system one, S will not make a good prediction of O's behaviour. This is equivalent to saying that there is a bias mismatch between S and O because system one is basically just a collection of biases. Biases are ubiquitous in human decision-making which is why understanding them is central to making accurate predictions of behaviour.

The two causes of bias mismatch can also both operate together. Gladwell (2009b, pp. 263–279) describes episodes of a tennis player 'choking' in a grand slam final. He characterises what happens as extreme stress causes the player to return to system two – i.e. explicit and deliberate – movements in relation to hitting the ball. This of course works very badly, because the player has thousands of hours of experience of hitting the ball automatically and effectively using system one and no recent experience at all of how one explicitly hits a ball using system two. Those of us who have never played a grand slam final might find it hard to understand how debilitating such stress can be, in an example of affect mismatch causing system mismatch between S and O, which leads to bias mismatch. Therefore we make the Theory of Mind error of predicting that professional experienced tennis players will continue to be able to hit the ball unless they are injured.

Our insight into how our Theory of Mind works is fairly poor, which explains why it can be a live debate as to whether we are doing it using simulation or theory. We are also strangely blind to its failures, which explains why we can continue to run it using biases that throw it off without ever applying a correction. As an example of how we miss Theory of Mind errors, consider the copious evidence (Konnikova 2016, pp. 36–42) that we cannot detect lying and the equally copious evidence that we think we can. If our Theory of Mind could accurately place S in the position of O who can gain from lying, we would surely pick it up more easily.

The alert reader may wonder how this can be squared with the claim above that we are good at reading emotions since it is advantageous to be able to do so. It would be equally or even more advantageous to be able to detect lying. I think the answer here is that there is a kind of 'arms race' going on with liars, which they have won: they have been able to suppress the signs of lying successfully to the extent that very few of us can detect them. On the other hand, suppression of the signs of emotion is less frequently done – since many people have no problem disclosing their true emotional state, while all liars are motivated to suppress the signs of their lying – and it can also be true that we detect emotion falsely when someone is trying to deceive us in this connection. The answer given by Konnikova (2016, p. 41) is that we do not evolve the ability to detect liars because most people are not liars.

All of these effects arise just as much in markets, peopled as they are by actual humans, as in other arenas. And even though a great deal of trading is now done by computers, that applies only in short-term trading and the computers are programmed by people. My aim in this book is give readers as much as they need to understand how biases can drive much that is perplexing about behaviour in markets and how that can benefit traders by giving them insights into the behaviour of themselves and others.

There have been claims that biases do not operate in financial markets. I dispute those claims; I see them as on a parallel with the now largely defunct idea that market participants are perfectly rational or nearly so. Seybert and Bloomfield (2009, p. 739) report a list given in the literature of various ways in which "economic forces that might allow markets to eliminate decision-making biases observed at the individual level. These forces include the presence of incentives, the ability of unbiased traders to discipline price errors, and the ability of biased market participants to extract information from the activity of less-biased traders."

I think there are serious problems with all three of these proposed mechanisms. We know that cognitive biases are very deep-seated in our mental architecture; Tversky and Kahneman (1974, p. 1130) report that "several of the severe errors of judgment reported earlier occurred despite the fact that subjects were encouraged to be accurate and were rewarded for the correct answers." Similarly, Dunning et al. (2003, p. 84) found that the Dunning-Kruger Effect (cf. §7.2) persisted "unchecked [even] after participants are promised up to $100 for accurate assessments of their performance."

On the second line, there is evidence that rational traders gravitate in the direction of irrational traders, as is to some extent rational (Wang 1993). If you reasonably expect everyone to bid up a stock beyond its real value, you should participate in bidding it up providing you are certain that you can get out before everyone else. (This is not an approach I commend; I merely point out a way in which it can be rational to partly join the irrational.) This means we cannot expect the rational traders to force the irrational ones from the market any time soon, and there are new persons joining the investment fraternity every year and they are of various degrees of rationality.

The third response is technically possible, but the biased traders do not know they are influenced by biases and the other traders are not − if there are any such unbiased traders. All they will see is other people taking different views to their own. They are then as humans much more likely to use a bias such as Confirmation Bias to conclude that they are right and that the other traders are wrong. So I also do not see how this third mechanism can work to force markets in the directions of much greater efficiency.

Interestingly, the reverse of the third line is true to some extent: after all, what I am proposing in this book is precisely that investors should seek to maximise their understanding of biases in order to reduce their influence in their own thinking and include them as an important missing factor in predicting the behaviour of other market participants. So this is, in a way, less biased traders extracting information from the activities of biased investors.

Finally, Seybert and Bloomfield (2009, p. 738) "identify a bias (wishful thinking) that is weak, if not nonexistent, at the individual level, and show how interaction in financial markets can amplify the bias, causing strong effects on prices and belief." Given how strong cognitive biases generally are, an example where even a weak one is amplified so as to cause strong price effects is rather compelling. Seybert and Bloomfield (2009) also found that wishful thinking was contagious in a laboratory market, which provides further confidence that biases are not eliminated in markets. Theory of Mind abilities are closely related to counterfactual reasoning abilities (Riggs and Peterson 2000). Arguably, predicting the behaviour of someone else is actually a species of counterfactual reasoning: what would I do if I were in their circumstances? Svetlova (2009, p. 154) records that "financial market professionals regularly question the mainstream scenarios because they can make money only by deviating from them [and] [t]hey use counterfactual thinking for this purpose." Her argument, which is plausible, notes that it is only possible to beat the market by deviating from the market. Identifying appropriate such deviations involves counterfactual thinking because one must consider scenarios different to those which the market expects. This is, in fact, more precisely described as counterfactual reasoning combined with a Theory of Mind input. One must use Theory of Mind to establish what the market expects – which may be very different to what it says it expects, since participants are motivated to avoid disclosure of their actual beliefs – and then examine counterfactually whether changing an element of what the market believes results in a different share price in future than the market currently expects. Again – this is the only way to make money in markets: Svetlova (2009, p. 153) reports a fund manager stating that "[o]ne can generate an added value only when he makes a non-consensus call …". So we can see that understanding Theory of Mind is central to the generation of added value.

Having now outlined why Theory of Mind is important and suggested that biases are the primary reason for Theory of Mind to fail, I will spend the rest of this book outlining the biases and how they play out in markets.

4

BELIEF-FORMATION BIASES I

4.1 Belief Perseverance Bias And Correlation

This bias describes the reluctance we all have to changing our beliefs. Basically, we seem to hold on to our beliefs even when we no longer have evidence for them. The bias is closely related to another bias I will discuss in §5.1, Confirmation Bias. Confirmation Bias – looking only for evidence supporting our current beliefs – is one method we have of avoiding changing our beliefs, so you could regard the Belief Perseverance Bias as a consequence of the existence of Confirmation Bias. There are other methods though, so Confirmation Bias is just one route to belief perseverance. As is often the case, there is some reason why applying a bias is a sensible approach.

We are constantly becoming aware of new information, which could potentially require us to update some of our beliefs. However, it is often appropriate for our beliefs to be somewhat 'sticky,' meaning that we should not allow our existing beliefs to be instantly overturned by some new information which appears to contradict the belief. The amount of stickiness is probably judiciously determined by attempting to make some consideration of two factors: how pressing and plausible the new data is, and how much disruption would be caused by changing the questioned belief.

Changing any of our beliefs will have ramifications which will be widespread and potentially significant. Sometimes the changes will not matter even though the number of beliefs changed is large. For example, if I persuade you that the moon is less than 100 million miles away from the earth, you will now also believe that it is less than 101 million miles away, and less than 102 million miles away, etc. I have therefore changed an infinite number of your beliefs, but it does not seem very significant. Other times, it will be much more significant. One picture of our belief set, known as the 'coherentist' (Quine 1951) account, sees it as a web which hangs loosely together and can be pictured as a sort of sphere. There are core beliefs which are hard to change and would have dramatic effects if they were changed. An example might be the belief that gravity exists. Further out, there are non-core beliefs, the changing of which would do nothing very much to how we saw the whole belief set. This might be something like which brand of toothpaste is favoured by Donald Trump. Clearly you will require quite extraordinary evidence to change your belief in the existence of gravity, but you will not care much about Donald Trump's toothpaste choice, and so if that information is presented to you, you will likely accept it and move on. So we can see Belief Perseverance Bias as a mechanism which adds efficiency to our methods of updating our belief set. It begins to look reasonable, but let us look at the other side of the picture.

Nestler (2010, p. 35) gives the formal definition when he notes that "belief perseverance has been observed in social perception [...] and self-perception [...] and it is robustly shown that individuals cling to beliefs even when the evidential basis for these beliefs is completely refuted." This is rather remarkable. We do not expect people often to believe claims for which they no longer have any evidence. Our failure to expect this is of course a systematic Theory of Mind error on our part, which will lead to widespread error in predicting the behaviour of others. I will now outline the experimental results that have been obtained on Belief Perseverance Bias.

The seminal experiment is a slightly macabre one involving testing people on the detection of fake and real suicide notes. Ross, Lepper, and Hubbard (1975) asked their subjects to say whether each one was fake or real. After 25 trials, subjects were given feedback indicating that they were either good, bad or indifferent at the task. After receiving this feedback, the subjects were left alone for either five or 25 minutes (Ross, Lepper, and Hubbard 1975, p. 883). Then, subjects were then told that the success, average or fail feedback had in fact been false, and that the "score had been determined randomly" (Ross, Lepper, and Hubbard 1975, p. 883). Surprisingly, subjects continued to think that they were good or bad at the suicide assessment note task. As Ross, Lepper, and Hubbard (1975, p. 884) summarise, "even after debriefing procedures that led subjects to say that they understood the decisive invalidation of initial test results, the subjects continued to assess their performances and abilities as if these test results still possessed some validity."

This is quite striking. One point to note is that people will quite probably be unaware of this bias; if they were aware of it they would alter their beliefs. After all, in the experiment they are shown to believe something about themselves to some extent with *no evidence at all* for that belief. The slightly strange task was chosen partly to ensure that people's views about their relevant abilities were uncorrupted by extra-experimental experience: few people have actually seen a fake or a real suicide note.

There are obviously many scenarios in which this bias will present problems and opportunities in markets. Investors will retain a certain measure of belief in a stock even when the original evidence supporting that belief has been discredited. A more important variant of the problem will arise when attempting to judge when to shift asset classes, which I suggested in Chapter 2 was important in beating the market. Getting the timing right is the hard part; though as I mentioned, one only needs to be approximately right. It is still difficult because one needs to do what everyone else is not doing: i.e. sell equities and buy bonds just when equities are highly valued by irrational exuberance. Clearly Belief Perseverance Bias will tend to make one wait too long.

Similarly, an important parameter of which one should be aware is correlation. One seeks a diversified portfolio which ideally will not have much correlation between its elements. This in principle means that one should have some protection against all of the assets declining at once. This idea has been shown to be lacking by the 2008 crisis, however. Prior to that, sales brokers would often hype exotic asset classes such as wine or fine art on the basis that they lacked correlation with the stock market. So one could assume that wine would not decline when the S&P 500 did and thus safely invest in both. Unfortunately, the 2008 crisis dealt this idea a fatal blow since it transpired that if a crisis is severe enough, all assets decline together.

The mechanism driving this is fairly straightforward. Some investors need to generate cash, either to meet running costs or to meet margin calls if they are leveraged. If they face declines in value in one part of their portfolio, they may well seek to generate liquidity in currently unaffected areas of their portfolio. They may sell wine in order to avoid crystallising losses in their equity portfolio. This, of course, causes the wine market to decline – assuming that we are talking about large enough investors or a relatively illiquid market such as wine. So these investors now face declines across the board, which was exactly the situation the investor was trying to avoid by choosing supposedly uncorrelated asset classes.

Indeed, during the recovery period from the 2008 crisis – and I am tempted to understand this recovery in the same way that one does in relation to 'recovering' alcoholics – trading days were characterised as 'risk-on' and 'risk-off.' This occasionally still happens as late as 2016. It means that *all* risky assets either appreciate or depreciate together in a highly correlated manner. This makes it harder to establish when one should switch from equities to bonds because there is no clear signal when equities rise and bonds fall as there was in the past. I think the only way to address this is to wait for a full recovery from the 2008 crisis – let us hope that this day eventually comes – which will mean that correlations decline and indeed negative correlations between equities and bonds return. Note that this return does not need to be permanent; it just needs to be the case at the time you make the switch.

Worse even than this is that correlation measurements are not stable even when considering past data. Taleb (2012, p. 453) notes that as a trader, he saw that "correlations were never the same in different measurements [...] 0.8 over a long period becomes −0.2 over another long period." This means that two assets can be highly positively correlated in one dataset – meaning that they both go up and down together – and then weakly negatively correlated in another dataset – meaning both that they now move in opposite directions and that they only tend to do so sometimes. So they no longer appear to have much to do with each other. This is very hard to deal with.

I am sure that Taleb (2012) is right about this type of observation, partly because it is within his speciality as a former quantitative options specialist and partly because I have seen it myself. It is visible in the way the prior anti-correlation between equities and bonds became a strong correlation in the immediate post-crisis 'risk-on' and 'risk-off' days. Combining this data problem with Belief Perseverance Bias can mean that one assumes wrongly that correlation remains roughly the same. That could be disastrous. The answer is to be data-driven. While I think it is dangerous to assume that correlations remain stable, I think it is reasonable to act in the belief that they will return to previous states in the future. Bonds will again be anti-correlated with equities at some point. This will, in itself, be a sign that normality has returned to some extent: it is effectively a bet that the business cycle has not been abolished. Another valuable point made by Taleb (2012) is that we can expect characteristics and objects that have been around for a long time to continue to be around for a further long time. We do not need to fear Belief Perseverance Bias in relation to that type of claim because the evidence has not been removed; but in general it is another bias to be avoided in our own thinking. Evidence is decisive and so is the elimination of previously used evidence.

So much for our own performance. On the other side of the coin, we may also expect other market participants to continue to hold on to their prior beliefs longer than they should do if the evidence for them has been weakened or eliminated. This may in part be behind the continued appeal of momentum trading: stocks overshoot both to the upside and to the downside. This effect will only be exacerbated if people have invested money on the basis of prior beliefs which are now outdated. One could look for opportunities in areas where something dramatic and salient has occurred for a particular stock, which has caused it to drop sharply. Market participants will, in some cases, be too slow to return and too cynical in relation to whether the stock can recover from its difficulties. Sometimes this will be correct of course; but we can assume that participants' beliefs will nevertheless be too 'sticky.' That sort of factor may have led to the fact that few people participated in the long post-2009 rally in the S&P 500; a corollary of the fact that few people did it is that doing so was immensely lucrative.

4.2 Representativeness Heuristic

This bias is similar to what is sometimes colloquially expressed as if it looks like a duck and walks like a duck and sounds like a duck, it's a duck. That phrase is almost a heuristic on its own, expressing as it does a fairly useful approximation which is valuable in many everyday situations and wrong in others. For our purposes, we are, of course, much more interested in the occasions when heuristics produce wrong answers. The grain of truth in the phrase lies in the idea that if item X has two or three key characteristics which class Y of objects typically exhibits, then X is a Y. So if you see something feathered that waddles and quacks, you can assume that you are looking at a duck. And most of the time you can, of course. Part of the appeal of this heuristic lies in its repetition of the term 'duck,' which gives its conclusion 'it's a duck' a certain inevitability and persuasiveness. It is known that people can remember phrases that rhyme much more easily than non-rhyming phrases. There is even a Rhyme as Reason Effect where people go even further and decide that rhyming statements are more likely to be true – which I will be discussing later (§4.3).

Tversky and Kahneman (1974, p. 1124) formally define the Representativeness Heuristic[1] as occurring when "probabilities are evaluated by the degree to which A is representative of B, that is, by the degree to which A resembles B." Intuitively, we may regard this as stereotyping, because a typical application of the heuristic will involve people deciding that someone is a librarian because they fit the stereotype of a librarian. The error is also known as 'base rate neglect.' Subjects fail to take account of what should be a much more significant factor in the probability estimate viz. the number of people in the population who are librarians.

This is one example of a theme which will be common throughout this book; how bad we all are at making estimates of probability. As Pinker (2015, p. 334) points out, "many social psychologists have concluded that the mind is not designed to grasp the laws of probability." This is a severe disadvantage in markets and is to be struggled against at all costs. Intelligence and education do not make one immune to these errors. I have two PhDs and I make probability estimation errors all the time. My approach to the problem in this book will be to illustrate many examples of when probability estimates are likely to be wrong so that we can look out for those situations and see what the dramatic effects would be of using a bias.

The Representativeness Heuristic was investigated by giving subjects descriptions of the personalities of a group of persons. Tversky and Kahneman (1974, p. 1124) write that "subjects were told that the group from which the descriptions had been drawn consisted of 70 engineers and 30 lawyers" or vice versa. The subjects were then asked to assess the probability that a given person was an engineer or a lawyer. The descriptions were slanted to be engineer-like or lawyer-like. For example, a stereotypical engineer will enjoy fixing his car at weekends while a stereotypical lawyer will be tenaciously argumentative in personal situations.

Tversky and Kahneman (1974, p. 1125) found that subjects ignored the population probability data. If given an engineer-like profile, they said the person was probably an engineer, even when they had also been told that the sample consisted of 70% lawyers. This is quite a striking result. Ignoring a piece of data which is of great importance is a much stronger and more unexpected result than just according it insufficient weight. The fact that the subjects knew that 70% of the sample were lawyers should have dominated their assessment of the profiles. Optimally, they would have started from the 70% number and adjusted it slightly given the profile.[2]

This takes several forms in real life markets. It has been argued that the Representativeness Heuristic is implicated in bubble-generating investor behaviour. The mechanism is explained by Shiller (2003a, p. 94) as occurring when "people may tend to match stock price patterns into salient categories such as dramatic and persistent price trends, thus leading to feedback dynamics." This means that investors will tend to trade momentum, assuming that moves up or down are similar to previous longer-term moves up or down and thus are new examples of the same sort. This leads to a false prediction of a continued move in the same direction. Note, also, the importance of the term 'salient' here; I will be arguing in §4.4 that salience and vividness also lead to exaggerated probability estimations.

Several unhelpful market effects of the Representativeness Heuristic have been noted by one author who studied the effects by means of an investor questionnaire. Jordan (2003, p. 275) notes that investors perceive a direct connection between "listed on the New Market" and "high growth rates,"[3] neglecting the risk of loss, because some high-growth stocks do, in fact, choose to list on this market. Even if it were the case that many of the stocks on such a junior market have previously been high-growth, this is no reason to skip the analysis of a new potential purchase.

Investors also prefer to invest in companies that have "a good reputation and a good image and thereby neglect or underweight fundamental data and market comparators" (Jordan 2003, p. 275). Reputation and image are at best a fair proxy for the latter, more important factors and in no case a substitute for them.[4] Here we can see how the Representativeness Heuristic can mislead in that factors that can be readily identified are considered in the investment decision to the exclusion of the harder to determine fundamentals. Jordan (2003, p. 275) is also wise to object to "betting on trends" and "naive extrapolation," both of which can be seen as aspects of the Representativeness Heuristic. The mistaken reasoning runs approximately: if a stock has done x, then it is the sort of stock which does x, so it will continue to do x.

The worst problems are found in the arena of funds. The largest amount of fund flows from private investors goes to mutual funds, but investors assess these "by extrapolating past performance into the future uncritically and intuitively" (Jordan 2003, p. 276) as a result of the Representativeness Heuristic. Such an assessment, though, is "extremely questionable" (Jordan 2003, p. 275). Although that is quite a strong statement, I would go even further: such extrapolation is not just questionable, it is so inaccurate as to be downright dangerous.

Funds often come with a star rating from rating agencies; these are unfortunately of little value in predicting future performance. Jordan (2003, p. 283) reports the results of her questionnaire as follows: "only incompetent investors estimated future value fluctuations as clearly lower when a rating was part of the advertising, while competent subjects were not significantly influenced by the ratings." Competence was measured by self-assessment among the subjects who completed the questionnaire; the sample was composed of 263 economics students. This is important, I think, because it means the sample will contain a wide range of competence from individuals with very little, to quite a lot of relevant experience; Jordan (2003, p. 285) confirms in her footnote [1] that some of the students have investment experience. Critically, Jordan (2003, p. 283) concludes that "this shows that in this particular case, the competent subjects are not subject to heuristic influences." That means that avoiding the Representativeness Heuristic is the difference between competence and incompetence, here.

It also means, in the approach I take in this book, that taking account of the Representativeness Heuristic in one's simulation of other investors is crucial to making accurate predictions of their behaviour. In other words, on the line of Short (2015), eliminating bias mismatch is the key to accurate Theory of Mind. This can be done here by matching the bias of O. By that I mean simulating the Representativeness Heuristic and using it to predict the behaviour of others; it remains crucial not to let the Representativeness Heuristic form an element of one's own decision-making in relation to one's own actions.

Similarly, Barberis (2013, p. 16) suggests a mechanism by which the Representativeness Heuristic can lead to bubbles: investors "expect even small samples of data to reflect the properties of the parent population [so] they draw overly strong inferences from these small samples, and this can lead to over-extrapolation." In other words, a period of three days of rising prices in a stock – the 'three white soldiers' of technical terminology – can cause investors to expect that to continue indefinitely and buy accordingly. If enough investors follow that line, the price will rise and they will be encouraged further in an unstable positive feedback loop. Similarly, very large numbers of people think that house prices can only go up in future; this is especially remarkable given that we have recent, striking evidence of the opposite occurring.

The Representativeness Heuristic has been implicated in the extraordinary story of the South Sea Bubble of 1720. This saw four subscriptions for stock trade at wildly inflated prices to the underlying stock value and even more extraordinarily, at inflated prices to each other. This should not have occurred, because the subscriptions had value only derivative on the stock price and there was no rational reason for the different subscriptions to differ in price. Dale, Johnson, and Tang (2005, p. 260) note that the promoter of the scheme made it mirror a lottery he had also promoted, such that "successive issues of subscription receipts mirrored the successive draws of the lottery, which the population had associated with increased excitement and higher prizes." While that was true of the lottery, it was not at all true of the stock subscriptions. We may then now predict that clever marketing and pizzazz can lead to excess valuations and trouble down the line.

There is some scope here to object that the public is more sophisticated today than in 1720, but I think there are significant limits placed on the power of that objection by what one observes of investor behaviour, and the ongoing prevalence of bubbles. Dale, Johnson, and Tang (2005, p. 261) conclude that the "'representativeness heuristic' might well have caused investors to expect the later subscription issues to produce greater returns than the earlier issues." Dale, Johnson, and Tang (2005, p. 261) also note that the "central role of excitement in changing behaviour within speculative markets is well established."

Nofsinger (2016, p. 84) cites some hard data on how much damage is done to investors by succumbing to pizzazz-driven representativeness. He notes that investing in what he calls 'glamour stocks' – which he defines as companies with high growth rates or high P/E ratios – returns on average 11.4% p.a. while investing in unglamorous value stocks returns 18.7% p.a. That is an enormous difference which, moreover, continues to be seen over five years. Note how strange it is to consider a high P/E ratio stock attractive. The P/E ratio or price/earnings ratio is, oversimplifying slightly, how many years you would to wait to get all of your money back if all the company's earnings were paid to you. You want that number to be closer to 10 than 20. If it is closer to 20, the market has priced the stock for very high growth which had better be delivered or the stock will tank. Incidentally, using a P/E ratio discipline would have kept you out of the dot.com bubble because few of those firms had any earnings. Hirshleifer (2001, p. 1569) points to a further market application of the Representativeness Heuristic when he notes that if "investors see a sequence of growing earnings, they tend to conclude (wrongly) that the firm is in a growth regime, and over-extrapolate trends, which is arguably reminiscent of representativeness." If a series of growing numbers for earnings is considered, it appears to be representative of an infinite series of growing numbers and the probability that the earnings will continue to grow indefinitely is over-estimated. In fact, it is impossible for any stock to increase its earnings indefinitely and so that probability must be assessed at zero. This tendency to extrapolation is always wrong, not just because no company can increase earnings forever, but also because of the phenomenon of regression to the mean, which is more likely to be an early cause of dismay.

Many press stories achieve excess impact by virtue of relying covertly on aspects of the Representativeness Heuristic. For example, Soros was quoted in the press as saying that when he looks "at the financial markets there is a serious challenge which reminds me of the crisis we had in 2008."[5] This was widely reported because it is arresting for investors as a result of the Representativeness Heuristic. The chain of thought is approximately as follows.

1. Soros is a skilled and successful investor
2. Skilled and successful investors will make true statements about investment
3. Soros says 2016 has characteristics that 2008 had

4. 2008 was a catastrophic scenario for equity investors
5. 2016 is also a catastrophic scenario for equity investors

Note that there are potentially two uses of the Representativeness Heuristic in the chain here; as well as some influence of the Halo Effect (§8.2). The less significant one, which nevertheless opens up a way of questioning the validity of the argument, is related to the assessment of the truth value of the initial claim. It appears in item 2, above. The class 'statements by Soros' is accorded a high truth value merely because Soros has made them. Any given statement by him is seen as stereotypically true since much of what he says about investing is true. Now I am not suggesting for a second that we should ignore anything said by Soros or other specialists. But we should certainly examine it carefully rather than assume it is correct because it is said by someone famous. Note the affective import of the claim. Is it possible that some investors will trade on the basis of the immediate negative impact – the fear, in other words – and are we certain already that this is the right trade? If not, then consider trading against it.

It is also perhaps relevant that Soros is reported at the time of writing (May 2016) to own more than two million bearish put options on the S&P 500. It must afford a man singular pleasure to be able to short an asset and then disparage it in public, secure in the knowledge that such public disapprobation will alone suffice to cause the asset to depreciate. Note again that it is not enough to make Soros *right* that the S&P 500 declines from here. It has to decline and do so for the reasons he gives.

The other, more significant application of the Representativeness Heuristic is seen in the final item, 5, above. This says that 2016 is the same as 2008 because it shares some characteristics with it. So this is what we want to examine carefully. What are these shared characteristics? Soros's underlying point is that China is grappling with a difficult transition period to somewhat lower growth and a consumption-led rather than investment-led model. This seems true; it is at least widely accepted in markets.

So the first test is passed: the argument appears to have a sound premise. The second premise in this sub-argument is that 2016 is the same as 2008. But which of those statements about China was also true in 2008? None of them, on the face of it.

Now, the question as to what actually caused the post 2007/2008 crisis is an exceptionally complex one; I have seen probably a dozen candidate groups of explanations, any one of which could be true. Worse, it could also be a complex weighted combination of several of the different candidates. Even worse, there is nothing empirical or otherwise that can be done which will answer the question decisively. (Though that means you do have to look at events with the sort of analytical approach I am aiming to exemplify here; demonstrating that reading this book is a valuable use of time.)

One of the major candidate explanations does invoke China. It notes that social security spending is relatively low in that country and that this results in a high savings rate there as people look after their own futures in the expectation that the state will not do it for them. This resulted, according to the explanation, in a 'wall of money' in search of a safe and remunerative home. It found that home in the open US real estate markets, as a result of which there was an asset price bubble accompanied by declines in mortgage underwriting standards. There is no need to be very careful making mortgage loans when house prices are rising dramatically, if you also make the error of assuming that such a situation is irreversible. As a general rule, all situations are not just reversible but must be reversed; this applies to bad news as well as good. When that bubble burst, the adverse effects were transmitted globally via the mechanism of price-declines in mortgage-backed securities, and this caused the crisis. (For what it's worth, I think this is the most plausible explanation of the origins of the 2008 crisis.) But note that beyond the involvement of China in both accounts, there is nothing in common between the 2008 account and the 2016 account. So we do not yet have reason to accept the claim that 2016 and 2008 are the same. And even if we did, we would be falling into using the Representativeness Heuristic if we agreed that 2016 was like 2008 just because we found one of the same processes going on both times in China. Two items might quack and waddle, but that is nowhere near enough to say that they are both ducks.

At this point, a natural objection is to think, again, that I am saying that Soros is just wrong here and we should ignore him. That looks dangerous, because Soros is a much better investor than any of us. My response is to say that we need to look deeper. It might be that Soros has a better argument than the one I have outlined above. It might just be that Soros's only aim in invoking the 2008/2016 comparison was to underline his view of the gravity of the situation, rather than their similar origins and causation. Fine, but let us look deeper than just trading off the initial emotional impact.

Note that I am using the phrase 'chain of thought' loosely here. I do not claim that anyone need go through this step-by-step argument explicitly. But if your initial reaction to Soros's remarks was concern, as mine was, it is likely that you have implicitly gone through the stages without any of what is termed 'phenomenology.' Phenomenology is a term used in philosophy and psychology to mean something like 'what it was like for you.' For example, there is something it is like to taste strawberry ice cream and something it is like to taste vanilla ice cream, and the two things are different and hard to describe in words. They have, in the jargon, 'distinct phenomenology.' In the case of the above chain where you just got to the answer, there was no phenomenology associated with the chain itself, and your only phenomenology was the affectively negative outcome.

I think that the Representativeness Heuristic could be the cause of some of the common and dangerous phenomena of bubbles in markets and stocks. As Marks (2011, p. 38) puts it, investors can have "psychology that is too positive" and they can "associate exciting stories and pizzazz with high potential returns." This is a kind of reverse and inaccurate association effect. It is clear that actually obtaining high returns is going to be very exciting every time. So, there is a tendency to associate the two. And any time two things – A and B – are associated or correlated, someone will get the idea that A causes B, or vice versa. This is another exemplification of the sort of pizzazz bias I mentioned above in the context of the South Sea Bubble.

This sort of causation argument is often false and always unprovable since we cannot observe causation (Hume 1739); and dangerous because we have the illusion that we can observe causation (Taleb 2012, p. 199). The association of A and B could be random, or it could be that unknown event C causes both A and B, making them look correlated. We could also be observing causation in action, but be completely mistaken about what the underlying causes are. Hirshleifer (2001, p. 1560) reports that "cloud cover in the city of a country's major stock exchange, is associated with low daily stock index returns." This suggests that it is the mood of traders that is the causal agent, but this is not what most people would expect. Alternatively, this is, itself, a further example of the 'causation illusion.'

In this case, the problem is that since high returns are always accompanied by excitement, people can come to think in a logical fallacy that excitement must always be accompanied by high returns. To see why this is false, note that the fact that all snow is white does not entail that all white things are snow. I will first discuss the logic involved here and then look at a real case.

Also, as Taleb (2012, p. 200) reminds us, selection bias in reporting, or 'cherry picking' is widespread, which is another "reason why one should trust the disconfirmatory rather than the confirmatory." There are clear links here to Confirmation Bias, of which there will be more in §5.1. Traders look very good when they only report their winners. It is important to be wary of cherry picking in one's analysis of one's own results, just as much as those of others. There can also be what we might term 'lemon picking;' one could make one's own performance look relatively better by comparing it to a disadvantageous selection of trades concluded by others. All of this is to be avoided in the interests of an objective understanding of the data.

One valuable approach is to start with the fundamental idea that confirmation of a hypothesis can only be made by trying to break it. When you have tried extremely hard to break it and have failed, you can work on the basis that the hypothesis is true. Better yet, negate the hypothesis and try to find counterexamples. For example, say your hypothesis is that stocks sometimes rise on a Tuesday. Negating it gives you the strong claim that stocks never rise on a Tuesday. Look for Tuesdays when stocks rise. That should be quite easy and you have falsified the negative hypothesis: it is false that stocks never rise on a Tuesday and so you have proven the – admittedly weak – hypothesis that stocks sometimes rise on a Tuesday. I will return to this question of strong and weak hypotheses in §5.1.

For a more sophisticated example, consider the hypothesis that cold weather makes people depressed. Depressed people become risk averse (Kramer 2008,

p. 129) and sell stocks. Look for periods when cold weather is accompanied by rising stocks. This, by the way, is a serious claim; it is behind the idea that one should go long Swedish stocks in the European Spring and then sell them all and go long Australian stocks in the European Autumn, as Australia starts to warm up. If you want to run with that idea, you had better try to break the hypothesis first. Another hypothesis is the one that says that Apple stock always rises sharply around the release of a new iPhone and declines in the interim. By now, it should be clear that you are much more interested in finding occasions when this is false. That might lead you to a restated hypothesis, perhaps 'Apple stock rises 75% of the time when a new iPhone is released.' That might be harder to falsify – what percentage of actual years in which AAPL falls on new release dates is *inconsistent* with a 75% overall probability? – but more tradable.

I now turn to a real case where the logical error of 'A therefore B, B; conclude: A' can lead one astray in the incarnation of the purported two-way link between excitement and returns. To spell it out, let us call A high returns and B excitement. High returns will be accompanied by excitement – this is true. One error is to think that this rule means that all high returns will be foretold by excitement. The other, even more dangerous error is to think that if B – excitement – is present, high returns are guaranteed. Plenty of investments that eventually produce high returns will be accompanied by excitement, but plenty will appear quite dull to begin with. I used to be in a private equity arm of an investment bank. The arm specialised in buying stable, dull companies in unexciting industries. The point was that these companies were excellent bearers of debt. They could be securitised – meaning that their cashflows could be parcelled up and sold in slices to different investors in tradable bonds. Illiquid assets became liquid ones, meaning that the illiquidity premium was eliminated and the value of the cashflows more nearly realised – "Dull, ignored, possibly tarnished and beaten-down securities [...] are often the ones value investors favour for high returns" (Marks 2011, p. 38).

The private equity outfit which I worked for was more-or-less the first to apply this technique widely in the UK. As a result, it was able to buy some 'boring' assets at prices the market thought was fair, without much fanfare. Sure, it was exciting enough to be involved in the deals, but to the average investor, there would have been no excitement. These would have been companies that were clearly not going to double their revenues every year, like the tech companies that, at the same time, were about to enter their most frenzied stage in the dot-com bubble.

Nevertheless, one major asset was securitised for more than the purchase price. This means that the equity was free, or even had a negative cost. Let me spell out what that means. Since the debt amount raised was more than the purchase price of the asset, no additional funds were required to buy the company. There was also a surplus which meant there was an immediate return on owning the asset. But best of all, we owned the equity or future cashflows of the company over and above what was needed to service the debt. Normally one calculates a return on capital for an investment. 10% is, I suspect, a very good return nowadays. At the time in question, in the late 90s, private equity firms were aiming for something not too far short of 20% a year, with the idea being that in a great investment, you would more than double your money in a standard five-year holding period. The return on investment for the company I have just described was infinite, because there was no capital at risk – at least after the period of about three months that it took us to get the securitisation away. Many deals were less successful. None were as successful as the one I have just described, though there was one I looked at, again in the late '90s, which I understand has just been exited in 2015. That is a very long holding period, but I think most investors could cope with that if they obtained the reported return of 8× or 9× the initial investment. The point is that none of these transactions involved exciting assets. They were companies that owned fairly down-at-heel barracks, or service stations serving tired sausages to equally jaded drivers. There need be no excitement about a great investment opportunity, and an affective involvement will cloud your judgment. As for pizzazz – any sales pitch which needs that to get you interested needs to be treated with extreme caution. People like pizzazz. It attracts them for no intellectual reason; it is just fun. There is nothing wrong with that in many contexts – but do you want to make your investment choices that way?

4.3 Rhyme As Reason Effect

We have all heard the phrase 'Sell in May and go away.' There are many phrases like this in life, generally and in the markets. The Rhyme as Reason Effect is observed when a subject acts as though a piece of action guidance which rhymes is more valuable than one which does not. The rhyme then *becomes* the reason, as opposed to remaining where it should: as an aid to remembering the reason.

Such tags are highly memorable as a result of the rhyme, and this tends to make them frequently said and frequently paid attention to. They are, in the terms of Gladwell (2000, p. 25 et seq.), "sticky," or just more likely to stick around in our memory whether we like it or not. It may be fine to pay attention to such rhyming ideas just in case there is a grain of truth to them; though even this carries a risk because mere consideration can result in infection. But relying on them solely on that basis is a mistake. Since whether a heuristic is useful or not is orthogonal to whether or not it rhymes, stickiness is more likely to benefit the heuristic rather than the host. Sometimes rhyme will suffice to make the tag sticky even if it harms the host. For example, Gladwell (2000, p. 25), mentions a successful advertising line from 1954, "Winston tastes good like a cigarette should." The year 1954 is quite early on in the debate about cigarettes and health; this discussion scarcely remains a debate today. This is also an early example of extra stickiness being added to a tag by its lack of grammar – technically it should have been as a cigarette should. So, for those who think grammatical standards should be maintained, there is additional damage done by the tag beyond its obstruction of the effectiveness of health-related anti-smoking campaigning. Gladwell (2000, p. 25) notes that most Americans today can complete the line, which is remarkable. What other ephemeral artefacts of US culture from the mid-50s are still extant in everyone's mind? It is not a counter argument here to mention products such as, for example, Coke, which were available then and are available now. Coke is still a widely-known product because it is still sold and much-advertised today. One reason that rhyming claims look more convincing to us could be extrapolated from evidence noted by Wright *et al.* (2012, p. 253) to the effect that repetition "has proven effective in bolstering the believability of product claims." We have all had the experience of a song lyric repeating in our head for no apparent reason, which is beyond our control and can be quite annoying. Part of the stickiness of such lyrics is drawn from their rhyming nature, and so it could be that rhyming tags are repeated more often, conceivably subconsciously, and thus gain plausibility from mere repetition.

Another possibility is shown by evidence gathered by McGlone and Tofighbakhsh (2000) who conclude that rhyme, as well as repetition, "affords statements an enhancement in processing fluency that can be misattributed to heightened conviction about their truthfulness." This means that our mental dealings with rhyming statements are easier than with non-rhyming statements, and this makes us more likely to think they are true. What McGlone and Tofighbakhsh (2000, p. 424) measured was that "rhyming aphorisms in their original form (e.g., 'What sobriety conceals, alcohol reveals') were judged to be more accurate than modified versions that did not preserve rhyme ('What sobriety conceals, alcohol unmasks')." This is irrational because the truth probability of the two statements must be independent of their phrasing – in fact, arguably we have only one statement here in two forms. Helpfully, for our purposes, McGlone and Tofighbakhsh (2000) also found that warning their subjects to assess truth value of aphorisms by their propositional content rather than on their aesthetic qualities including, primarily, rhyme, had a salutary influence with a substantial attenuation of the Rhyme as Reason Effect.

J. Sutton (2010, §3.5) includes rhymes in "various kinds of memory scaffolding" along with diagrams, sketchpads and rituals among "artificial memory techniques" which aid recall. The distinction, of course, is that we only choose to draw a diagram, or make a sketch, or engage in a mnemonic ritual when we want to. This will optimally be when we have correctly decided that what we want to recall is worth recalling. We are aware of the great mnemonic boost given to a tag by making it rhyme. We may on occasions use that deliberately by making up and repeating a mini-rhyme to ourselves a few times. But we can lack the choice about whether a rhyming tag sticks. I suggest that the line I gave above about Winston cigarettes is sticky enough to persist in the memory irrespective of whether you want it to. This will be true even for UK resident non-smokers, who presumably have little interest, and receive little benefit from recalling such a line. Try the experiment of getting someone to ask you to complete 'Winston tastes good ... ' in a year from now and see if the rest is still there.

Poole (2008, p. 208) notes that sometimes memories which have been repressed in wider society, perhaps in relation to shameful topics like slavery, will nevertheless leave traces in nursery rhymes. This provides a further example of the extra stickiness of rhyme. Even when a society has made strenuous efforts to eliminate consideration or discussion of certain topics, they can persist in the form of rhyme. There is a further indication here that rhyme can be bad for you, because you cannot get rid of it whether you want to or not (and quite irrespective of whether you should want to or not: I make no point here in relation to slavery).

Very often, there will be a grain of truth in a rhyming tag; after all the relevant 'meme' had to stick around, and an element of truth could have been what made the difference. The term 'meme' was introduced by Dawkins (1976) and refers to a replicator similar to a gene but in the space of ideas or culture. Successful memes reproduce themselves and are, therefore, still here. Sometimes a meme or idea will be successful because it is true. But there are many other mechanisms by which a meme can reproduce itself in human society when it is not true, and even deleterious to the host. One characteristic a meme could have could be avoiding making any testable predictions. That makes it unfalsifiable and, therefore, not a basis for useful hypothesis. This is one way in which religious beliefs persist (Dennett 2007), though it also seems to be true in some religions that they make testable predictions which do not transpire but this is not seen as a problem by adherents.

As said, another way for a heuristic to survive is for it to rhyme. That is a useful characteristic for a 'selfish meme' to have in that it will aid its replication, but it does nothing for its likely truth value. The use here of 'selfish' by Dawkins (1976) has been much misunderstood. The apparent surface meaning to the effect that people have genes that make them selfish is not what Dawkins (1976) intended; it is, in fact, almost the opposite of what he intended. He meant that the genes or memes were, to some extent, metaphorically self-interested. This is a much more subtle and interesting idea. It has also received criticism, however. For example, Midgley (1979, p. 439) has alleged that "[g]enes cannot be selfish or unselfish, any more than atoms can be jealous." I think this criticism is true but unhelpful.

I agree that Midgley (1979) is right to think that genes and atoms are structures of DNA, or protons, neutrons and electrons that are not the right type of item to which we could sensibly ascribe personality traits such as self-interest. But this is only right if we are using a 'thick' understanding of the term self-interest, which includes some sort of self-awareness. Being selfish in the way I am sometimes includes being aware of myself and being interested in fostering outcomes which benefit that self. This though is not what Dawkins (1976) means. He intends to argue for the much more pure and simple evolutionary claim that the memes and genes which survived are still here because they had characteristics that helped them survive. It seems to me that this simpler claim is very hard to argue against. It looks as though objecting to it would involve suggesting that fitness for survival is not an aid to survival. With this in hand, it becomes clear that what has helped a meme survive is just self-identical: i.e. characteristics that help a meme survive are just characteristics that help a meme survive which, importantly, are not identical to characteristics which help the host survive or prosper.

To illustrate this, I will consider a bad argument against natural selection on the basis of the existence of homosexuality. It will not matter for our purposes that the argument is bad. I will also not consider why the argument is bad; it seems to me that there are obvious good objections. The argument runs as follows.

- Homosexual people are less likely to have children
- Natural selection means that only traits which do not make people less likely to have children will be selected
- Natural selection means that there are no homosexual people
- Contrary to this, there are homosexual people
- Conclude: natural selection is a false account

As said, there are many problems with this argument. What is interesting for us, though, is one attempt to provide a genetic response, because it illustrates the distinction between gene characteristics that help the gene survive and gene characteristics that help the host to reproduce. The genetic response aimed to show that there was a genetic basis to male homosexuality and that this gene was multifunctional. It had the effect in female relatives of increasing the number of children they had. Again, I will not opine on the quality of this argument or the science underpinning it. The point for us is that, if this response is correct, we can clearly see how gene or meme characteristics which benefit the gene or meme are distinct from gene or meme characteristics which benefit the host. The gene or meme had, overall, characteristics which ensured it would be more widely replicated even if that meant that some hosts did not reproduce themselves.

How should we respond to this? We should examine the meme critically to establish what has helped it replicate. To what extent has its survival depended on truth and value to the host – which may well be separate questions – and to what extent has it depended on purely 'selfish' characteristics, which only aid the meme in replicating? As discussed above in §4.2, the wider point is to try to break the hypothesis represented by the meme. We should try to find an occasion when selling in May would have been a bad idea. And we may safely assume that it is impossible that the fact that a heuristic can be stated in rhyme can make it more likely to be true, while it is highly likely that it can contribute to its survival in the evolutionary marketplace of ideas.

Consider other non-rhyming heuristics to examine the converse question: if rhyming makes a heuristic better, then non-rhyming should make it relatively worse. A couple of sample heuristics often heard in the market would be 'never fight the tape' and 'never fight the Fed.' These both encapsulate ideas which have been pursued with some success. The first is a slogan for momentum traders, who trade on the basis that what has just been happening will continue to happen. A rising stock will continue to rise. The answer, of course, is that it will continue to rise until it stops rising, which is not useful. The second heuristic expresses the idea that the Federal Reserve is more powerful in the markets than you are, if you are an individual investor. If the Fed is trying to keep long bond yields down, then do not trade on the basis that they will fail.

So we have one rule of thumb which looks false, and one which looks true. Would either be more true, or more compelling, or more valuable if they rhymed? They might be more compelling, but they would not be more true if stated as 'always gape at the tape' or 'always bed the Fed.' (I appreciate these are terrible rhymes; the point, though, is that introducing rhyme does not alter the effectiveness or otherwise of the rules.) Since "usually people who pay less attention to information tend to be more likely to use heuristics to simplify decision making" (Labroo, Lambotte, and Zhang 2009, p. 1517),[6] the answer here as elsewhere will be either to acquire information to support the heuristic, or replace it, or reframe the question so that it becomes simple enough to answer formally.

The same authors make another useful point in the context of 'rhyme as reason' when they note that "people hold the 'what is memorable is important' illusion" (Labroo, Lambotte, and Zhang 2009, p. 1517). This could explain what is behind the Rhyme as Reason Effect. Since we can recall rhymes very easily, we believe that they must contain important information.

Stated this way, the idea looks ludicrous. But do not estimate the insidious effects that such a meme might have; which might also be unknown because they are subconscious. There is no way to be sure that it is not affecting a trading decision. What you can do is to write down all the reasons you have for conducting a particular trade. None of them should rhyme. You can also expect that market participants will be influenced by the Rhyme as Reason Effect even though they will deny this. McGlone and Tofighbakhsh (2000, p. 426) asked their subjects whether they held the "explicit belief that rhyming aphorisms are more accurate than non-rhyming ones" to which all subjects responded "'no' (and many gave us quizzical looks)." The "quizzical looks" element of the response suggests that subjects found the hypothesis involved – that the Rhyme as Reason Effect exists – highly implausible, so it can for that reason be highly unhelpful for market participants. This suggests that if rhyming statements have been found wanting under analysis, it is worth considering trading on the basis that they are wrong but that some market participants will act as though they believe them without actually admitting that they believe them.

4.4 Availability Heuristic

This heuristic also looks plausible at first glance, as many of them do. People use it when they assume that the probability of an event is to be estimated by how much difficulty one has in thinking of an example of the event in question. This is going to be a lot better than nothing, as can be seen from the following two examples. What is the probability that a green dragon will be observed in Manhattan? What is the probability that a yellow cab will be observed in Manhattan? Searching one's memory extremely hard will reveal no occasions of the former type, while one will be overwhelmed with many examples of the second type of event; it may, in fact, be hard to tell them apart, but that is not a problem here. In both of these cases and in a large array of other ones, the Availability Heuristic gets the probability estimates exactly right. There is a 0% probability of observing a green dragon in Manhattan and an extremely high probability of observing a yellow cab.

Where the Availability Heuristic breaks down is in relation to probability assessments of events where they are harder or easier to think of for reasons unrelated to how often they have occurred. Some events are simply easier to recall. They might be more vivid or salient than others, or they might have other characteristics which make them memorable. Perhaps they are stored in the form of narratives that occurred to a friend, or maybe they are phrased in rhyming terms (§4.3). This is consistent with evidence noted by Wright *et al.* (2012, p. 254) to the effect that marketing claims "are rated as higher in validity when they are written concretely rather than abstractly." Hirshleifer (2001, p. 1546) notes that "people may overreact to information that is easily processed, that is, scenarios and concrete examples," thus suggesting that the over-reaction comes about simply because the information comes easily to hand. The corollary, naturally, is that abstract information may be used less even if it is more useful.

Formally, Tversky and Kahneman (1973, p. 208) write that "[a] person is said to employ the availability heuristic whenever he estimates frequency or probability by the ease with which instances or associations could be brought to mind." For example, "one may assess the divorce rate in a given community by recalling divorces among one's acquaintances" (Tversky and Kahneman 1973, p. 208). This is reasonable as a first approximation, but will be subject to inaccuracy depending on the events of one's life. If one happens to know many divorced people, one will likely over-estimate the prevalence of divorce in wider society.

Tversky and Kahneman (1973) measured the Availability Heuristic by asking subjects to rate the probabilities of certain syllables occurring in words. They found that the subjects' responses were driven by the ease with which they could think of examples, rather than the actual probabilities, even though subjects obviously had a great deal of experience of words in their native languages. Tversky and Kahneman (1973, p. 212) found that subjects "erroneously judged words beginning with re to be more frequent than words ending with re." This came about because it is easier to think of words beginning with re than ending with re, because it is generally easier to think of words with a specified beginning than with a specified ending. This means the words beginning with re were much more available and this produced the faulty probability estimate.

Two further factors feed into availability: salience and vividness. Simply put, salient and vivid events are much more available. Salient, here, means conspicuous or noticeable, i.e. we are highly likely to notice something which is salient. Vivid could mean visually striking or bright, or it could indicate those same terms in a non-visual metaphorical sense. We are also likely to notice anything which is vivid. Items can be both salient and vivid; they can be salient without being vivid though, so we need both terms. Something cannot be available if it is not noticed, so we have an initial explanation as to why salience and vividness increases availability. It could also be true that salient and vivid events are more available because they are more memorable, but we do not need to adjudicate on that separable question here. Hirshleifer (2001, p. 1543) notes that "salient cues weaken the effects of less salient ones" irrespective of which of the cues carries most importance.

The source of irrationality here is that the Availability Heuristic will cause errors in probability estimation, which is highly likely to result in sub-optimal performance in markets. These errors will derive from the excess availability of salient and vivid events as compared to equally instructive but less salient or vivid events. Highly salient or vivid events will warp probability judgments via their increased availability. Taleb (2008, pp. 79–80) gives several examples of this form, including a story of someone who heard of someone's relative who was mugged in Central Park. This is likely to be much more salient for them than the statistics relating to muggings in Central Park and therefore much more available. It will also be much more vivid because we can easily imagine the terror of being mugged and indeed will automatically do so when hearing the story. This is especially true if one has spent time in Central Park: it is easy to 'paint' the story on to a known background. Persons hearing such stories will likely greatly overestimate the probability of being mugged in Central Park.

So, such a story is highly vivid, and a vivid story can enhance noticeability and hence availability, but the vividness of a story is different to the vividness of being present. This vividness of actually being the mugging victim in Central Park is so high that we can easily imagine someone vowing never to enter the park again, whatever one says to them about the statistical probability of being mugged. Neither type of vividness – that attaching to the story or, even more so, the extreme vividness of a memory of actually being mugged – does anything to the actual probability of being mugged in Central Park. That, however, is the only relevant calculation in deciding whether to enter Central Park again.

Similarly, we may consider the highly salient and vivid example of shark attacks. We have all read about these a lot and they sound awful; the film *Jaws* with its apocalyptically threatening music cannot have helped. This makes estimates of the probability of shark attacks highly inaccurate on the high side. Levitt and Dubner (2010, pp. 14–15) note that the "media hysteria" obscures the fact that there were only 68 shark attacks *globally* in 2001 of which four were fatal. They also mention that elephant attacks killed 200 people that year but there are no media reports or scary movies.

We may also consider air crashes. These are salient and vivid enough to be the subject of a popular and informative TV series with many episodes, called 'Air

Crash Investigations' or 'Mayday.' People are, wrongly, more afraid of planes than cars (Pinker 2015, p. 343). One might think that the chances of being in a plane crash are high, and the chances of dying in one also very high. In fact, you can get on a plane every day for 10,000 years without being in a crash and even if you are, you have more than a 50% chance of surviving. There will probably also be an element of selection bias here in that we do not see documentaries specifically about planes landing safely, or crashes which cause no injuries. Shiller (2003b, p. 88) makes a similar and telling point when he notes the "famous example of overreaction to vivid images" seen in "the public's interest in insurance against their death in a crash of an airplane they are about to board, even if the insurance is wildly overpriced."

Finally in this context, we may consider the at one time prominent and notorious claim that "an unmarried American woman over 40 is as likely to be killed by a terrorist as to experience matrimony," a claim which rose to some prominence in the late 80s. This claim has a number of properties. It exhibits vividness, salience, and falsehood. The origin of the claim was a *Newsweek* article published in 1986. It reported accurately on the findings of a Harvard sociology professor in relation to the probability of future marriage. Cherlin (1990) writes: "those who remained single until age 35 would have only a 5% chance; and at age 40 the chance would be a mere 1%." The claim that this was less than the chance of being killed by a terrorist was added in a soundbite summary of the *Newsweek* article, it is said, as a joke. Later studies made very different predictions because they used a better statistical approach, finding "a 40-year-old had a 17% to 23% chance" of marrying later.

As we have seen, there are a number of explanations available for the prevalence of the 'terrorist' claim. It is highly salient to women who want to get married, which is a fairly large group. Its vivid nature is another reason for it to be highly available. It has immediate implications for action – get married early, rather than late, if you want to get married. More people will have heard the soundbite than read the *Newsweek* article; more people will have read the *Newsweek* article than the Harvard study it was based on; very few people will have also noticed the follow-up studies discrediting the initial claim; many people overestimate the chances of terrorism because terrorist acts are so salient and vivid – arguably, that is their aim.

It is also very easy to forget that the sample of women of 40 who are single is composed more heavily than a random sample would be of women who have chosen to remain single until that age. This is a smaller group than those who have married between 30–35, 35–40 and it is much more likely to remain single because after all, this is the subset that has not wanted to get married thus far, it appears. There is also a group of women who have not married but can also not be well described as single against their wishes because they have been in long-term relationships without marriage. There are also lesbians, since the data relates to a period before same sex marriage. All of these women are not single against their wishes.

The root problem here is the automatic and spurious extrapolation to the two salient but false claims that the 40-year-old single group is composed largely of women who spent the entirety of their 30s trying and failing to get married and also that the 40-year-old single group is not much smaller than the 30-year-old single group. There is also likely a propensity to hear 'will never marry' as 'will always be single' or 'will always be alone,' neither of which is at all entailed. All of these types of error are best avoided. All of these unhelpful effects are exacerbated by the fact that we "judge information that feels easy to recall as important" (Labroo, Lambotte, and Zhang 2009, p. 1517) so salient factors are even given excess weighting in our judgments.

In outlining vividness, Evans (1990, p. 27) credits Nisbett and Ross (1980) with the observation that in our reasoning, we "overweight vivid, concrete information and underweight dull, pallid and abstract information." This is intuitively plausible, just from considering that we prefer the vivid to the dull. More vivid information is more available. Evans (1990) again relies on Nisbett and Ross to supply three characteristics of vividness, which are "(1) emotional interest; (2) concreteness and imageability and (3) temporal and spatial proximity." Nothing which is abstract can meet these three characteristics: not (1) because the abstract holds little emotional interest – and if you think that politics, for example, is emotionally engaging and abstract you have forgotten the rule that the political is personal; not (2) by definition and not (3) because the abstract has no temporal or physical location and so cannot be proximate on either measure. So for these reasons we can understand an observation made by Taleb (2007, p. 37) to the effect that as a derivatives trader he "noticed that people do not like to insure against something abstract." Quite so: because they cannot persuade themselves that anything abstract is real and probable. Taleb (2007, p. 37) continues to note that "the risk that merits their attention is always something vivid" which underlines the point.

So, salient and vivid items are more available and receive higher probability estimates. One message here would be, I think, to avoid taking bets where the outcomes are particularly salient and vivid. Or, at least, only to do so when you have some alternate handle on the probability of the outcome than how salient and vivid it is. For example, you will often see football bets offered in betting shops of the form 'Arsenal to win and Sanchez to score first.' This is a combination of two events with a fair probability. Arsenal are a top team and win a lot of matches; though obviously our assessment of whether they will win any given match should be adjusted for the quality of their opponents. It remains true, though, that Arsenal winning a game is a highly available, vivid outcome and anyone falling prey to the Availability Heuristic will likely over-estimate the probability of an Arsenal win.

This same effect is even more striking in the case of the second element. Sanchez scores a lot of goals and every time he does so, it is a highly vivid event, especially for the sort of people likely to be considering betting on Arsenal. It is very easy to imagine Sanchez scoring a goal, which will appear very similar to the probability of Sanchez scoring the first goal, if we are not careful. Actually, of course, the probability of Sanchez scoring the first goal is much less than the probability of Sanchez scoring a goal. It is nevertheless highly emotionally interesting and imageable, which gives it high vividness according to the first two of the Nisbett and Ross criteria. Note that there is no difference in salience and vividness between the idea of Sanchez scoring the first goal and Sanchez scoring any goal – these are the same image – which could easily lead to mistaking two very different probabilities as being similar. It is unclear what value we should assign to the third criterion, but it might be that people who have watched Arsenal play live – again, likely to be a fairly high proportion of people who might make a bet on Arsenal – might feel a spatial and temporal proximity to the relevant action. And anyone who has seen a street full of locals in Thailand clustering around a Premier League broadcast knows that spatial proximity may become delinked from geography and boosted by the excitement of others. All of this will cause people to over-estimate the probability of the two events needed to win, and will mean that one would be better off taking the bookmaker's side of this bet. As is always the case, of course, it is their profession to get it right and they go bust if they do not.

One might also think that the Availability Heuristic lies behind what Taleb (2008, p. 50) complains of: our tendency to focus on "too specific a list of Black Swans (at the expense of others that do not easily come to mind)." A Black Swan is a rare and unpredicted event which is, in the compelling analysis of Taleb (2008), extremely dangerous for persons using bell curve statistics on past data. It might also be termed the 'fat tails' problem since, in distributions which actually are well-described by bell curves, extreme events are very rare. The central point of Taleb (2008) is that financial markets are not governed by bell curves. Worse, there is nothing in the past that can prevent the occurrence of a future event which is ten times worse than any prior event. Firms run stress tests asking questions like 'how would this portfolio perform in another 2007–2008 scenario?' which is an interesting question, but does not address the possibility of a much worse outcome. So, ignoring this sort of possibility is a mistake.

The first line of defence of someone who has listed some Black Swans and ignored some others that are harder to think of, is simply that since they are harder to think of, they have not thought of them. This, of course, will not do. But the Availability Heuristic also undermines the likely second line of defence, which would be that the investor will claim that they have 'thought of everything that is likely to happen.' That would be a form of the Availability Heuristic because it assigns a probability estimate of an event X based on how easy it is to think of an example of event X. That is a bad way to estimate a probability and, therefore, a bad way to decide what is worth worrying about.

We can now understand why Taleb (2008, p. 107) says that he never reads newspapers. He says that he has ceased to do this because the information contained in them is not useful. I think he is right to think that often the information includes dubious arguments, especially about the causation of events in the financial markets, but I disagree that this means you should not read newspapers. You should read them less in order to find out what is happening but, rather, to find out *what people think* is happening. After all, it is a rare day when a bad news story does not move a stock and, if the story is as often wrong as right, that has to represent a frequent source of opportunities.

I now turn to the effects of the Availability Heuristic in financial markets. As one example, Hirshleifer (2001, p. 1560) points out that "[i]rrelevant, redundant, or old news affects security prices when presented saliently," which is remarkable. It will always be worth asking whether some salient re-presentation of news which should not now affect prices has been so re-presented by someone with an axe to grind. The next question will be for how long the market will labour under the influence of the salient but invalid.

Evidence has been provided to show that such effects are notable under simulated market conditions. Ackert et al. (2009) designed an intelligent experiment in which students participated in a market for stocks which had a 2% chance of paying a dividend of $20. This, of course, is worth $0.40 in a one-shot simulation. Nevertheless, Ackert et al. (2009) found dramatic bubbles developing in half of their experimental runs in one version of their experiment. This version had ten trading sessions, so there were ten 2% chances of obtaining the $20 payoff. Since each chance is worth $0.40, the 10 chances are worth $4.00.

Despite this, Ackert et al. (2009, p. 729) report bubble patterns developing in 6 of their 12 reported experimental runs. In one, the remarkable price after the first period exceeded $20 or, in other words, exceeded the intrinsic value by a factor of more than five. In all of the other bubble runs except one, the first period price was well above $4. As the run progresses, the value of the stock declines since there are fewer of the ten chances remaining. So the intrinsic value of the stock declines on a straight line basis until the final period, in which it reaches the single-shot valuation of $0.40. In all of the bubble runs, the market price is significantly above the intrinsic value line throughout. Moreover, the market price sometimes shows increases, which should never happen since the intrinsic value is only decreasing linearly as time progresses.

It is also interesting that "bubble and crash patterns" were typical of the six bubble runs, while in the non-bubble runs "prices [...] were close to their risk-neutral values throughout" (Ackert et al. 2009, p. 726). This suggests that bubbles never end well, as we would expect. For the avoidance of doubt, I recommend never participating in them, even if you are certain that they will persist for some time and you could safely exit before everyone else. The problem is that many, if not all other participants will also be looking to get out at the last possible moment, which can make the crash extraordinarily precipitous.

The authors had two asset types in their experiment, 'un-truncated' and 'truncated.' The un-truncated asset could pay out an unlimited number of dividends, still at the 2% probability per period. The truncated asset could only pay out three times. For all practical purposes, this makes no difference since there is a vanishingly small probability of the un-truncated asset paying out four or more times. However, the un-truncated asset traded above the truncated asset throughout, on average. Thus, Ackert et al. (2009, p. 729) have confirmed that their results mean that "participants were susceptible to irrationality associated with probability judgment errors."

Naturally I would also step back one level and explain that they made such probability judgment errors in relation to the lottery-like payoffs because the idea of the payoffs was vivid and, hence, available. This was likely enhanced or invited by the instructions given to participants: these included the observation in the ten-period version that "[un-truncated] shares can receive as many $20 dividends as there are periods [while truncated] shares can at most receive three $20 dividends" (Ackert et al. 2009, p. 729). This makes the extremely improbable possibility of the un-truncated shares paying out more than three times highly vivid and thus the possibility is accorded a much greater probability than is warranted by the set-up.

One might think that it is also possible to say that what has happened is speculation in that participants were paid more than the intrinsic value in the expectation that other participants would pay them even more in future rounds. As I said above, I would not recommend that, but I would also not characterise speculation as always irrational. So there might be scope to say that the results do not show irrationality, if one believes such speculation is rational. Doubtless there was some speculation contributing to the bubbles, but it is also true that nine out of 12 runs show a market value above $0.40 in the final period, whereafter there will be no further trading and thus no more can be realised from the asset than its intrinsic value. That does not look like speculation.

I think we can also draw from this the interesting observation that if participants only have one salient feature to distinguish two otherwise identical assets, they will fixate on the salience of the distinguishing feature much more than the intrinsic value. Maintaining the 'correct' price differential between the two assets takes on more importance than the intrinsically justified price: participants are seduced into thinking that a price differential between the two asset types represents an opportunity whereas a differential between the price of the asset and the intrinsic value of the asset is where the focus should more appropriately be.

There are two caveats that the authors make to their conclusions which I think are worth noting before we leave this experiment. The first is that what Ackert et al. (2009, p. 737) have established is that "aggregate irrationality measured in one dimension (probability judgment error) is associated with aggregate irrationality measured in another (bubble formation)." The fact that the two items are associated does not prove causation by one of the other, though it does suggest it. In particular, it does not show the direction of any causation. We cannot see from these results whether probability judgment errors cause bubbles or bubbles cause probability judgment errors. My view is that both directions are entirely plausible; we could then develop an explanation of the sudden and dramatic nature of some bubbles from positive feedback effects. But in either case, this just serves to underline the inadvisability of participating in bubbles if one can detect them.

Secondly, Ackert *et al.* (2009, p. 737) canvass the possibility that some of their data can be explained by the House Money Effect (Nofsinger 2016, p. 37). This is a bias in which participants regard cash at risk differently depending on its source, which, of course, is not rational. If you had to earn some dollars, they are 'hard-won' and you might be very careful about risking them. If, on the other hand, you have just won some dollars in a casino or in the simulated trading experiment, you might now be more inclined to have a flutter in an 'easy-come, easy go' approach. This would also explain why prices in the simulation became more bubbly after a payout. This is especially plausible given that the participants could 'go bankrupt' in the course of the simulation, i.e. if their losses at any point became greater than the promised attendance allowance of $15, they were sent home empty-handed. So a dividend payout creates distance between them and that unattractive outcome, thus perhaps sponsoring risk appetite. However, such an explanation should not figure in the real world, where it is also important to remember that money is fungible. It simply does not matter when you take a risk whether the dollar you risk was earned, or won, or found in the street; the house money illusion is to be scorned.

It has plausibly been suggested that the Availability Heuristic is implicated in causing the type of recessions that involve credit crunches after a period of irrationally exuberant lending. Guttentag and Herring (1984) observe that the Availability Heuristic means that events will be regarded as less probable the more time has elapsed since an event of the type in question occurred. This will be a natural consequence of the tendency for events to be forgotten as time passes. In benign credit market conditions, it will have been a long time since the last default and so the probability of a default will eventually be assessed as much lower than it really is. Eventually, this probability falls so far below the real probability that ought to be assumed in considering lending decisions that the situation becomes highly vulnerable. I suggest, then, that when the first default occurs, the Availability Heuristic switches around very suddenly. A default is now salient and highly available and the assessed probability of further defaults swings from unrealistically low to unrealistically high. This, of course, means that lending conditions will disconcertingly switchback rapidly from too lax to too severe. That is a description of a canonical credit crunch of the sort from which we are still in 2016 attempting to recover. So a great deal more knowledge of the Availability Heuristic among borrowers and lenders would be of great value to society.

Away from the laboratory, I think there is good reason to suppose that vivid storytelling can lead to bubbles. One of the most famous bubbles in financial history was the Dutch tulip bubble of 1637. Many people made spectacular fortunes and then lost them again and, indeed, lost everything. Shiller (2003a, pp. 91–92) gives a very vivid example of how this could happen. He canvasses a 'price-to-price' feedback mechanism – which is obviously unstable due to runaway positive feedback effects – which is passed by word-of-mouth. Shiller (2003a, p. 92) provides a translation of a contemporary fictional dialogue between two Dutchmen, one of whom is in the market and the other who remains to be convinced. In response to the sceptic's query as to how it can be known whether it is too late to join the frenzy, the participant uses very vivid terminology: "Look at all the gardeners that used to wear white grey outfits, and now they're wearing new clothes. Many weavers, that used to wear patched up clothes, that they had a hard time putting on, now wear the glitteriest clothes. Yes, many who trade in tulips are riding a horse, have a carriage or a wagon, and during winter, an ice carriage." Note that this does not address the question, but we can be so caught up with the vividness of the response that this does not matter. We can see the newly suited weavers and gardeners, we can see the plush carriages with a direct and vivid intimation that this could also be us. The Availability Heuristic is almost being deliberately employed by the participant to convince the sceptic. Here are some vivid examples of what happens if you win in this market; forget the question as to how we can know when the bubble will end – and the sceptic will conclude that if it is vivid, it is probable. A sufficient volume of people talking like this and acting accordingly is enough to create a bubble. This might be an opportune moment to make one of the few cast-iron guarantees that I will state in this book: anyone who tells you that any particular market can only go up is *always* wrong.

One important question to ask when someone tells you something like this is *why* are they telling me this. You should not need me to tell you to avoid such yarns, but if you do need convincing, consider whether you are being recruited because obtaining new blood is the only way a bubble can continue. Another point to keep in mind is what we might term anti-bubbles. Returns in the S&P 500 have been excellent after 2009 since so many people got vividly burned in the crisis. Many investors were so shocked by their losses that they have never returned, meaning the stocks were very cheap. Others who may have lost nothing have vivid memories of others losing everything and apply the Availability Heuristic to produce an exaggerated forecast of the likelihood of a repeat which says it is a near-term certainty.

Stories which are vivid are assessed as more likely to be true. As an example, consider Lewis (2014), which offers a highly readable, informative and entertaining story of High Frequency Trading (HFT). This book has been presented as another instalment in the long-running saga of Wall Street scandals, and is widely-accepted as another piece of evidence showing that everyone on Wall Street is a crook seeking to rip-off the innocent member of the public. In the context of the Availability Heuristic, everyone is easily able to call to mind examples of Wall Street scandals and so everyone will make unrealistically high estimates of the probability of such negative outcomes. On the other hand, there is nothing that falls into the category of a vivid image of a Wall Street scandal failing to happen, and so the assessment of the probability of such an outcome is even further lowered.

Looking at the HFT story in more detail, it seems to me that the key facts are as follows: Lewis (2014) describes how HFT works and how it depends on the existence of multiple exchanges. Major traders route orders to several exchanges with the aim of obtaining the best execution. HFT firms see the order beginning to be executed. Perhaps the first 100 shares go through on one exchange. The HFT firms, who are able to obtain trade information and react by placing trades in microseconds, are now in a position to move *before* the remainder of the large order has gone through. If the large order is for 100,000 shares in Microsoft, the HFT firms can buy all of the stock in Microsoft that is available for sale on the other exchanges before the rest of the large order goes through. They can then immediately sell those shares into the large order, exacting a small turn on the way.

This does indeed mean that many trades are conducted on slightly worse terms than would otherwise be the case. However, my view is that portfolios should be traded much less than they are: one should generally aim to be an investor rather than a trader. And overall, the position may, in fact, be greatly improved from the investor perspective. As Lewis (2014, p. 107) concedes, prior to computerisation of the markets, bid/offer spreads were typically 16 bps and afterwards they had fallen to about 1 bp in the more active stocks at least. This means that the situation has changed from one in which one is worse off by an overt 16 bps, to one in which one is covertly worse off for an amount 16 times smaller. Similarly, Barber and Odean (1999, p. 46) report that at a discount (!) brokerage house between 1987 and 1993, the "average commission on a sale was 2.76 percent," which is an extraordinarily high number. Transparency is good, but I do not think we should pay that high a price for it. So what seems to be happening is that a widespread application of the Availability Heuristic to the idea of conniving Wall Street bankers has created a problem from a benefit.

Moving on to another real world example, let us consider a recent trade of mine. Last week, I decided that Deutsche Bank stock was trading too cheaply. This was 12 May 2016, when the stock was trading at $15.85 or 32% of book value and at 30-year lows. Book value is somewhat subject to manipulation, as are all accounting values, but the magnitude of the mismatch looks so dramatic that there seems little scope for a mis-valuation to alter the ratio significantly. There was some speculation that DB would not be in a position to pay the interest on a class of hybrid bonds. Such an event is highly likely to mean instant death for a bank. All of this was topped off by someone showing an overlay of the DB stock price over Lehman Bros. immediately before the latter firm became insolvent. They matched. I thought that this, as an argument, combined interesting characteristics of being utterly without force but extremely vivid.

We can 'see' very easily the situation where the pictures of people carrying their boxes out of Lehman as it implodes transfer over to DB. Those images of newly unemployed bankers are very vivid and cause us to overestimate the probability of such an event. By contrast, there is nothing particularly vivid about a solvent DB continuing in business. There is no 'hook' to this; it is just the persistence of the status quo which has nothing vivid to it all, which is relevant. Taleb (2008, p. 77) points to a similar vividness asymmetry when he notes that "lottery [ticket] buyers overestimate their chances of winning because they visualise such a potent payoff." Naturally, the idea of holding a losing lottery ticket produces no vivid imagery to visualise.

But the idea that this is more likely because the stock price has described a similar early trajectory to Lehman is ludicrous. It is more likely that DB will become insolvent if its stock price has declined rapidly, but it is not certain. I will later discuss Hindsight Bias (§5.5) which makes it look as though past events were inevitable. This is why it looks like events which are similar to the precursor events of an insolvency must also inevitably presage doom for DB. Moreover, there is a clear affective overlay on such vivid imaginings. We can also imagine very easily how we will feel if DB becomes insolvent after we have bought the stock. And the negative affective forecasting gives us very clear and likely fallacious action guidance.

Keep an especially sharp lookout for regulatory stories. The Financial Conduct Authority (FCA) announced this morning that it had issued a s166 notice in respect of DB and its Anti Money-Laundering practices. This looks terrifying, and it has caused the stock to drop by 3%. A s166 notice, also known as a Skilled Persons Review, is basically a supervisory – rather than enforcement – action which involves ensuring that the relevant staff have the appropriate training. For sure, this is not good news, but it does not warrant a 3% drop in the value of the company unless it eventually leads to enormous fines. That is possible, but since the market capitalisation of DB is $25.4bn, those fines would need to exceed $750m to justify the drop. That is not impossible, but I judge it improbable.

Of course, from the time perspective of the reader, DB may have famously become insolvent and sparked off a new Eurozone rout, in which case I will look wrong. I would still suggest that it was the right trade, because 0.32 is very cheap for a solvent bank and I do not believe that DB will actually fail to make any payments. The stock appreciated by 8.5% the day after I bought it on leverage, which obviously is a pleasing result so far. Time will tell whether the trade comes good, but I will not be accepting any blame for making a bad trade if it does not. There is room for a speculative element in a portfolio and being aware that one side of an argument may have spurious but salient characteristics makes it harder to focus on the numbers as one should.

What to do? It is not useful to give advice to think harder about the hard to think about, though one will still be better off in realising that one's initial probability estimate will be biased by vividness. So look out for that. Note how courting vivid yet improbable disaster can really be seen as the core of the contrarian approach. Consider total disaster scenarios. In the case of the DB trade mentioned above, I suppose that the absolute worst case is an insolvency event which causes total elimination of the equity value. This could happen in a bailout situation which is certainly conceivable after 2008 but I currently believe improbable. How would I respond to that situation? I would in this case be relaxed because I am also holding a diversified portfolio and this was a speculative trade within that context. There is another, wider, worse case. This is where correlation spikes up and all of my stocks decline seriously at the same time. This would feel a lot worse. I believe one might consider an array of stop losses at say 50%, so limiting the downside. My personal choice would be to hold under those circumstances and I recommend that approach. This also suggests, again, that one should never trade the rent money, as is plain.

If anyone thinks that this is all too unscientific, I would commend the position taken by a practitioner. Taleb (2008, p. 285) recommends we prefer "a sophisticated craft, based on tricks, to a failed science." The claim that risk can be measured seems to be falsified by the observation that the hedge fund LTCM saw some events that were massively improbable by their measures to the point of practical impossibility – 'eight sigma' in the jargon – before they went bust. Evolving such a sophisticated craft will largely be a matter of surviving in the real world of trading; this can include a lengthy period of running dummy portfolios or low-value test portfolios. One could also learn a lot from studying famous disasters (Leeson and Fearn 2000). I think that Taleb (2008) is largely right that financial markets are not governed by bell curves, though they may be 'good enough' as an approximation for short periods. The problem is that we have no way of knowing what a 'short period' means, and also that the deviations from the Gaussian may dominate eventual outcomes.

I think Taleb (2007, p. 242) is unfair when he says that the fact that the LTCM gurus speak about 10 Sigma events[7] means that they must either know what they are talking about at an impossible level of perfection or that they do not know what they are talking about at all when they speak of probability. It could also be that they understand what, externally, seems to be the best interpretation of these events. This is not to say that such hugely improbably events occurred of that level of improbability, which should only happen a few times per universe, actually occurred.[8] The best interpretation is that the models employed by LTCM were inadequate; they assigned much too low a probability to the extreme events which occurred. This, of course, is just the 'fat tail' ignorance of which Taleb (2008) complains, so he should be happy to accept that explanation. My view is that the LTCM principals were well aware of this when they spoke of 10 sigma. None of this means that their modelling methodology is the way forward, of course. It is very interesting that Taleb (2007, p. 243) proposes the alternative explanation that the principals took this line in order to avoid killing their self-esteem. If so, what we see here would be a variety of Self-Presentation Bias (cf. §8.3).

Overweighting the wrong information is another way of stating the problems caused for investors by the Availability Heuristic. Investors often look to other successful investors to see what can be learned from them. This whole approach needs to be conducted with some caution. One potential difficulty relates to survivor bias, or what I have termed in the past the 'cat in a box' mistake. Imagine we have a million boxes and we randomly place a cat in one of them. It turns out to be box number 463,734. The cat, whom we are assuming to be sentient for the sake of the illustration, is highly likely to conclude that there is something deeply significant and special about the number 463,734. There is not, of course: it was randomly chosen. The error derives from the confusion between the probability of a very unlikely event occurring and the probability of a single *particular* and previously specified event occurring. The probability of box 463,734 being chosen is extremely remote: it is, in fact, one in a million. However, given the fact that we have placed the cat in a box and it has not escaped, the probability that the cat is now in a box is very high: it is certain, in fact. It is important to distinguish between these two probabilities. Very improbable events happen all the time: we just do not know which ones they will be.

I do not intend to suggest that Warren Buffett is a cat in a random box. But imagine we started off with 1,024 proto-Buffett neophyte investors.[9] Let us say they all gain a respectable amount of seed capital and begin investing. They have an investment career which lasts ten years. Each year they make a binary investment decision of the type, for example, that USDGBP will increase or not during the year. They invest their entire capital accordingly. Each proto-Buffett makes ten such binary decisions over the ten years. Let us also say that no two of them make exactly the same ten decisions; though plenty of them will make many of the same decisions. Ignoring the possibility that USDGBP remains unchanged, there are only two possible outcomes in relation to this and all of the other investment decisions: either USDGBP increases or it does not. Either the investment was successful or it was not.

How many decision trees are there? $2^{10} = 1,024$. This is equivalent to the question of how many possible investment careers are there. There will also be exactly one optimal path through the decision tree: one in which all ten of the decisions were 'correct,' which here means borne out by the outturn. Plenty of other decision paths were likely pretty good: anyone getting nine out of ten investment decisions correct would be very happy with that outcome, unless they were risking total loss of all accumulated capital on each of the decisions. But for clarity, let us say that each correct decision results in a 100% return and each incorrect one results in a total loss. So what do we have after ten years? We find that of our 1,024 proto-Buffett investors, all except one have at some point been wiped out and are now holding zero capital. The other one has made ten correct decisions and, as a result, is now holding 1,024 times his initial capital. Who do you think is in the papers?

To think that Buffett is a magical talent under these circumstances would be a mistake. In just this toy example, Buffett is just the cat in one particular box. In real life, of course, there is plenty we can learn from Buffett. We can usefully assess how he makes his decisions such that they ideally have a better than random chance of being successful. We can aim to absorb some of his wisdom such as the idea that if you are disturbed by losses, you should take a long-term view and you might be aided in that by not checking your portfolio every day.[10] But do not be seduced by the idea that Buffett's success was inevitable given his undoubtedly special talents and that the only way to be successful is the way that he did it. Do not be drawn into this error by the undoubted availability of Buffett's great success, which is of course both salient and vivid.

Also remember to look at the whole picture. Another virtue of Buffett's that we could all emulate is tight risk control. As I have said elsewhere, you need to look at how much return you have made for a certain level of risk, and not just the return alone. A small return with no risk is, in fact, a terrific result, especially if it can be replicated, but makes no headlines. As Marks (2011, p. 57) puts it, high "absolute return is much more recognisable and titillating than superior risk-adjusted performance." This is absolutely correct, and could be restated as the claim that the Availability Heuristic, with 'recognisable' standing in for 'salient' and 'titillating' standing in for 'vivid,' is tailor-made to make us look at returns and not risk-adjusted performance. This will be as true when we assess the performance of other investors as when we examine our own performance.

This is one occasion where I think that a particular cognitive bias can, to some extent, be avoided – and should be. We need clear eyes when we assess any performance, especially our own, in order to draw the appropriate lessons from that performance. Simply making it habit to consider all relevant data, not just the salient and the vivid and also always to consider risk-adjusted returns would go a long way in this regard. It might be to go too far to suggest that we can attempt to observe in a way that does not favour the salient – indeed, it looks potentially impossible by definition – but we can at least try to be careful to notice the elements that others seem to be missing.

So I have now twice suggested that 'seeking dullness' can pay off. It was one way of countering the Availability Heuristic bias described in this section and also the Representativeness Heuristic described in §4.2. This can obviously be quite hard work. Even Taleb (2008, p. 17) says that he initially avoided the minutiae of the business world since he found the details "inelegant, dull, pompous, greedy, unintellectual and boring." I think this needs careful interpretation and is only partly correct. Certainly, I concede that reading interviews with CEOs who are explaining why their share price has declined can be unhelpful. It reminds me of football commentary. It is rather superfluous and involves listing a set of unconvincing reasons that could explain what has just happened. But it could be useful in that we can look beyond what the CEO says to why he is saying it, and how he is saying it. Is the CEO retreating into pomposity because it would be too dangerous for him to be straightforward and transparent? That is exceptionally interesting, I maintain.

Everything can become interesting if we are following it for the reason that we expect to make money from knowing it. You might think that taking this approach renders you open to another of Taleb's criticisms: that of being greedy. My response to this is: so what? I see no demerits in seeking to make money. I might if that was one's only objective and one continued beyond the point where enough was obtained. But no-one else's opinion matters here. It cannot be the case that investing in stock markets and spending time reading about how they and the corporate world work is greedy just because one wants to be successful in investing.

Similarly it may well be boring to study the details of an annual report. But this is exactly why you should do it. Look for the apparently dull. Often it will be dull because it is generally uninteresting; at least you will know that no-one else is looking. So if you find something it will be all yours.

It is appropriate here to mention briefly the bias of the next section (§4.5), which is the Gambler's Fallacy. This is the inverse of the idea that lightning does not strike twice, or that the probability of an event is altered by whether it has previously occurred. I will discuss this in more detail in the next section, but for now let us just note that it may form a component of the behaviour of the person above who vows to avoid Central Park. They may be thinking that the probability of being mugged is higher after having been mugged. It has not changed. What may have changed is the state of their knowledge about their own probability of being mugged, but that is something very different.

4.5 The Gambler's Fallacy

This is the illusion, as mentioned briefly above, that the probability of an event is altered by whether or not a similar event has already happened. For example, we may wrongly think that if a coin has landed heads up ten times in a row, we ought to see it come up tails next – because we 'are due' some tails, or heads next – because that seems to be what the coin is doing.

As so often, it is the contrast between the "heuristic reasoning that makes the gambler's fallacy appear plausible and the sometimes psychologically less compelling controlled reasoning" (Nagel 2011, p. 20) which gives the effect its potency. We get the results of the heuristic immediately and without effort – 'what has been happening will continue to happen' – while to counter that, we have to think hard about probabilities, which is exactly what we are bad at.

The actual probability of an event ought to be sharply distinguished from the state of our knowledge of the probability, which can legitimately change our *assessment* of the probability without meaning that the probability has itself changed. The classic example of the Gambler's Fallacy occurs in coin-tossing, where, crucially, the coin is a fair one. The probability of obtaining heads is always 50%. It never changes. One of the items that does not change it is whether the last result was heads. Further, it is still 50% even if the last 100 throws have been heads. (You might, of course, start to be suspicious about the coin under those circumstances, but it remains true that whatever the probability is of obtaining heads with even a suspect coin, it remains fixed and unaffected by how many throws have been made.) It is also still 50% if the last hundred throws have been tails. These two situations illustrate both sides of the Gambler's Fallacy, which are wrong in different directions. The gambler who thinks that if it has been heads a hundred times it will be again makes one sort of mistake – it will stay the way it has always been. The one who says that since there have been so many heads it must now be time for tails makes the opposite error.

One particularly difficult aspect of this fallacy is that it is closely bound up with another common error, which can tend to make the Gambler's Fallacy even more appealing. The other error which exacerbates the Gambler's Fallacy involves a failure to properly appreciate the phenomenon of Regression to the Mean. What this means is that results will generally *tend* to move back towards the mean. It is obvious that this must be true, because the mean simply is the most probable result or the average among them, depending on what sort of result we are talking about. We know that if we toss a fair coin a very large number of times, we will end up with approximately the same number of heads as tails. As the number of trials increases, the closer we should in fact get to 50%. The probability that we have a large preponderance of heads decreases as the number of trials increases. It is somewhat unlikely that we could have more than 90% heads in a series of ten trials; it is very unlikely that we would in 1,000 trials and extremely unlikely that we would in 100,000,000 trials. But, the probability of obtaining more than 90% heads never actually goes to zero, however many trials we have – as long as the number remains finite. (Our assessment of probabilities in this sort of arena is further weakened by the Clustering Illusion; see §5.2.)

Despite all of this, we know that normally, we are increasingly likely to move towards a 50/50 split between heads and tails if we have a large number of trials. So we can be tempted by the idea that if we are in one of the unusual scenarios where there has been a preponderance of heads, there must now be an increased probability of tails in order to shift us back to the 50/50 split. This is the error. The mean 50/50 split *emerges* from the coin tosses: it does not result from the probabilities shifting in response to the current split. How could the probabilities shift? Short of someone modifying the coin, it will continue to have a 50% chance of showing heads every time forever.

None of this theory, which is undeniable, does anything to shift the power that the Gambler's Fallacy has over us. Sometimes circumstances conspire against us in this connection as well; and sometimes it is arranged that those circumstances will so conspire. For example, Lewis (2010, p. 147) describes how casinos place screens above roulette tables showing the outcome of the last 20 spins. Since the wheels are completely random, this information cannot be useful other than to the casino: it plays to our tendency to succumb to the Gambler's Fallacy. In its grip, we now 'know' that the next spin will come up black and bet accordingly. The casino wins, on average, because it loses almost half the time, wins almost half the time, and also wins on the one green slot. The green slot is analogous to the bid/offer spread on financial assets.

It is notable that Goldman (1989, p. 166) uses the example of the Gambler's Fallacy as being so egregious an error as to cause a problem even for understanding others, on the assumption that they are rational. We generally need to assume that they are to some extent rational when we interpret their words and predict their actions, because otherwise we lack a constraining factor, and the number of potential interpretations becomes unbounded. The answer that Goldman (1989) gives to this problem is to suggest that we are all irrational in this and other ways together. This is a consequence of the general Simulation Theory approach to Theory of Mind supported by Goldman (1989) and, indeed, Short (2015). It is congenial because it allows one to assume that S can understand O and predict O's behaviour when O exhibits the Gambler's Fallacy because S will, explicitly or implicitly, also exhibit the Gambler's Fallacy. What we need to do here is to take explicit advantage of our Theory of Mind. We can use our abilities to predict scenarios in which others will commit the Gambler's Fallacy but then, if we avoid committing the fallacy ourselves in such scenarios, we will be in an economically more optimal position. Note it is useful on its own to avoid the Gambler's Fallacy; it becomes doubly valuable in a scenario in which others are not avoiding it because their money will flow in our direction.

It might be hard to believe that investors will actually risk money based on assertions deriving from the Gambler's Fallacy. Evidence shows that money follows the fallacy in lotteries, however. Clotfelter and Cook (1993, p. 1521) studied the Maryland daily numbers game and found "a clear and consistent tendency for the amount of money bet on a particular number to fall sharply immediately after it is drawn." Precisely, what Clotfelter and Cook (1993, p. 1523) found was that, expressed as a ratio to the money wagered on a number on the day it was drawn, bets fell from "1.00 on the drawing day to 0.64 after three days, then recovered gradually to reach 0.93 after 84 days." This means that there was a 36% reduction in money wagered on a winning number three days after it won. I expect that playing lotteries will never be a good move, but if you insist, you could bet on numbers that have just come up coming up again. The probability of this is, of course, not changed, but you will be sharing your winnings with fewer others.

Clotfelter and Cook (1993, p. 1521) also note previous data from Metzger showing that betting on the favourite in horse races becomes more popular after a "series of races have been won by long shots." My view of betting on racing is similar to that of casinos or lotteries, but I am prepared to believe that someone spending their 10,000 hours on studying horses, form and tracks could outperform. Such a person should, of course, never back favourites after several long shots have won because the odds will have shortened; the odds will have lengthened on further long shot victories and that is where money is best placed.

Cowan (1969, p. 250) suggests that the Gambler's Fallacy arises partly because "especially where evidence is lacking as to the way things actually are, people will tend to picture the world according to their hearts' desires," which makes it a variant of wishful thinking. This seems plausible, and leads to the straightforward ideas that seeking evidence is useful, avoiding situations in which no evidence is available is desirable and replacing missing evidence with desired states of affairs is a mistake. I state banal precepts here because I think we can expect plenty of behaviour in the markets, which flouts these precepts. One sort of example will be people who buy stocks for emotional reasons, perhaps because they support a sports team or they like a local brewery which is going to do an Initial Public Offering (IPO). There is every possibility that a listed football club or brewery is a sound business, but also every possibility that the stock price is inflated by emotionally attached buyers. Examine the financial evidence and be on the lookout for opportunities to short the stock.

Cowan (1969) has also anticipated in one way the Goldman (1989) problem as to how we can understand and predict persons exhibiting the Gambler's Fallacy if we are assuming that they are rational. Cowan (1969) suggests that when people commit the fallacy, they are not engaged in an 'argument,' or at least not in the technical way that a logician would understand this term. I think this is probably correct as an explanation: people do not generally construct good philosophical arguments. This is an opportune moment to examine what a good argument looks like.

Such an argument needs to have some premises and a conclusion and be what is termed 'sound' and 'valid.' If it is valid, then the conclusion is entailed by the premises. If it is sound, then it is valid and the premises are true. The classic example of a syllogism, which is sound and valid, is as follows.

- Premise 1: Socrates is a man
- Premise 2: All men are mortal
- Conclusion: Socrates is mortal

This is a good argument since it generates knowledge. We can deduce the truth of the conclusion from the two premises. Often there will not be a way to construct a good philosophical argument like this in markets. There may be something more complicated we can do with a chain of maybe a dozen premises. This is difficult to get right and often it will not be possible to show that all or most of the premises are true, perhaps because they relate to the future. For example, the argument below is also a good one.

- Premise 1: GM will sell more cars
- Premise 2: The GM stock price will go up if it sells more cars
- Conclusion: The GM stock price will go up

Obviously the problem is showing that P1 is true or will become true. If you see any opportunities to construct good arguments like this, then go to it. But I think that using the framework set out to check the vast array of what passes for published argument is much more likely to pay off. Sometimes the premises will be false. Sometimes the conclusion will not be entailed by the premises. Sometimes, remarkably, financial market commentators will argue from premises that are false to a conclusion that would not be entailed even if they were true. All of this represents opportunities to consider the merits of the opposing view, especially if an obviously unsound or invalid argument is obtaining a great deal of attention. To extend the example above in a way which exhibits the Gambler's Fallacy, one will find suggestions that GM will sell more (or fewer) cars next year because it sold more cars last year. Check how that happened and whether it can continue.

There are occasions when something like the Gambler's Fallacy becomes true, because it is only a fallacy in relation to events such as fair coin tosses, which are truly independent of each other, and not where probabilities are path dependent. Some events really are more likely if they have already occurred; this is what is behind 'momentum' trading where one trades on the assumption that a stock which has appreciated will continue to do so. The problem, of course, is that this is only true until it becomes false. Conversely, Pinker (2015, p. 346) recalls an occasion where he upbraided his father for predicting a clear day after several days of rain, accusing him of committing the Gambler's Fallacy. His mistake here was to fail to consider that the probability of cloud is not completely independent of whether there was cloud the previous day, because cloud cover must have some finite scope, and also, presumably, mechanisms like rain which can reduce the amount of further cloud to be expected. I make no claims at meteorological expertise: all I require here is the idea that whether there is cloud tomorrow can be linked to whether there was today in a way that is not the case with sequential coin tosses.

But this is not the case in the stock market. As Pinker (2015, p. 346) notes, an "efficient stock market is another invention designed to defeat human pattern recognition." As I noted before, the Efficient Markets Theory can be questioned but it is still at least a good first approximation. Any deviations from efficiency in asset prices should be quickly exploitable by traders who will, therefore, tend to remove such deviations. So, the view Pinker (2015) argues for here constitutes a confirmation that the stock market is one place where the Gambler's Fallacy is to be avoided. The seductiveness of the fallacy means that it rarely is avoided, however, and therein, I underline again, lies opportunity. As Cowan (1969, p. 251) concludes, "the same bit of discourse might often better be understood not as argument at all, but rather as sheer dramatisation." Quite so: a dramatic piece of discourse can be vivid, and hence 'available' in the sense of §4.4, and yet still not be a good argument. Bet against the drama.

I mentioned a market simulation experiment in the previous section. Ackert *et al.* (2009, p. 737) also found that "bubbles occurred more often in the multi-period markets in sessions where there was a successful dividend draw" early on.

This looks very much as though participants were succumbing to the Gambler's Fallacy in that they now assigned a higher probability to future dividend payouts having seen one early on. It would, I think, be too much of a stretch to say that the bubbles were caused by sophisticated speculators expecting other participants to exhibit the Gambler's Fallacy because the participants had not had the benefit of reading this book. The 'priming effect' of seeing a dividend also, of course, remains entirely consistent with the Availability Heuristic explanation of the previous section, since the idea of a payout will only be made more vivid by seeing a payout.

Notes

1. Cf. also Nofsinger (2016, pp. 83–85)
2. Even making this small adjustment assumes that there is some validity to stereotyping, which is itself questionable.
3. Most of the quotations I will provide from this paper are translated by me from the original German. The New Market is where higher-risk stocks are listed in Germany.
4. Here, as elsewhere in this section, there are links to the Halo Effect (§8.2).
5. Javier Hasse, Yahoo Finance, January 7, 2016: "George Soros Says We're In A Crisis Like 2008", http://finance.yahoo.com/news/george-soros-says-were-crisis-212013913.html
6. It must be conceded that Labroo, Lambotte, and Zhang (2009) are actually arguing against this point under specific circumstances.
7. It is not important whether we are discussing 8 sigma or 10 sigma events; both are dramatically improbable.
8. Shull (2011, p. 12) claims that the CEO of Goldman spoke of a "25th deviation event" in the wake of August 2007. I cannot think of a better reading of 'off the scale' than that.
9. An example of this type is outlined by Taleb (2007, pp. 152–153).
10. Nofsinger (2016, ch. 11) includes this as one of his tips for beating biases.

5

BELIEF-FORMATION BIASES II

5.1 Confirmation Bias

Confirmation Bias, put most simply, is the tendency people have to look for evidence that confirms what they already believe. There are several definitions of Confirmation Bias because the bias is evident in several distinct but linked forms. The most important definition refers to the "fundamental tendency to seek information consistent with current [...] beliefs, theories or hypotheses and to avoid the collection of potentially falsifying evidence" (Evans 1990, p. 41). This is the form of Confirmation Bias which involves differential *evidence-seeking*. The other forms of Confirmation Bias involve differential *treatment* of evidence.

For example, gamblers exhibit an unexpected form of Confirmation Bias. We know that gambling in casinos or betting shops is generally a poor idea without special, perhaps inside knowledge because the casinos and betting shops are profitable. So, one would need to believe that one had a particular edge over other customers; such an edge is not to be found in games of chance and is still very difficult to obtain in scenarios like horse-racing – though conceivably a great deal of knowledge about horses and conditions could pay off. So we might predict that gamblers continue to patronise casinos and betting shops because they forget about all their losses, and thus flatter their own performance statistics.

Contrary to this, Gilovich (1993, p. 32) found that gamblers pay *more* attention to their losses than to their wins. What they do is work hard to construct stories in which their losses were 'near wins.' For example, they would have won but for some freak incident involving an injury to their team's star quarterback. Or, that stock would have gone up but for climatic factors, which could not have been foreseen. There are parallels here to what Taleb (2008, p. 151) describes as the tendency for financial forecasters to explain their failures to predict market outcomes by saying 'I was almost right.'

Many excuses of this type are made in quarterly results and some of them are reasonable. We may assume that this type of behaviour is just as prevalent on the trading floor as in the betting shop and so it is worth looking out for. This, though, is differential treatment of evidence depending on *for what* it is evidence. There is no real justification for looking harder for evidence that tends in any one direction rather than other ones: we should try to seek and treat the evidence even-handedly. Otherwise, if that is fair game, then so ought to be constructing 'near-loss' stories.

In fact, that might even be a useful discipline. We may see that a particular stock we hold has gone up, but we ask ourselves the question: 'if it had instead gone down, what would have been the three most likely reasons?' This sort of 'counterfactual post mortem' could be even more potent if we asked what could have caused the stock to decline by 50%. If we find any of these scenarios plausible and probable, it might be time to sell the stock.

The point remains that there should be even-handed and dispassionate treatment of all evidence, no matter in which direction it points. This needs to be combined with an equally even-handed search for evidence rather than a Confirmation Bias driven openness only to evidence that supports our current views. Perhaps one useful discipline is to always try to look for the evidence that we do not want – try to disconfirm one's favoured hypothesis. If we own a stock, what will make it go down? If we do not, what will make it go up? Taleb (2008, p. 59) mentions expert chess players who, it has been shown, distinguish themselves from rookies by their "focus on where a speculative move might be weak." Focussing on the negatives, then, can be a way forward. Hirshleifer (2001, p. 1549) notes evidence that "individuals more subject to this Confirmation Bias lose money in an experimental market to those who are less subject to it," so it is certainly worth the effort.

We are generally very poor at the sort of logical analysis that overcomes Confirmation Bias; it rivals probability estimation for inaccuracy. The rule for hypothesis confirmation is that we should accept as true any hypothesis which we have tried hard to falsify but have failed. How people test hypotheses is investigated using a Wason test. In the Wason test, subjects are given some cards showing 'D,' 'F,' '3' and '7.' They are asked to check whether the rule 'if a card has a D on one side, it has a 3 on the other' is true, and asked which cards they turn over to check.

Most people, including myself, feel an irresistible pull to turn over the 3 card to look for a D. The feeling is that if we see one, we will have confirmed the hypothesis. What we will have done, however, is provide only confirmation in the limited sense of increased confidence by having elicited data consistent with the rule. That could be a very limited confirmation since there could be a million cards with 3 on one side that do not have a D on the other side, and this one card is the only one that fits the rule. Most people also turn over the D card because anything other than 3 will kill the hypothesis. This gives a clue to the correct answer: the two cards to turn over are D and 7, for the reason that both can kill the hypothesis. If the D does not have a 3 on the other side the hypothesis is dead. If the 7 card *does* have a D on the other side, the hypothesis is dead. We learn almost nothing from turning over the 3 card; no-one has said anything about the prevalence of 3s. It might be that all other letters always have 3s on the back. We should not care because that is not the question which has been asked.

Taleb (2008, p. 58) discusses another illuminating experiment in which Wason presented subjects with the sequence of numbers '2, 4, 6 …' and asked them what rule governed the sequence. The subjects were allowed to ask any question with a yes/no answer. We feel a natural pull to extrapolate the pattern and say that the rule is 'even numbers ascending.' Very few subjects established what the correct rule was – simply, numbers ascending – because they tended to ask questions which had confirmatory answers but lacked precision. The questions were focussed on trying to confirm the rule 'even numbers ascending.' A step on the way to find out that the true rule is 'numbers ascending' is to ask whether '7' would be allowed by the rule and receiving the surprising response 'yes.' This answer is negative – because it breaks the obvious hypothesis that the rule is 'even numbers ascending' – and therefore powerful. But the key test is to ask whether '2, 4, 3 … ' is allowed. Receiving a negative answer to this is the only way to get to 'numbers ascending.' There is even a question as to whether we can ever know what rule is being followed. I will discuss this 'rule-following question' briefly below.

Taleb (2008, p. 56) is very slightly too bold with his claim that seeing "white swans does not confirm the non-existence of black swans." His statement is true if we read 'confirm' in a very strong sense similar to 'prove.' However, in real life there are few proofs of anything. If we read 'confirm' as more like 'tends to confirm,' then there is a very limited but non-zero extent to which seeing a white swan does, indeed, tend to confirm that there are no black swans. This is because both a black raven and a red herring tend to confirm the claim that all ravens are black, in a very weak sense (Hempel 1945). That is because there are two ways to prove that all ravens are black. The first way is to find all the ravens and see that they are all black. The second way is that we could look at everything that is not black and see how many ravens are in that category. Both methods are impracticable, because of the large number of ravens and the even larger number of non-black items. But finding just one instance goes a non-zero, if infinitesimal way towards completing the task.

Taleb (2008) is still right for all practical purposes to say that if one observes a turkey, then a thousand instances of it being fed by the farmer does not prove that the farmer will not kill the turkey at Thanksgiving. But observing a thousand non-killing instances does go *some distance* to confirming that.[1] Again, Taleb (2008) is right to say that the negative instances are vastly more powerful than the positive ones. Thus a single observation of turkey-killing falsifies the hypothesis that the farmer will never kill the turkey, while 1,000 instances of not killing the turkey are insufficient to prove the hypothesis. But what about a billion samples? What about a googolplex of data points?

Naturally, the number of data points would need to be on a footing with the timescale of interest. It would not be useful to obtain billions of data points over a thousand days showing that the turkey was alive on each of them by simply dividing the turkey's lifetime up into nanoseconds. But imagine that we have daily data on a million turkeys all of whom are alive until they die after their full natural lifespan. Thus, I think, we can say that we have obtained good corroborative evidence for the hypothesis that none of the turkeys *in this sample* will be killed by the farmer. Care is then needed in extrapolating this result. Are these turkeys representative of all turkeys in the world? Apparently not, because some turkeys are, indeed, killed by the farmer. So we want to know what makes these turkeys different, and to try to be sure that the turkey population to which we have risk exposure is relevantly similar to the one for which we have obtained evidence that the farmer is unlikely to kill them. Naturally, it is very possible to make a serious and expensive mistake in conducting either of these tasks, but that does not change the point that we have a counter-example to the claim of Taleb (2008, p. 59) that there is "no such animal as corroborative evidence."

Taleb (2008) might respond here that there can be corroborative evidence in scientific fields, especially in areas governed by bell curves, but that financial markets are not governed by bell curves and therefore there can be no corroborative evidence. He is right that financial markets are not (always) governed by bell curves, despite the common assumption, often implicit, that they are. A bell curve, or Gaussian, is the sort of curve you would get from throwing two dice a large number of times. Central values are more likely, because there are more ways of obtaining them. You can get a total of six on the two dice in the following ways: 5 and 1; 4 and 2; 3 and 3; 3 and 3 (again); 2 and 4; 1 and 5. Extreme values are less likely since you can get a total of 2 only in two ways: 1 and 1 and then the same again backwards.

The likelihood of obtaining outcomes far away from the central values is described by the standard deviation, or sigma. Two-thirds of outcomes lie within one sigma of the average. 95% of outcomes lie within two sigma of the average. This continues indefinitely. Turning it around, outcomes more than 2 sigma away from the average only occur in 5% of outcomes for regimes governed by bell curves. Anything beyond about 5 sigma is extremely unlikely to occur by chance. For this reason, discoveries in particle physics are not accepted until they reach 5 sigma, meaning that the probability of observing the signal randomly must be less than 5 sigma.

We know that market returns are not completely governed by bell curves. LTCM was a hedge fund that became insolvent after seeing a series of events which would have been immensely unlikely if financial markets were governed by bell curves. Gladwell (2009b, p. 60) reports the results of Fama[2] to the effect that if markets were governed by bell curves, one would expect to see a five-sigma event every seven thousand years, but, in fact, "jumps of that magnitude happen in the stock market every three or four years." Black Monday, on which the DJIA declined 25% in a day, was a 20 sigma event (Bogle 2008, p. 32). These points together are, I think, conclusive. But further argument is needed to show that there can be *no* corroborative evidence in financial markets.

Since I have introduced a graded concept of confirmation above, we can say that the fact that a stock price has not declined to zero in any trading day in the last 60 years *tends to confirm* that it will not. Taleb (2008) is, of course, right to say that this is not proof that it will not decline. But it does represent corroborative evidence of non-zero value that it will not do so. Otherwise we would have to say that we can be no more confident that a stock with 60 years of history of trading above zero will continue to do so, than that a stock with one day of history of trading above zero will continue to do so. Even though there are famous examples of companies like Kodak, which traded for many years and then had their entire business model removed by technology, there are others where threatened incumbents responded and adopted new technology. Nokia famously was a paper company before rising and falling in the fast-changing world of mobile phone handsets. Again, I think we can say that there is some legitimate increase in confidence well short of that required to move to certainty when we consider a stock that has traded for many years. There is some corroborative evidence for the claim that a company will be able to survive technological changes that threaten its business model if it has already done so in the past. Data on this will only tend to become more available as time progresses in the internet age.

One experienced trader identifies Confirmation Bias as a primary cause of losses, since traders often trade their last mistake, rather than update their beliefs for the current market situation. As Williams (1998, p. 9) puts it, "when reality does conflict with our belief systems, we will deny reality and distort incoming information to keep our unquestioned beliefs intact." Although he does not use the term, this is clearly a very good definition of Confirmation Bias and the problems caused by it in markets. It is also worth noting that the final chapter of Williams (1998) is devoted to the importance of mastering one's own psychology. This is perhaps significant because the book is a technical work on trading chart patterns, which ought to allow one to escape psychological factors.

An experiment has been run to investigate what biases might be apparent in assessment of the profitability of a company. More precisely, Corcos and Pannequin (2006) told their subjects that a company fell into one of two categories: a strong financial performer or a weaker one. They then gave their subjects a simulated sequence of earnings announcements that made it look more-or-less likely that the company fell into one or other category. The topic of inquiry was how quickly the subjects adjusted their initial views to the truth, given the unclear data they were receiving. Corcos and Pannequin (2006) found evidence for what they term 'conservatism,' meaning that subjects were too slow to update their initial beliefs given the data.³ I think we can equate this conservatism with Confirmation Bias. The implication is that investors will likely be too slow to change their minds once they have decided that a particular stock is strong or weak. It will take a longer sequence of countervailing results than would usually be the case if they were optimally updating their beliefs based on data. So, as usual, avoid this, but expect it in others.

I think that Confirmation Bias, possibly in combination with the Conformity Bias⁴ (§7.4) is behind the invariably cyclical nature of markets. At all previous high points in the credit cycle, there have been arguments to the effect that this time is different and the cycle has been abolished. This has been shown to be false by subsequent developments on 100% of occasions. Investor psychology can drive the inevitable recurrence of the cycle. Marks (2011, p. 74) notes that "investor psychology seems to spend much more time at the extremes than it does at a 'happy medium'." By this he means that investors in general tend to swing between euphoria and despair on occasions, but once in either state, they will tend to stay there for a long time. This is because Confirmation Bias will reinforce their views, whether they are currently highly positive or highly negative. As ever, the smart place to be on this parameter is wherever everyone else is not. I do not mean adopt the opposite emotional state so much as adopt the opposite trading posture. Buy when everyone wants to sell and vice versa.

We should be concerned if our positions are exposed to major adverse events for which the only suggestion of low probability is an inadequate sample. The problem here is that we are very bad at knowing what an adequate sample size is. Even professional psychological experimenters are massively over-confident about what sample size will be necessary to show that an effect in an experiment is real and not a fluctuation. So I suggest that the answer as to what is an adequate sample size is almost always going to be much more than you think. If you can obtain such a large data set, that is the way to go. Another heuristic might be to consider an event twice as bad as the worst one seen in the last century. If you find the effects of this unacceptable, it is probably time to rebalance, taking less risk or increasing diversification.

Even this can be tricky. Lewis (2010, p. 71) suggests that one issue behind the 2007–2008 crisis was what one might regard as false diversification. Portfolios were created of US mortgages and it was argued that they would be diverse portfolios if they included mortgages from a wide geographical spread within the US. I recall this argument being accepted generally in the markets and at the rating agencies, who were therefore prepared to accord high ratings to such portfolios. The idea was that not all parts of the US could experience house price declines and increased default rates at the same time, based on the fact that this had not happened for 60 or more years. This seemed convincing enough to me at the time, although Lewis (2010) suggests that it was obviously false. I contend that 60 years of data is good enough to believe that something which has not happened in that period is unlikely. One reason to say this is that you simply are never going to get any more data than that – often you will have much less – and so if you insist on more, you will be unable to take any risks. Now, though, it is incumbent on me to provide an alternative explanation of the 2007–2008 crisis, since I am suggesting that it was reasonable to rely on the fact that there had not been a concerted geographical decline in US house prices for 60 years. In fact, 60 years is probably already too much to ask. It is not usual in financial forecasting to use scenarios dating back from the Second World War, or even the period of recovery afterwards, because these times are just too unusual. Imagine if you were to use such data and it showed dramatic, negative effects on the predicted outcome, as one would expect. It would be natural for any client, internal or external, to ask what sort of event could cause models to make substantial negative forecasts about an asset value. It would be unhelpful in the extreme to explain to such a client that these outcomes last occurred in 1939 when Poland was invaded, because it tells the client nothing much about how probable such an outcome is in the future as seen now.

The suggestion made by Lewis (2010), that it was obvious that house prices could decline in all US locations at the same time, is itself an instance of Hindsight Bias (of which more in §5.5). We now know that it was, in fact, possible and therefore believe that it was obvious at the time that it could happen. I can tell you as a securitisation professional, it was extremely non-obvious; no-one saw this crisis coming and they would have done if there were obvious clues. Clearly, it was not obvious unless you want to believe that the market and the rating agencies were deliberately negligent. Believing that, I contend, takes you into the realm of conspiracy theories. The existence of some people who bet against the market, as outlined by Lewis (2010), not only does not support the idea that simultaneous house price declines were obviously possible, it falsifies it: because such people were so few. They were not relying on anything obvious; they each had specific psychology which meant that they made a different prediction to everyone else. If it was so obvious, why were they not joined by everyone else in making enormous and easy profits?[5]

What seems of much more consequence to me is that Lewis (2010, p. 71) also discloses that portfolios went from 2% subprime mortgages to a majority, without anything much happening to the market value of those portfolios or, more precisely, the amounts being charged to insure them against default. This strikes me as very odd and constitutes the root of the problem. In the UK securitisation market in which I was a specialist, there was little subprime lending and hence little subprime mortgage securitisation. But it was a central tenet to getting anything rated that if you allowed in the legal structure for the collateral quality to decline, the rating agencies would assume in their modelling that the collateral would, in fact, deteriorate to the maximum possible extent at the first available opportunity. For this reason, there was little point in allowing much of such scope because it would just harm the ratings and, thus, mean that the bonds would have to pay more interest.

One result of this was that there were enormous profits available in the UK mortgage securitisation market in the immediate post-crash environment, in which anything labelled 'securitisation' was toxic. (This continues to be largely the case.) B pieces – being the subordinated elements of securitisations which were in a higher risk position than senior A pieces – were trading at 5c on the $. I know of one trader who put a high six figure sum of his own money into such paper at that sort of rate. What happened next was not very much. These bonds were backed by prime UK mortgages. Default rates ticked up a minor amount, but culturally, people in the UK pay their mortgages.

Culture seems very important to this story. Lewis (2010) also points out several times that major buyers of US subprime mortgage securitisations were German regional banks. In Germany, there is no house price inflation, most people rent and those people who do have mortgages have very high credit quality. There is an instrument called a Pfandbrief in Germany, which is basically a mortgage securitisation. I understand that these instruments have a 200-year history without defaults. If that is the culture you are from, maybe you scrutinise less thoroughly a product which carries apparently the same risk. If those investors started examining US subprime mortgages carrying through some Pfandbrief-inspired hypotheses strengthened by Confirmation Bias, we have an explanation for the problem which is valid even if those investors knew they were not actually buying Pfandbrief.

UK house prices declined over about two years from 2007 by about 16% but that just took them back to 2004 levels and was, in any case, not savage enough to do much damage to securitisations. And there was no particular reason to expect rapid repayments or other quick changes, unlike the case in the US. Once it became apparent that the B pieces were going to more-or-less come out fully paid, they traded back up to 95c on the $ which obviously represented a major profit for my former colleague. What this tells us is that it will be worthwhile avoiding allowing your Confirmation Bias to appear to confirm the hypothesis that 'all securitisations are bad investments,' even if it looks that way initially from where you are standing.

Returning to the rule following question and going even further, Wittgenstein (2001, §201 et seq.) shows that we cannot even in principle show what the rule is to arbitrary precision. For example, we would be very unlikely ever to distinguish between the candidate rules 'numbers ascending' and 'numbers ascending up to a googolplex and then all Xs' because hardly anyone would think of testing the region of numbers beyond a googolplex. There would likely be little practical value in doing so but, of course, the same argument works just as well if we set the change point to a small distance beyond whatever is tested. This work of Wittgenstein (2001), which is known as the rule-following paradox, was aimed at showing that we would never know which rule was being followed.

It may look like philosophical hair-splitting to say we cannot tell the difference between '2, 4, 6 …' being 'even numbers ascending' and 'even numbers ascending up to point X' but there are, I think, real practical applications here. That is so because Wittgenstein (2001, §201 et seq.) can also be read as reminding us that there are plenty more hypotheses out there that can explain the data. And, of course, the key point is that the harder it is to find the correct hypothesis, the fewer people there are who will have been able to follow you and find that correct hypothesis, and the more valuable the information is.

The vignette about 'numbers ascending' illustrates how insidious Confirmation Bias can be in that the true hypothesis is simply invisible to us. If you are one of the few people who are very good at hypothesis selection, you will be able to avoid the problem. For the rest of us, maybe the answer is to make bold or even random claims and see if you can break them. There is no shame in proposing a radical hypothesis for test purposes. Note that the negation of a weak statement is a strong statement. For example, a weak statement in philosophical terms would be 'some cars are yellow.' The negation is 'no cars are yellow,' which is a strong statement. By 'weak' and 'strong' here, I simply refer to the amount of evidence that would be required to prove the statement. In order to prove a weak statement like 'some cars are yellow,' we just need to find a yellow car. By contrast, to prove a strong statement like 'no cars are yellow,' we would have to examine all the cars in the world.

Transferring these ideas back to the example, a relevant weak statement would be 'numbers ascend' while the stronger one is 'numbers ascend evenly.' Inverting this, we find that the negation of the weak statement is strong: 'numbers do not ascend,' which is, in fact, already ruled out by the initial sample. Inverting the strong statement produces a weak one: 'numbers do not ascend evenly.' Trying to break that involves finding an odd number which is unexpectedly allowed by the hidden rule, which is again the exact question to ask to figure out the puzzle. So one approach would be to try to break weak statements because that is easier to do, and to negate strong statements to find a weak one for this purpose if a weak hypothesis does not present itself.

All of this is very hard to get right even for college-educated people, and even those who have studied logic. Again, if you can do it reliably, good luck and stick with it. There are some occasions when we can do it well: when rules for detection of cheats map on to logical rules. Since we are very good at detecting cheats, on these occasions we will perform well on logical tests (Pinker 2015, pp. 336–337). So for the rest of us, let us now look at a cheater detection version, which is much easier for us to handle correctly. Pinker (2015, p. 336) restates the first Wason problem with cards by asking subjects to imagine they are a bouncer in a bar. Subjects are charged with checking whether everyone drinking beer is over 18. Alternatively put, they are testing the hypothesis that 'if someone is drinking beer, they are over 18.' The people to be checked, standing in now for the cards, are: 'drinking beer, drinking coke, aged 25, aged 16.' It is immediately obvious that the people to be checked are the 16-year-old and the beer drinker. We, in the role of bouncer, simply do not care about the person drinking coke or the 25-year-old because they cannot break the rule; they cannot falsify the hypothesis. On the other hand, the 16-year-old must be checked to be sure he is not drinking beer and the beer-drinker must be checked to make sure that he is over 18. So this tells us that we can greatly aid our clarity of logical analysis and avoid some instances of Confirmation Bias by restating the question in terms of people. We are better at making predictions about people than about numbers, but as this book shows, making predictions about people is a Theory of Mind task and bias mismatch is a major cause of Theory of Mind errors. Watch out for them.

5.2 Clustering Illusion

We see patterns where none exist. We find faces in cliffs and toast. We tend to think that any run of similar items looks pattern rich even when it is random. When we look a random stream of noise, it is perhaps natural to try to make sense of it by focussing on where it seems to fall into a pattern. With any stream of random numbers, we find nothing to look at apart from where, say, three fives occur together. We will then start looking for other multiple occurrences of five, and soon we have convinced ourselves that there is something interesting going on with the fives. We tend to jump to this conclusion much too easily.

Gilovich (1993, p. 16) defines the Clustering Illusion as occurring when we believe falsely that "random events such as coin flips should alternate between heads and tails more than they do." For example, in a sequence of 20 tosses of a fair coin, there is a 25% chance of a sequence of six heads, which seems to us far too ordered to be random. Alternatively, consider the probability of the two sets of results of coin tosses: HHHTTT looks much more pattern-rich and therefore improbable than HTHHTT but they actually have the same probability. The reason for this may be that we can easily mix up two probabilities. The probability of getting six heads in a row at a defined location – say, right from the start – is quite low. If you see six heads from the first six throws, you can certainly take some notice and suspect something is going on. However, the probability of seeing six heads sequentially *anywhere* in the 20 tosses is much higher. This is because there are many more ways of getting six heads than one; it could start on toss one, on toss two, or on any of them. We miss this, because we just see the six heads straight away and start from thinking that it looks improbable, whereas as said, it is only improbable if the start point is forecast in advance.

The Clustering Illusion is this tendency to see patterns in data that are not really there. Gilovich (1993, p. 15) provides further examples including a belief that the random pattern of bomb sites in London actually shows a pattern; this effect is due to selecting the quadrant frame almost in order to arrive at the view that some quadrants of London were more heavily bombed. Very few people would turn the map of London on its side to see if the effect is still visible – it is not – but this, of course, should still work if one had successfully identified clusters.

It seems to me that the effects of the Clustering Illusion in markets will primarily be to bolster the malign effects of the Gambler's Fallacy (§4.5). Not only will the latter bias cause participants to act as though the probability of an event is increased by its previously having occurred when this need not be so, but they will be starting with probability estimates that are distorted by seeing patterns that may not be there. As Gilovich (1993, p. 10) notes, "gamblers claim that they experience hot and cold streaks in random rolls of the dice, and they alter their bets accordingly." There is no way that this can be an optimal or rational way to proceed unless the dice are fixed, and if they are fixed, we can be sure that they will not be fixed in favour of the gambler.

This type of combined effect may explain part of the popularity of the so-called technical analysis or charting that I mentioned in Chapter 2. While I think that there is some value in this approach, to the extent that sometimes it may reflect the momentum generated by investor psychology, I think it receives somewhat more attention than it should, because adherents are falling victim to the Clustering Illusion. They see patterns more than they should and they think they will continue or repeat themselves.

Hirshleifer (2001, p. 1575) reports evidence showing that "people misperceive random walks to be shifts between continuation and reversal regimes," which could be an illustration of the Clustering Illusion in action. As I mentioned above, it could also work with the Gambler's Fallacy to create excess momentum in stock prices. It may also lie behind excess momentum in mutual fund prices. Investors are bombarded with data about the past performance of such funds, presumably because they often make buying decisions based on them, and yet as Wilcox (2008, p. 58) notes, "the bulk of evidence about the mutual fund market strongly suggests that past performance is a miserable predictor of future performance." Mutual fund selections, if you insist on having them, as with stock selections, should be made on fundamentals.

The Clustering Illusion will work with another cause of market underperformance: that deriving from the 'illusion of control' (Nofsinger 2016, p. 18). Experiments were conducted by Langer on coin-tossing and people's beliefs about their ability to predict them. Coin flips are random and cannot be predicted by anyone, ever. Skill, experience, and what has just happened are all irrelevant. Konnikova (2016, p. 276) notes that despite this, people "treated it like a skill instead of dumb luck;" they thought that they would improve with practice. She concludes that "we think we are in control even when there is no way we can be."

The analogy here in markets will be seen when traders sit hunched over screens, attempting by force of will to change the GBPUSD data point in the direction that favours their trade. This is much more common than you might think, in the same way that you might be surprised at people thinking that they can get better at predicting random events. Both of these surprises are, of course, systematic Theory of Mind errors caused by failure to take account of biases, which is the major underlying theme of this book. The Clustering Illusion makes the illusion of control worse because it amplifies it; traders in the grip of both will imagine whole patterns that are not there and that they are controlling those patterns. Avoid all of this, and expect excess momentum. Konnikova (2016, p. 278) observes that "traders with the highest illusion of control performed the worst" as measured by compensation and evaluation.

As ever, the direction of causation is unobservable and may be the inverse of what we intuitively expect. Prima facie, it looks like what is happening here is that the illusion of control causes poor trading performance. That may well be true, and it remains a good idea to avoid it. However, it can also be the case that being a poor trader causes the illusion of control. In other words, only the poor traders *need* the illusion of control. In that case, if you notice yourself exhibiting it, it is worth re-evaluating what you are doing. Your strategy must be wrong. Ditch the Clustering Illusion and the illusion of control and do something else.

5.3 Position Effect

This is a rather strange bias which has received a great deal of attention in the literature, partly because of its oddity. People seem to select from a range of similar or identical options based more on the location of the object rather than aspects of its quality. Even odder yet, they fabricate reasons for their selection and vehemently deny that it had anything to do with the placement of the object. I have included this brief section because the Position Effect is very heavily discussed and potent, even though I am unfortunately not in a position to offer cast-iron trading strategies based on it.

There does not seem to be a settled name for this bias in the literature, so I have adopted Position Effect since that was the term used by the pioneer investigators. An experiment was run using some stockings in a shopping mall, so some commentators have referred to 'the stockings experiment' and others to 'the shopping experiment.' The shoppers were asked to choose between some pairs of stockings which were, in fact, identical. One might expect that the choices would be random, since there is no basis on which to differentiate between the stockings, and since the choice does not really matter. However, Nisbett and Wilson (1977, p. 243) report that they observed "a pronounced left-to-right position effect, such that the right-most object in the array was heavily over-chosen."

Note that the shoppers merely had to say which of an array of identical pairs of stockings was of superior quality. It is often mis-reported in descriptions of the experiment that the shoppers were given the pair of stockings they chose, which would have given them some interest in the selection. It could be that adding some level of motivation to the subjects weakened the effect; though as we have seen, biases tend to be robust against exogenous attempts to alleviate their intensity. Johansson *et al.* (2006) criticised Nisbett and Wilson (1977) for the strange and contrived nature of the task: when shopping, we are generally choosing between items of different quality. Moreover, we intend to take one of the items home with us, so we care about the choice.

Harris (1992, p. 133) attempts to explain the effect: "the shopping-mall experiment [...] I suspect, involves [...] faulty assumptions about what causes the [...] behaviour." The mechanism would be that the "action of choosing the right-most item is not governed by the decision-making system at all" (Harris 1992, p. 133). The original experiments also have a candidate explanation which is consistent with Harris's view. The authors say that it could be a 'last-seen bias' rather than a 'rightward bias.' This would add up in a shopping context at least; imagine you are out shopping for a particular item, and you have seen several that would do in shops you visited previously, and elsewhere in the shop in which you are currently. You would need a very good reason to go back to one of the previous shops to pick up an item and you would never rationally do so if the items were of identical quality and similar price. Note that no sales or ownership were involved in the experiment and so price does not feature as a factor. If this is true, then it means that we sometimes make choices where we think we have used our decision-making decision and we have not.

What might this mean in markets? I will concede that I find it difficult to operationalise a trading strategy based on the Position Effect; I would gladly consider possibilities if others can suggest them. I have included it here partly in order to request such ideas, but also because the Position Effect is so strong and so strange that its influences ought, somehow, to be tradable. It is also quite possibly the most discussed bias in the literature; Johansson *et al.* (2006, p. 673) note that Nisbett and Wilson (1977) has been "cited an astonishing 2633 times." I will offer some speculative sketches of what possibilities I can see below, and also issue a plea for some empirical work.

One way to try to trade the Position Effect might be derivable from consideration of what is driving the behaviour. If the 'last-seen' explanation given by Harris (1992, p. 133) is correct, and I suspect it is, we also need to decide whether it relates to the preferential direction in which people scan items. Last-seen only gets you right-ward if the usual scanning direction is from left to right. Nisbett and Wilson (1977) conducted their experiment in a US shopping mall; we may assume that all of their subjects were English speaking. English is read from left to right. If you were contemplating markets in the UAE for example, you might want to bear in mind that Arabic is scanned from right to left, which could reverse the Position Effect.

One difficulty arises from the paradox of trying to be a rational investor in a world packed with irrational ones. We have already considered how rational investors can be drawn in the direction of irrationality (Wang 1993). It can be rational to trade partly irrationally if one rationally expects irrational trades from others. In particular, in this context, a rational trader might expect stocks listed at the end of a section to be priced somewhat higher than they should be based on fundamentals. One rational course of action might then be to buy the stock on the basis that others will also do so. However, I suspect that a better approach would be to invert this and instead buy the potentially overlooked stocks that are 'first-seen' or left-most, or top-most. This would be especially valuable in a left-to-right listing of similarly valuable stocks. One would then be waiting for fundamentals to reassert themselves, which is a rational position. While it might also be rational to buy the unreasonably favoured right-most stocks, one would then be hostage to the reassertion of fundamentals, and that is the less optimal of the two possibilities.

Here, and with other biases, a germane question is as to how long it will take for rational investors to drive out irrational ones, and if, indeed, that will happen. It is, I think, clear that the Position Effect is completely irrational to first order in markets. I restrict the claim to markets because it is conceivable that the Position Effect has some value in decision-making processes – perhaps just to cut to the chase, as it were, in scenarios where the decision in question is low-impact – but I fail to see any way in which it can be rational as a part of a stock choice, other than with the caveat I will mention next. This one caveat relates to the idea of the previous paragraph: it could be rational to trade irrationally if one expects other investors to do so. More particularly here, it could be rational to trade assuming falsely that the Position Effect is a good guide to value in stocks if one expects that other investors will trade as though that assumption is correct. And this is why it becomes important to have an idea as to how long it will take before rational investors force out irrational ones.

Sandroni (2005) works with some equations which bear on this question. He simulates a market which includes some rational agents and some irrational ones. The rational agents change their estimates of the probability of an asset paying a high dividend based on applying Bayes's Rule and the irrational ones do not. It is actually controversial whether Bayes's Rule is the optimal way to update probability estimates or not; I favour the idea myself, however. I think Sandroni (2005, p. 742) goes slightly too far when he describes non-Bayesian estimators as not just irrational but as actually suffering from a cognitive bias. I can see the thought behind this, but this line would suggest that not knowing a fairly complex and difficult to use piece of mathematics means exhibiting a cognitive bias, while all of the other biases I describe in this book are involuntary and automatic rather than a reflection of not having attended a statistics course.

There is one way of reframing this failure to use Bayes's Rule, or an approximation thereof, in a way that makes it look like a bias. One major advantage of updating somewhat in line with Bayes is that it means avoiding 'base rate neglect.' This was the problem I discussed in §4.2 where subjects are likely to say that someone who has the stereotypical characteristics of a librarian is a librarian even if the subject knows that the person under consideration was drawn from a sample composed primarily of engineers. This is an application of Bayes's Rule because the rule tells us how to update our estimates of probability based on new information and a prior estimate of probability.

Just knowing of the existence of such a rule reminds us that, when assessing the probability that someone selected from a pool is a librarian, we need to consider and combine two underlying probabilities: how many librarians are there in the pool and how likely is it that someone who has the characteristics of a librarian is a librarian. It also raises the important question as to how certain we are that there is such a thing as a stereotypical librarian – of which I am doubtful, not least because of the way it relies on the Fundamental Attribution Error (§8.1) – and whether that should be an important consideration. One can have this realisation and make a much better estimate, which will make one a more Bayesian updater, without having an understanding of the exact formula. So while I argued in §4.2 that exhibiting base rate neglect was an example of using the Representativeness Heuristic, and that this is a bias to be avoided, there is nevertheless scope to avoid making the claim that failure to apply Bayes's Rule is a bias, because just moving in the Bayesian direction, without fully applying the rule, suffices to avoid or significantly reduce the effects of the Representativeness Heuristic.

Nevertheless, Sandroni (2005, p. 752) produces the following fascinating conclusions: "[s]urvival in financial markets requires fast learning" more than it requires a completely correct initial belief set. This is because there is, in the Sandroni (2005) world, as in real markets, a great deal of data available and a large number of possible reasonable beliefs about market developments. So since there are plenty of opportunities to fix sub-optimal beliefs quickly, the rate of fixing them is more important than how bad they are to begin with.

Accordingly, not only must the agents adopt Bayes's Rule, or a similarly optimal method of belief set optimisation, but they must do so quickly: "[t]he initial beliefs could be far away from the truth, but the speed of learning needs to be as fast as that of Bayesian learning [; in] order to survive, agents must quickly forecast close to the Bayesian paradigm." Non-survival of agents in the simulation means that they attain zero wealth and no longer influence prices. This means that prices are eventually set by the Bayesian agents in the experiment. Analogously, in real markets, sub-optimal agents will lose all of their investments and will exit stock markets.

Obviously, you do not want to be one of these sub-optimal agents. Any sub-optimal agent will fairly quickly exit the market, with the losses made constituting profits for the optimal agents. This would be a fairly short game, of course, except for the point observed by Sandroni (2005, p. 744) to the effect that "financial anomalies driven by cognitive biases can only persist if behavioural agents keep entering the economy bringing sufficient wealth from outside sources." We may, in fact, assume that this continues indefinitely. There are new sub-optimal non-Bayesian-updating agents born every minute, to coin a phrase. Some of them continue in sub-optimal behaviour because human biases are often ineradicable. And, of course, 'optimal' does not mean 'infallible.' Even if Bayes's Rule is the best method of estimating probability, it does not provide certainty about the future. Every time any of us makes a mistake in markets or trades based on a cognitive bias, someone else invariably benefits, sooner or later. And finally, there is room for doubt on the extent to which markets are described by mathematics. I regret to inform you that in my view, the answer is 'somewhat,' and I will be needing another book to expand on 'somewhat.'

Returning specifically to the Position Effect, a major objection to this entire approach involves observing that nowadays, a great deal of stock information is available on the internet in a wide variety of formats, which means that various stocks will be on the right, and on the left, or in the middle depending on which exact web page investors are contemplating. That could mean that the Position Effect is much weaker today than it was in the past, when stocks were listed primarily in the financial press and there was a dominant newspaper in each major market which printed stock prices in a very similar format every day. This, of course, is an empirical prediction, so experimentation would be valuable. While we cannot now test the strength of the Position Effect in the pre-internet past, we might be able to identify emerging market jurisdictions where there is a dominant web page or financial news sheet and look for the influence of the Position Effect.

One discussion of the Position Effect occurs in the context of a discussion of how we fall prey to confidence tricksters. Konnikova (2016, p. 161) notes that con artists "manipulate this all the time by placing objects or people they want you to gravitate toward in more privileged positions." This, I think, underlines the importance of the effect since it seems to be strong, non-transparent in that we are unaware of its influence and used for malign purposes. Again, it is difficult to operationalise this, since it is pointless for me to advise you to be wary of the Position Effect when being conned. Obviously, I want you not to be conned at all. I nevertheless hope that this section has given you some food for thought and at least alerted you to one of the odder biases. In addition, you would be wise to be suspicious if you suspect someone is using the Position Effect as a persuader because it suggests that they do not have anything more rational to employ.

5.4 Conjunction Fallacy

This error is made when assessing the probability of two events. The probability of two events cannot be higher than the probability of one of them alone, but we sometimes say this, though maybe not explicitly.

The probability of two events A and B is given by multiplying the probability of event A by event B. For example, if the chance of a coin toss coming up tails is 50%, then the probability of getting two tails in a row is 25%. The maximum probability of an event is 1, or 100%, for events which are certain to occur. A consequence of this is a law of statistics called the conjunction rule which holds that the probability of both events A and B occurring must be no greater than the probability of event B occurring alone. This is because the probability of A and B occurring will have a maximum value when A is certain and that maximum value will be the same as the probability of B occurring alone. As Tversky and Kahneman (1983, p. 298) state, "[t]he violation of the conjunction rule in a direct comparison of B to A&B is called the conjunction fallacy." In other words, the Conjunction Fallacy occurs whenever we assess the probability of two events as higher than one of them alone.

The canonical illustration of the Conjunction Fallacy is the famous 'Linda' experiment. Subjects are told that Linda majored in philosophy, is very bright and as a student "was deeply concerned with issues of discrimination and social justice" (Tversky and Kahneman 1983, p. 297). Subjects are then asked whether it is more likely that a) Linda works as a bank teller or b) Linda works as a bank teller and is active in the feminist movement. Subjects consistently state that b) is more probable, even though it is impossible that b) could be more probable than a) alone, since b) includes a).

The Conjunction Fallacy is closely related to the Representativeness Heuristic and the Availability Heuristic, since what is happening is that a reduction in extension is being combined with an increase in representativeness and availability. Thus it becomes easier to think of examples of a category even when the number of members of that category has decreased. This is what leads us to make the errors in probability estimation. There are also links to what Taleb (2008, ch. 6) calls the Narrative Fallacy, which combines our tendencies to remember facts linked by a story and over-attribute causation. It is much easier to construct a story about Linda being a committed social activist at college and continuing with those interests later. This is why Tversky and Kahneman (1983, p. 299) found that 85% of subjects rated b) more likely than a).

Taleb (2007, p. 205) observes that he is "glad to be a trader taking advantage of peoples' biases." This is an important point, which I have basically expanded into this entire book. It is worth pointing out, though, that in the same paragraph he mentions the Linda problem, which I am discussing here, but he ascribes it to part of the evidence for the Availability Heuristic. While I can see how the example of Linda relates to the Availability Heuristic, it is best discussed in its original context, that of the Conjunction Fallacy. So, while Taleb (2007, p. 205) makes a useful point about the benefits of understanding the biases of others when one is trading, he may not always be precise enough in situating those biases within the psychological literature correctly.

Another notorious example of the problem deals with the probability that someone who tests positive for a disease has the disease. The problem here is false positives. These may vastly outweigh the people who really have the disease for exactly the sorts of rare disease for which one will be tested. Imagine that the probability of having the disease is only 1 in 1,000 and the accuracy of the test is 95%. When one is asked the question: 'what is the probability that someone showing a positive test result for the disease actually has the disease, there is an almost irresistible pull to answer '95%." This is wrong though because many more people will test positive as a result of the 5% error rate – multiplied by the whole group, remember – than will test positive because they have the disease.

Pinker (2015) points out how this bias can be avoided or minimised. The line is based on the idea that we may have evolved our probability assessments to work over groups of people or events rather than single shot probability. There are parallels to the way that reframing the Wason test in cheater detection mode (§5.1) – i.e. making it about people rather than about numbers – made logical analysis much easier. Again, this should make no difference, but in practice it seems to make our lives much easier here if we consider groups of people. Pinker (2015, p. 348) notes that if the question is changed to the following, much better results are obtained: "[o]ne out of a thousand Americans has the disease; fifty out of a thousand healthy people test positive; we assembled a thousand Americans; how many who test positive have the disease?"

The right answer here seems to be much more readily found. The test will very likely (95%) find the one American in the group of 1,000 who has the disease. Another 50 will falsely test positive. So we have a group of 51 who test positive of which one is the person who really has the disease and 50 are false positives who are healthy. So the probability of having the disease given a positive test is 1/51 or just less than 2% – much lower than the 95% which is the accuracy rate of the test. This is why doctors often order tests to be performed again, because getting the same wrong answer twice requires being in the 5% false positive section twice – which is unlikely.

Taking this 'people based' approach makes up to 92% of people (Pinker 2015, p. 346) able to make good statistical inferences. So we should always try to think this way. In markets, avoid trying to compute multiple layers of probability but set the story up in a different way. Ask yourself questions like: 'if a thousand investors do X and some then do Y, how many have then done both X and Y?' Or: 'if one in a thousand investors is right about a positive property of stock X and 95% of them are wrong about it but have bought stock X anyway, what is the number of investors who have bought stock X for the right reason?'

5.5 Hindsight Bias And The Antifragile

Hindsight Bias, which might also be termed the 'I knew it all along' effect, arises when people think that they foresaw something which they now know to have happened. Alternatively, an attenuated form of the bias might be that people believe that they assessed the probability of an event which they now know took place as much higher than the actual assessment of the probability of the event they gave or assumed prior to the event.

In a related formulation, Bernstein *et al.* (2007, p. 1374) note that in "hindsight bias, one's present knowledge influences one's recollection of previous beliefs." This is true and consistent with the phrasing above, but it also suggests a mechanism whereby the shape and probability of the event before it happened are massaged in memory in order to appear as more probable than one thought prior to the event.

Put like this, the Hindsight Bias looks slightly confusing. Why should we need to think that we predicted unlikely events when we did not? Perhaps we want to give ourselves the comfort of thinking that the world is more predictable and controllable than it really is, a line which would accord well with the general approach of Taleb (2008).

One account of how Hindsight Bias arises sees it as resulting from the tendency to regard the past as fixed and the future as changeable. This state of affairs may well be true, but it is important to remember that at one point, what is now the past was still the future and so even if it is fixed now, it was not then. On this line, what has happened is that the past has *become* fixed. What has also changed is our state of knowledge. We have, arguably, no knowledge of the future, though often we can make predictions in which we can be highly confident. We can have knowledge about the past, however, and we can also take steps to improve such knowledge. None of this means that the past as we can now see it was inevitable. The failure to appreciate this results in Hindsight Bias.

You may recall the story in Chapter 2 about day traders and the error in Marks (2011, p. 18). I said that the error was to fail to appreciate that the day trader missed out on upside but also avoided risk. One way this can be seen is as an illustration of Hindsight Bias in action. Because, in actual fact, the stock went up, there is a tendency to think that it had to go up, and that no risk of it falling existed. That is why it was easy to miss the fact that this risk did exist, even though in the period under consideration, the risk of a fall did not eventuate.

In interesting research that supports my general line that biases cause behaviour prediction errors, Bernstein *et al.* (2007, p. 1374) study 3–5 year olds and find that their performance "on hindsight and [Theory of Mind] tasks was significantly correlated." It is also consistent with the idea that improved cognitive capacities result in both reduction in susceptibility to Hindsight Bias and improved Theory of Mind abilities, but that seems to entail that adults would be less liable to Hindsight Bias and that does not seem to be the case.

Bernstein *et al.* (2007, p. 1374) give the formal definition of Hindsight Bias: it "occurs when outcome knowledge influences the judgments we make for a naive other or a naive "prior" self." Specifically, we are unable to detach ourselves from our current knowledge of what actually happened when we try to determine whether we previously knew that what was going to happen was going to happen, or whether we thought it was probable. We believe wrongly that what has now happened was seen by us as probable before it occurred; it looks as though it was then probable because it is now certain that it happened. Making this type of judgment is, of course, a paradigm Theory of Mind task. 'What would O do given knowledge of the probability of event X occurring?' requires an accurate estimation of the probability of X as seen by O at the prior time. Starting with the incorrect assumption that O was certain that X would occur because S now knows that X has occurred will lead to systematic Theory of Mind error.

This can be quite frustrating if O is S's prior self. As I write in early 2016, the Chinese stock market has experienced a very substantial correction. It had been in a bubble for quite some time, with a 12-month gain of 140% in the year to mid-2015. Gains like this are always unsustainable. The Chinese market is not easily accessible to Western investors, and so I asked a colleague whether we should consider buying puts on the Hang Seng index in Hong Kong. The question was whether this was linked closely enough to mainland markets to benefit from the downside when it came. We never reached certainty on that and I did not make a trade. Sometime later, I heard of an individual who was a 'mid-level' employee in a major bank who had gone ahead and done exactly what I considered. He bought 25k worth of 25% out of the money put options on the Hang Seng in June 2015. Normally, this is just throwing away 25k, but in this case the person made half a million pounds and quit his job. Some people might think that this is not a sensible trade – for every person who got it right, there must have been ten who mis-timed it. This type of activity should definitely only be conducted with money that can be totally lost without adverse consequences. When I heard this, of course, I felt bad. Why had I not done the trade, when I had had the same idea? And after all, it was certain that the index would decline, and I knew that at the time.

The latter reasoning is, of course, false. I did not know that the index would decline. I thought it was probable, but I was not sure enough to commit money, and I did not know much about the timing of the crash. Timing is very important in purchasing options like puts because they have defined durations, and become more expensive with a longer duration. That makes perfect sense – if someone is offering you a bet that X will not happen, they will give you worse odds if you say X will indeed happen in the next six months as opposed to in the next three months. I made a reasonable decision under the true state of knowledge that I had at the time. So, succumbing to Hindsight Bias here is a way of becoming depressed about one's own performance. As we know from Kramer (2008), this is itself a hindrance to good performance because it will stifle one's risk appetite, as well as being affectively unpleasant. It also interferes with making a dispassionate post mortem assessment of what has gone right and what has gone wrong in reviewing our investment decision making processes.

As Taleb (2007, p. 56) notes, Hindsight Bias also makes it hard for us to remember that "a mistake is not something to be determined after the fact, but in the light of the information until that point."[6] What he means is that while it is fine to decide whether a particular decision was a mistake later on, it is not acceptable to do so using information that only became available after the decision. It is equally hard to avoid the negative emotional impact of making a mistake, but one way to minimise the problem is at least to reduce the incidence of genuine mistakes. It cannot be that 'all bad trades were mistakes,' it must be 'all trades I made, which I should have been able to see at the time were bad, were mistakes.' The latter category should have many fewer members.

A very interesting study showed that the effects are significant and damaging to financial market professionals, which underlines once again my general message that biases are a key issue for traders. Biais and Weber (2009) studied 85 staff from the trading department of two investment banks. They found that a major problem occurred in estimating volatility. Biais and Weber (2009, p. 1018) note that on "observing unexpectedly positive or negative returns, rational agents should raise their volatility estimates." These sorts of events are, of course, very frequent. However, agents exhibiting Hindsight Bias, who "knew it all along," "fail to understand that such returns were unexpected, and thus underestimate variances" (Biais and Weber 2009, p. 1018). This could be a major driver of a key source of poor portfolio performance. If investors are unprepared for sudden large losses, that would explain their propensity to sell in anti-bubble scenarios. Conversely, they will take less account than they should of sudden upside, seeing it as unsurprising and confirming their good judgment in buying the stock. It should be seen as an invitation to reconsider the investment case for the stock, without, of course, going too far and displaying the equally unhelpful Disposition Effect. This effect is a description of the way that fear of future regret causes investors to sell winners too early, among other deleterious effects (Nofsinger 2016, ch. 3). As an example of one type of this sort of problem, Biais and Weber (2009, p. 1018) observe that "hindsight-biased agents who underestimate volatility will underprice options and fail to hedge appropriately."

Biais and Weber (2009, p. 1018) also report that "hindsight-biased agents will form inaccurate beliefs about asset returns, leading to suboptimal trades and inferior financial performance." This is a more straightforward problem: it simply represents an inability to work on the basis of accurate returns data. The inability to be surprised about anything can only be obtained by massaging the facts about what one believed, sometimes quite dramatically so. Further, "[h]indsight-biased agents will also fail to question economic analyses that are at odds with the underlying facts" (Biais and Weber 2009, p. 1018), which would be especially dangerous when combined with Confirmation Bias (§5.1).

Crucially for my argument in this book that biases throw off Theory of Mind and that this is a key cause of trading underperformance, Biais and Weber (2009, p. 1018) conclude that investors suffering from Hindsight Bias "will fail to estimate accurately the difference between their information and that of other traders." This is basically a statement that the bias has, in fact, caused Theory of Mind errors, of a sort which bears comparison with the Curse of Knowledge bias I will be discussing later (§7.1). It means that extremely profitable trading opportunities will be missed, since knowing when one is better informed than others or perhaps when one is justifiably more confident than others is almost the best possible position to be in in markets. The line taken here by the authors – that a bias can cause a Theory of Mind error and that this is important – provides assurance that my project in this book is worthwhile. If one bias can do that, would not all of them do so?

The strength of this conclusion is reinforced by the conclusion of Biais and Weber (2009) that higher paid bankers of all types exhibited less Hindsight Bias irrespective of what department they were in, their age and experience, their seniority or any other factor. Notably, having a high Hindsight Bias score was a guarantee of not being highly paid in the research department. These results were obtained from professionals being asked questions about their specific areas of expertise and on which they were highly motivated, so one suspects that the market does not teach one to avoid the bias. My suggestion, then, as a rather glib rule of thumb, is that whenever one is asked to make a judgment relying on a volatility estimate, to consider the volatility estimate and then double the number you first thought of. It would at least be an interesting thought experiment to ask the question: what would happen to my proposed course of action if everything is at least twice as volatile as I think?

There are two candidate explanations for how Hindsight Bias can arise (Bernstein et al. 2007, p. 1375). On one view, memories are overwritten with new information. On the second view, the memories are retained but they are accessed in a biased way. My view, which is probably consistent with either of these two approaches is one of cross-talk between memories of data and memories of what one thought about that data. Bernstein et al. (2007, p. 1374) describe a situation where S has to estimate what O will say as the height of the Statue of Liberty. If S has the correct answer, 151ft, S will make a number of Theory of Mind errors about O's estimate of the height, even when O is S at a previous time. So, S's view of O's view of the height moves towards the correct answer when S has that correct answer. Before S is told the answer, there is much more variance predicted in O's answer. Since this applies also to O when O was S at a previous point, we can ask the critical question of S: What did you think the height was before? Now S will claim that S's previous estimate was much better than it was.

This does not happen immediately. Adults who said a second ago that the height of the Statue of Liberty was 200ft do not commonly claim now that they said 175ft. However, they will move towards claiming that they thought that once sufficient time has elapsed; Hindsight Bias is robust "from minutes to years" (Bernstein et al. 2007, p. 1375). In parallel, we can see this effect in a much stronger form in developing children. Those who are too young to pass the False Belief Task will be quite brazen in their assertions of what they thought and said a few seconds ago. If they now know that there are Smarties in the pencil case, they will claim that they knew that all along and that is what they said, even if they actually said 'pencils' not a minute before. The explanation for this is probably that they lack a Theory of Mind at the age of four and so they are incapable of ascribing false belief. That explanation, of course, will have to account for the challenging results of Onishi and Baillargeon (2005) who suggest that even infants can ascribe false beliefs.

The cross-talk idea of mine suggests that there is contamination between updating the memory of the data and updating the memory of what one said about the data. The first type of updating is unalloyedly positive. If one thought that the Statue of Liberty was 200ft high and now one knows the true value of 151ft, one is better off storing this new data. Obviously, in this particular example it will probably have to be conceded that few people will ever find it of critical importance to know the height of the Statue of Liberty, but that does not amount to an objection because the example generalises. Now, it is not the case that updating the memory of what one said is beneficial in exactly the same way. In fact, the opposite is true to some extent; one has a false belief if one believes that one previously said that the height was 175ft when one actually said that it was 200ft. There are two reasons this may be, I think. The first is the cross-talk idea. One has to update the actual information about the height, and the conceptually adjacent memory of what one said about the height can be updated in error at the same time, especially as time goes on. While this is an error, it might be one of the McKay and Dennett (2009) beneficial errors. It could even feed our own desire to look good; in other words our Self-Presentation Bias. I will discuss this bias in §8.3; it is a result of our desire to maintain healthy self-esteem. One can take spurious but no less beneficial self-satisfaction from the false belief that one gave a more accurate estimate of the height of the Statue of Liberty than one actually did. Again, it is important to recall here that the example generalises to all facts that one knows.

I think, in the trading context, what this also underlines is the need for accurate record keeping. Do not pretend to yourself that you bought a stock at $15 which has risen to $45 when, while it has done that, you did not buy it until it had got to $25. You must take a record of when you bought it and at what price; you will need this for tax purposes anyway. While you may pay a small price in terms of self-esteem, in the long run it will be more beneficial to have an accurate record. It will be better for your self-esteem if you can accurately state a smaller gain than make up an imaginary larger one. Overcoming Hindsight Bias will be crucial to this endeavour. Bear in mind that what you hear from other investors will be exaggeratedly positive for not just cynical reasons – i.e. they will lie about how well they have done – but for the arguably less objectionable reason that they have fallen prey to a bias about which they know nothing. (You no longer have this excuse!) Either way, do not be discouraged by tales of people making 40% a year every year.

Better yet, divorce your self-esteem from your trading performance. Do not involve yourself emotionally in the success or failure of your trades at all. This, of course, is easier said than done, but one way to do it may be via an extrapolation of the diversification argument. The benefit of diversification in a narrow sense just means that if you hold a reasonable number of stocks, maybe 10 to 15 or so, they should not all go down at once. This can also be read on a wider basis. If you hold a number of stocks and follow a number of strategies, you are diversified some more. Even more widely, there are other asset classes. Yet more widely, there are other ways of making money – you could pursue some of the other avenues open to you while you are waiting for your stock portfolio to perform or recover. This approach has the additional benefit in difficult market periods, because if you are distracted you are more likely to be able to avoid the error of selling low for affective reasons. Distraction techniques may help, but ideally you will not need them. You will instead have what Marks (2011, p. 26) describes as the two things you need to hold on in a crash and avoid selling at the worst of times: "long term capital and strong psychological resources." I suggest that many of the biases I describe in this book are a drain on psychological resources; knowing when they are whispering in your ear will help you to ignore the siren voices.

And most widely yet, you can recall that money is not an intrinsic good. It is merely instrumentally good: we value it for what we can do with it. It creates time to pursue other interests; right now I am taking piano lessons. You can even diversify your interests beyond finance, and you should. You should always be asking yourself three questions: 'What do I want?; Why do I want it?; How am I going to get there?' If you do not have three answers in relation to any area, forget it. You might even want to consult Aristotle (1998) on what constitutes a life worth living.

Some authors have concluded that Hindsight Bias is behind the persistence of some markets such as those for some mutual funds which continue to exist even though they generally lose money for investors. Somehow such markets must be able to continue to lure in new losing investors. Patel, Zeckhauser, and Hendricks (1991, p. 235) suggest that Hindsight Bias means that "participants examine past movements and convince themselves they would have made the right choices had they been involved, implying they could do so in the future." This will, of course, lead them to make investments which would have worked out had they made the right choices in the past based on an exaggeratedly high estimate of their probability of making the right decisions in the future. Patel, Zeckhauser, and Hendricks (1991, p. 235) also propose a commendable DIY experiment to confirm the prevalence of Hindsight Bias, which we can update for today when they suggest we "ask finance-oriented friends whether they sensed that the stock market was 'clearly' over-priced just before the October 1987 crash." This can be updated for the 2007–2008 crisis. Many will say yes, but we know that this is unlikely to be true because the absence of such a widely-held belief is a prerequisite for pre-crash bubble to exist.

Hindsight Bias has also been linked to investor over-confidence (§8.3.1). Over-confidence is already prima facie unhelpful to investors; it will also lead to over-trading which is known to be bad for investment performance. Malmendier and Taylor (2015, p. 6) suggest that "over-confidence might persist in part because of hindsight bias" since Hindsight Bias makes it look as though "something that has already happened was highly predictable." Thus investors can imagine as above that they would have been able to make predictions and they become over-confident about the quality of their future predictions. This will make them engage in bad trades.

Another area where the Hindsight Bias will cause problems is in assessing prior performance. Gladwell (2009b, pp. 244–262) is an illuminating account of how retrospective observation can make accounts of apparent intelligence failure deeply misleading. One example concerns the offensive launched by Syria and Egypt against Israel in 1973. When Gladwell (2009b, pp. 244–245) notes the extensive combat preparations made by Syria and Egypt, known to the Israelis, and the fact that the Israelis received an intelligence warning of an imminent attack, it seems extraordinary that the Israelis did not prepare. However, context is everything; Gladwell (2009b, p. 246) points out that the Egyptian army had mobilised 19 times between January and October 1973 without launching an attack. Similarly, Gladwell (2009b, pp. 247–249) notes that post-9/11 intelligence failure post mortems often criticise the FBI for not 'connecting the dots' on apparently obvious signs of the WTC plot; which does not take account of the fact that the FBI undoubtedly had a billion dots to connect.

This can also be seen in the context of a valuable distinction introduced by Gladwell (2009b, pp. 153–154) between a puzzle and mystery. A puzzle is a question we cannot answer because we do not have enough information; a mystery is one we cannot solve because we have too much information. For example, locating Bin Laden was a puzzle because no agency had relevant data. Deciding what would happen in post-Saddam Iraq was a mystery; many agencies had a great deal of data but no-one knew which was the most significant or how to combine it. Similarly, I suggest, the FBI has been criticised unfairly on the basis that it did not solve a puzzle when it received new data, when in fact, the FBI was facing a mystery when trying to predict terrorist assaults on the US. Adding new data to a mystery exacerbated the FBI's difficulties. I further suggest that one form of Hindsight Bias will be seen in scenarios which, in retrospect, look like puzzles when they were actually mysteries.

All decisions about what stocks to buy are mysteries rather than puzzles. Investors have an enormous amount of information about listed companies; no-one should be buying a company which is a puzzle because that would mean it is not known how it earns its revenues or what it does. Both of those are obviously unacceptable in an investment proposition. Gladwell (2009b, pp. 151–176) mentions the puzzle/mystery distinction in his insightful commentary on the Enron[7] collapse. He rightly claims that the problem there was too much information: all of the problems with the company were hiding in plain sight in the masses of financial market disclosure. The problems investors face are around obtaining the right subset of available information and weighting it appropriately. Hindsight Bias will make it impossible to learn from mistakes in this area. It will not be possible to determine subsequently that a trade was an error because the wrong data was weighted heavily or not heavily enough, and to therefore resolve not to make that particular mistake again – because the mysteries can look like puzzles. If only we had been told about the Enron Special Purpose Vehicles (SPVs), we might regretfully exclaim, when the problem was not that information about the SPVs was not disclosed. The problem was that that information was not interpreted correctly.

Perhaps expecting ordinary people to know about SPVs is too much. My experience as a former specialist complex securitisation structurer means I have a lot of familiarity with SPVs, so it would be a paradigm example of the Curse of Knowledge (§7.1) for me to exhibit that bias in my Theory of Mind judgments about investors. Today, also, in the wake of various books and movies like Lewis (2010), it can be hard to forget that the public knowledge of SPVs was for a long time zero. But Wall Street analysts should have no difficulty following such transactions and their implications for companies employing them, surely. So the task for the individual investor becomes gaining access to such reports and gaining the ability to understand them. The other option, of course, is to simply decide that this is too much complexity to be worth playing the game and simply avoiding any companies which make substantial use of SPVs.

Also, in market terms, Hindsight Bias will take another form when it obscures the reasons for stock performance. The facts that will become known will be the performance of each stock and the performance of the portfolio in percentage terms. Usually, some attempt can be made to say why this performance occurred, though we may here once more succumb to what Taleb (2008, ch. 6) calls the Narrative Fallacy. This is our tendency to construct and hold to simple explanatory stories, though in reality they may be partial, unfounded or completely inaccurate. Again, as Taleb (2012, p. 6) later writes, "[o]ur minds are in the business of turning history into something smooth and linear." This is partly useful – it simply makes events easier to 'understand.' That is why we retain the heuristic. But it also brings with it over-simplification and therein lies opportunity.

Hindsight Bias can also obscure a crucial part of deciding whether performance was good or bad. A return of 10%, while certainly encouraging, tells us nothing about whether it should be seen as good performance and whether the strategy underlying it should be replicated or emulated. This is because we need to know how much risk was taken: "Return has to be evaluated according to how much risk was taken" (Marks 2011, p. 44). If you put the whole portfolio on a horse which won, doubled your money and then lost 90% of the upside by betting the portfolio on other horses which all lost, you made 10% but you took an enormous amount of risk. If, as I have done twice, you made 10% in Treasuries over six-week periods by deciding that a temporary lull in the 2007–2008 crisis was indeed temporary, and that investors would shortly be looking for safety again, you can be happier with your performance. Note that a key underpinning of that particular idea was my comfort at holding the investment indefinitely, if need be. If I had been wrong about the temporary nature of the lull, I might have ended up holding the Treasuries until the depths of the next crisis. So what? I was taking either no risk or the lowest available risk in financial markets and I was getting a yield while I waited. I was so sure I risked my entire disposable net worth both times. That makes 10% in six weeks worth having.

Hindsight Bias will make it very difficult to make a good assessment of how much risk you took because it will make it look as though what actually happened was bound to happen. It looks now as though that horse which doubled your money was bound to double your money and so you were not taking much risk. You might conclude that continuing to bet on horses is a good investment strategy. It is not.

There is no empirical measurement that can tell you why a stock performed as it did. The Hindsight Bias will, in addition, make it look as though what happened was probable and so it will be very difficult to avoid concluding, if you bought stock X because you thought it would go up because of event Y, and it did go up and event Y occurred, that event Y caused stock X to go up. Perhaps, though, event Y had nothing to do with stock X going up and there was a secret buyback programme. If you are in the business of providing plausible explanations to others of why a stock did what it did, then a partial explanation may be good enough. If you are in the business of serious analysis of performance, you will need to allow for the fact that the performance of a stock over a year may have been caused by one hundred factors of which you have heard of ten.

It may even be true that a completely fictional explanation 'works' to some extent. You may decide that the reason a stock performed as it did was due to several properties that the stock had. It may, in fact, not have had those properties at the time in question, but it may now have them and so your prediction of the future performance of the stock has, despite your slackness, become well-founded. This is not to be recommended as an approach, but if judgment by results is the only yardstick, then the outcome is more important than the process. It may even be true that your story about the properties of the stock was and remains fiction, but the stock still performs as predicted. All of this depends on what the process is by which fictional entities gain their properties; I have addressed this question elsewhere (Short 2014).

This line might seem in tension with the warning I gave above to the effect that we should avoid the Narrative Fallacy outlined by Taleb (2008, ch. 6). I think the tension can be resolved in a useful way. Simply succumbing to the fallacy without knowing that one has done so is unambiguously unhelpful and it is this against which Taleb (2008, ch. 6) correctly warns us. I think, though, that explicitly using semi-fictional accounts can be useful. As Williams (2004, p. 172) argues, we can valuably construct a story which abstracts away from a "much denser and more complex set of historical contingencies." While this, if taken too far, does indeed lead to the over-simplification problem I mentioned above, sometimes it may be unavoidable. It may, in fact, often be unavoidable. It may simply be beyond our capacities to deal with a historically complete and comprehensive narrative of the reasons a stock went up. We may, nevertheless, gain something from a simplified story if it retails a key reason for why the stock went up, and that this can generate a hypothesis. We can then attempt to break this hypothesis by looking for counter-examples. We can retain in view at all times that our hypothesis is a simplified, greatly cut-down version of history and is to be treated roughly as a result; we must not slide across to the related view that even if we fail to break the hypothesis by back-testing it, it is therefore a complete view of history. We can then usefully look at the other elements of what happened and see if they inevitably accompanied a rise. This may be the best we can do.

I will now move on to a type of opportunity in which a potential consequence of Hindsight Bias can blind us. If we 'knew it all along' in relation to dramatically adverse events, then we can also imagine that if we are not predicting such events now, they cannot happen. This type of logical elision is very easy to fall into and can mean we miss the opportunity to profit from such dramatic events.

5.5.1 The Antifragile And Options

Taleb (2008) would at this point no doubt warn us that we should avoid assuming that the future will resemble the past, because that does not take account of the possibility that the future will be radically worse than the past. Here he is right, but we are entitled to ask on what else we should base our predictions. His response, which has much to be said for it, will be that we cannot: prediction is hopeless. What we can do is attempt to remain robust against catastrophes – or even better, become anti-fragile (Taleb 2012) and gain from disorder.

This looks like the right approach. However, I must confess I do not immediately understand how it can be done. Taleb (2012, p. 390) writes that betting against "a portfolio of financial institutions because of their fragilities [...] would have cost you pennies over the years preceding their eventual demise in 2008." It is certainly true that making such a bet would have been extremely profitable. However, I am not sure how it could be done cheaply. The obvious way to do it would be to buy put options on the securities.

Options have a number of properties. They are, as suggested by the name, the option to trade rather than a trade. A put option is the right to sell a stock at a particular price. A call option is the right to buy a stock at a particular price. Options are cheap in relation to a stock price. They have an expiry date and a strike price. They are worth nothing if you do not exercise them, so you can lose all of your money. This is in contrast with owning a stock, which will always be worth something provided the company does not become insolvent.

As I write, the market price of a put option with a strike price of $33 in Citigroup and an expiry date one month hence is $0.13c i.e. much cheaper than the stock price, which is currently $42.06. Remember that the option expires and is worth nothing if it is not exercised. You will not exercise it unless it becomes valuable to do. Obviously, selling a stock for $33 is a bad idea unless you can buy it for less. The current price of $42.06 is much higher than your strike price, so it is unlikely that the stock price will decline below your strike price in less than a month. This is why the option to do so is available cheaply: it is unlikely to be exercised and therefore unlikely to be valuable and therefore unlikely to cost your counter-party much money. This put option may become valuable over a longer period because there is more time for the stock price of Citigroup to decline, but you will pay for this extra value, since there is no such thing as a free lunch. Just adding a week to the duration of the put option increases its price to $0.16c, which is quite a large increase compared to $0.13c.

As I said, it is true that the rewards will be outsized, and perhaps it is this that Taleb (2012) has in mind. If the stock price of C declines to $30 within this duration of the put option, you now have the right to sell a stock at $33 which you can buy in the market for $30. Thus, each option becomes worth $3. This is an enormous profit on the initial investment of $0.13c. Bear in mind that you will probably deal not in single put options, but in perhaps 100,000. In the scenario under discussion, this means that an investment of $13,000 would now be worth around $300,000. This is a stunning performance inside a few weeks and so Taleb (2012) can certainly say that pennies have been spent in order to realise riches.

However, the problem is that you might have to wait a long time for the downturn to materialise. So you will have to keep putting in the $13,000 every month or so. While it is true in this scenario that you are anti-fragile in that you cannot lose more than $13,000 and you can gain $300,000, you will only do so on a monthly basis. Over a year, you would lose $156,000 and over two years, you would lose more than you would gain. So another possibility that Taleb (2012) may have in mind is a magnification of even these dramatic performances. After all, a decline from the current value of C from $42.06 to $33 is dramatic yet mild in comparison with what happened in 2008. On 01 May 2007, C opened at $538.[8] There were a great many periods between then and 01 February 2009, when it opened at $33.90, in which one would have realised extraordinary profits with a short options trade. I do not know what put options with a strike price of $25 would have cost in May 2007, but I imagine it would have been less than 1c, even for quite long durations. That was just 5% of the stock price at that time. Currently it costs $0.75c to buy the lowest strike price put at $20 – which would represent a decline of over 50% from the current stock price even with a long duration out to January 2018. That represents almost two years from the time of writing.

Taleb (2012) also writes that his major exposure was to a portfolio of financial stocks, which might have made it cheaper for him since his counter-party might assume that there was some diversification benefit in a set of stocks, even if they were all in the same sector. While such a reduction in expense would be of great benefit to him, it would not be available to anyone not in a position to take sector-wide exposures.

It is also possible that the trade was done on a Credit Default Swap basis. This is a derivative whereby one party effectively buys insurance from a counter-party against the default of a third party. Having such insurance would be very lucrative in the 2008 scenario even when the financial institutions did not actually default, but came close to doing so. One problem I can see, though, is that the likely counter-parties to such derivatives are the very financial institutions against which one is betting: it would be ironic and unprofitable to be holding a winning bet against a counter-party which was a winning bet partly because that counter-party had defaulted and was no longer able to honour the bet.

Lewis (2010, p. 113) suggests that in 2002 it was possible to pay $3 for an option to buy Capital One stock at $40 over the next 2.5 years. This may have been specially cheap since the company had experienced regulatory difficulties which meant it had crashed 60% to $30. So there do seem to be some long options available, but it should be pointed out that this one might have only been affordable because the market was not priced for a strong recovery of a stock with regulatory trouble. It may well also have been true that prior to 2007, the market thought that a group of major investment banks was very unlikely to get into trouble – or certainly not as much trouble as they did in fact get into – and that, therefore, betting on that would have been cheap even over a long period. I do not see evidence of this in Lewis (2010), however, which discusses at length the difficulties investors had who wanted to bet against subprime mortgages and the banks securitising them.

I am sure that circumstances will again arise in which trades of this type will be highly successful once more. I go into some more detail about how the trade might have been done below. In the meantime, I can only suggest that the type of options trade I have outlined will only be valuable in circumstances where there are good prospects of a sudden change within the duration of the options. Or alternatively, the extra duration can be paid for by predicting a more extreme change. Again, there is no free lunch here, but there may well be a lunch that is well worth paying for.

We know something of the approach that Taleb's fund Empirica was taking in 2000 because he gave interviews. The central motivation for the approach is to avoid destruction from negative Black Swans and gain exposure to positive ones. He adopts a 'barbell strategy' for both his personal funds and for Empirica. There is a large low-risk element to the portfolio and a small high-risk. I do not know what the proportions are, but I would estimate that they are 80% to 20%, partly from judgment and partly because we know of the fondness of Taleb (2008) for Pareto's principle that 80% of the effects come from 20% of the causes.

The low risk element of the portfolio is invested in USTs (Gladwell 2009b, p. 62). It is fair to say that USTs are still the lowest risk investment we know of, even if they are today regarded as less solid than when their yield indisputably provided the 'risk-free' rate of return. Prior to 2008, no-one considered the possibility of a US Government default, though nowadays that possibility, while remote, must still be considered. Moreover, as of early 2016 we are at the start of what appears to be a Fed tightening scenario which, if it continues, will cause UST prices to fall. Taleb may be using an alternative safe form of investment today such as gold or cash. The large low-risk element of the portfolio is designed to avoid damage from negative Black Swans and may even profit somewhat from them as investors seek safety.

To construct the high risk element of the portfolio, Empirica buys options and never sells them (Gladwell 2009b, p. 62). This means that, again consonant with the Black Swan considerations, Empirica will pay a premium in order to benefit from drastic moves. If it had sold options, it would be receiving premia in order to take the risk of drastic moves. Empirica does not buy equities at all (Gladwell 2009b, p. 62) so it is probably buying options on equities and perhaps indices as well. The options are "on both sides" (Gladwell 2009b, p. 62) meaning that they pay off if the stock in question goes up or goes down, but not if it stays still. The options are all dramatically "out-of-the-money" (Gladwell 2009b, p. 62) meaning that the strike price is a long way away from the current market price. Thus, for example, Empirica may be buying options on GM at strike prices of $20 and $80 when GM is trading at $40 and so GM stock would have to move a very large amount for the options to be worth anything. The fact that they are so far out of the money will make them cheap, because the counter-parties consider that there is a very low possibility of any of the options being exercised.

Buying a pair of options of the same sort on the same stock is called a 'straddle' if both options are at-the-money, meaning that the strike price is close to the current price. It is a long straddle if both of the options are call options, because the trader is betting that he will eventually want to own the stock. This position is effectively long volatility, meaning that the trader will profit if the volatility of the stock increases. Betting on increased volatility is basically the idea of betting on Black Swans because they will cause a whole lot of volatility. One problem, though, is that the value of the options declines as volatility declines – if it does in the short term – and also the options become worthless as the expiry date approaches. Naturally it is not a solution to buy longer dated options, because that just makes the options more expensive. Moreover, Empirica is buying options on "hundreds of different stocks" (Gladwell 2009b, p. 62). Another problem is that since the strategy equates simply to 'long volatility,' volatility declines hurt the position even if the underlying stock prices do not change. This represents a significant friction cost – though it would have to be conceded that implied volatility could also increase beneficially without underlying stock prices moving. A final problem with using options is that they are restricted to specialised investors who have one of four option approval levels. Obtaining such clearance is not straightforward for the very good reason that it is possible to lose a great deal of money very quickly and, indeed, much more than one has staked.

Taleb (2007, p. 209) discusses the difficulty of maintaining such a long volatility position. While this does not constitute a confirmation that long volatility is basically his favoured position, it does suggest it. He is certainly right to think that our psychological setup, including primarily biases, and the affect flowing from them, make holding a long volatility position emotionally difficult. And it is certainly consistent with what we know of the author's personality, so far as it can be divined from his books, that he would think that a difficult position is nevertheless worth holding. I certainly agree.

A further alternative would be to trade the Chicago Board Options Exchange's (CBOE) Volatility Index (VIX) which is colloquially and aptly known as Wall

Street's fear index. It is a measure of market expectations of near-term volatility in the S&P 500 index, which is derived from option prices in that index. Unfortunately this also has some disadvantages. One of these is tracking error; this occurs when a derivative fails to match exactly the underlying asset to which it is designed to give exposure. It can occur that if mathematical volatility in the index rises, the VIX will rise but not by exactly the same amount. The other issue is that because gaining exposure to the VIX is done using options, value tends to decay somewhat in the way that option values do as time goes on. Neither of these are fatal objections, but they do somewhat detract from using the VIX to form an entire investment portfolio.

There is a further problem to do with how long one has to run the strategy. Such a strategy will, I expect, produce regular small payoffs as individual stocks depart dramatically from their previous prices in either direction. But the major payoff will occur in severe crashes. These are not frequent. Taleb (2008) did well in the Black Monday crash in 1987 and in the 2007–2008 crash. I am not sure whether he benefitted also from the dot-com crash of 2000, but I expect he did. But that is all of the serious and broad crashes; other events like the Savings and Loan crisis were certainly not positive, but relatively contained. So this suggests that we can expect a crash or a cycle maybe every ten years. While that also means we are possibly 'due' one soon, as I write in 2016, it may be the case that cycles do not die of old age but of a cause. If that cause is irrational exuberance, that is scarcely to be seen. Note that I do not make a prediction here that stocks will continue to appreciate strongly – that would be a very dangerous prediction – but the opposing corollary that it would be equally risky to bet on the timing of the next crash.

It may be that this line works for Taleb (2012) because, as Gladwell (2009b, p. 75) notes, the "financial crisis of 2007–2008 made a staggering amount of money for his fund." I am sure that this is true. One will have to handle a high burn rate to pay all of the option premia. Or it could be that the interest income from the UST portfolio pays the option premia. That, if so, would be an excellent position to be in, but requires starting with a major portfolio. As of Spring 2009, Empirica had "billions under management" (Gladwell 2009b, p. 75) and prior to the 2007–2008 crisis, it had "hundreds of millions" (Gladwell 2009b, p. 62) of reserves. Retail investors will not have this. So for all these reasons I think it will be difficult for a retail investor to pursue this approach.

Notes

1 As Shull (2011, p. 16) notes towards the beginning of her book and in a prefiguring of her argument in response to Taleb (2008), probabilities "tell us something – just not everything."
2 This 'fat tail' effect is explicitly described as meaning market returns are non-Gaussian as early as Fama (1970).
3 Interestingly, Corcos and Pannequin (2006) did not find evidence supporting the claim that the Representativeness Heuristic (§4.2) was a factor in these precise circumstances.

However, they do see the anchoring and adjustment bias (Tversky and Kahneman 1974, pp. 1128–1130), which I lack space to consider in this book.
4 Cf. Marks (2011, p. 84).
5 Wilkin (2015, pp. 185–186) presents a much more even-handed exposition of the securitisation market.
6 Cf. also Graver (2007, pp. 193–194).
7 I cannot mention Enron without underlining another obvious diversification point. If you work for Enron, do not fill your 401(k) with Enron stock.
8 This is an adjusted price taking account of a subsequent stock reverse split.

6

QUASI-ECONOMIC BIASES

6.1 Certainty Effect

This bias is approximately summed up by the saying 'a bird in the hand is worth two in the bush.' One point I will be making throughout this book is that we should be highly suspicious of such folk wisdom. As ever, these sayings do not arise from a vacuum and they are not completely without value. Risk reduction is definitely valuable, and possession of an item avoids the risk involved in attempting to possess an unpossessed item. But there should be a very important caveat: A bird in the hand is only worth two in the bush if the risk involved in moving the two birds in the bush into the hand is not adequately compensated for by the value of an extra bird! Kahneman and Tversky (1979) wrote a seminal paper on 'Prospect Theory' in which the authors identify three deviations from Expected Utility theory. In the Certainty Effect, "people underweight outcomes that are merely probable in comparison with outcomes that are obtained with certainty" (Kahneman and Tversky 1979, p. 263). I will discuss the Reflection Effect next in §6.2 and then the Isolation Effect in §6.3. The problem that results from the Certainty Effect is that it "contributes to risk aversion in choices involving sure gains and to risk seeking in choices involving sure losses" (Kahneman and Tversky 1979, p. 263). It also looks as though it is irrational, since Expected Utility theory looks like it ought to be true at first glance, as I will now explain.

Expected Utility theory basically formalises the common sense view that people will try to maximise their assets. Put like that, it looks as though everyone will try to maximise assets all the time. Why would anyone throw assets away? However, you may already be wondering whether this is too strong. It is not the case that everyone establishes what activity will create the most (financial or other) value for them at a given time and conducts only that activity. Also, it is generally the case that going to university is a very good investment, depending on what you study and where you study it. But not everyone who could benefit goes to university, and some who do study subjects that will lead to less lucrative careers. This, of course, could be absolutely fine if people have correctly observed that there are other types of value beyond financial ones, and have made a choice accordingly. So it can already seem as though the scope of the theory should be restricted to a domain of pure financial decisions. Trading falls into that domain, so we can now consider whether assuming that other market participants will seek to maximise their assets works in financial markets.

Kahneman and Tversky (1979, pp. 263–264) set out three axioms of Expected Utility theory. They all look highly plausible, initially. They are:

1. "the overall utility of a prospect [...] is the expected utility of its outcomes;"
2. "a prospect is acceptable if the utility resulting from integrating the prospect with one's assets exceeds the utility of those assets alone;"
3. a rational person "prefers the certain prospect (x) to any risky prospect with expected value x."

Axiom one says people should assess prospects by looking at how well they do in the various possible outcomes multiplied by the probability of each of those outcomes. A prospect is a set of outcomes weighted by probability. If I offer you a bet in which I will pay you $10 if I throw heads and you pay me $4 if I throw tails, you have two outcomes to consider. The bet, or prospect, has a 50% chance of paying you $10 and a 50% chance of costing you $4. That adds up to an expected utility of $(0.5 \times \$10) + (0.5 \times -\$4) = \$3$. Since that is positive, you should accept the bet. (People are strangely reluctant to take this bet, however because they focus on the loss more than the profit. This is an early indication that Expected Utility theory may have problems.) Axiom two says you should take bets that are likely overall to make you money. It also says that you should consider this in the context of your overall asset position. (This, again, is infrequently done. People rarely think about their total net worth when deciding whether to bet on a coin toss. When they do that, they realise that the potential loss of $4 is insignificant in comparison to their net worth and so losing it would not be as much of a problem as they think.)

Axiom three is called 'Risk Aversion.' Note that it is a very carefully defined type of risk aversion. It says that the rational person, when choosing between two outcomes with a positive pay-off, should prefer one which certainly pays $10 to one which only has a probability of less than one of paying $10.

These axioms have varying levels of initial plausibility. Axiom one looks fairly convincing. It does not seem to say much more than if you give people a set of choices where they have some chances of good outcomes and some chances of bad ones, they should consider how good the outcomes are and how likely they are in making their decision. Since we are frequently called upon to make some estimates of what might happen and how good it would be in many spheres of life, we ought to be pretty good at it. Note that making the observation that we often do not have a good measurement of the probability of an outcome does not constitute an objection here. While that is true – we do not know exactly how probable it is that we will find a job with an electrical engineering degree – the axiom just says that the rational person should take account of his estimate of the probability, however rough, in making an assessment. Axiom two likewise looks plausible in its approximate formulation, though we will be wondering the precise meaning 'overall' is doing and the extent to which someone thinks of their total net worth. But even that last caveat has some responses that can be made on behalf of Expected Utility theory. We can imagine that everyone has an amount of money they consider 'insignificant' in some contexts. Anyone faced with a risk of losing an insignificant amount of money will not worry about it too much. What constitutes an insignificant amount of money will be different for a poor person, a college student and a wealthy businessman. Axiom three looks unassailable. It can never be rational to prefer risk to uncertainty – unless one is paid extra to accept that risk, of course. But that is excluded from the axiom as specified.

With these axioms in hand, we can turn to the evaluation made of them by Kahneman and Tversky (1979). Do these axioms describe well how people behave? The answer is a clear no.

Kahneman and Tversky (1979, p. 264) offered people a choice between two options:

- A: 50% chance to win 1,000, and 50% chance to win nothing;
- B: 450 for sure

The currency involved was Israeli Pounds ('I£') at a point when the median net income for a family was I£3,000. (This currency was replaced by the Israeli Shekel ILS – soon after the experiment was conducted.) So these are clearly significant amounts of money. We can immediately appreciate the pull of option B, even though we can see that option A is more valuable. The problem seems to derive from an asymmetry in affective forecasting. We often conduct affective forecasting to help decide our future options. It involves nothing more complex than forecasting how good or bad we will feel in the future given different outcomes. It transpires that we are particularly bad at making these forecasts. In this case, the regret we forecast if we take option A and receive nothing seems to look incredibly large. It looks as though we will be horrified if that is the outcome, whereas the happiness involved in winning the I£1,000 looks less than equivalent to the regret of obtaining nothing even after we make the sign change, or multiply through by -1 as the experimenters effectively do. We need to make the sign change because the point is not that losing is bad and winning is good; the point is that losing is worse than winning, even when the amounts involved are the same. To see this, note that we can analyse option A as being equivalent to starting with I£500 and then either gaining another I£500 or losing I£500. It even seems as though we were foolhardy in taking the risk of option A. Even if we win, we risked getting nothing in order to obtain the I£1,000. How can that be better than just walking away with the I£450, and avoiding all of the risk and all of the calculations?

The problem, of course, is that this is all wrong and irrational. The I£500 value of option A *just is* worth more than I£450. One way to see this is to consider the game above not as a one-shot option but as one of a lengthy series of trials. If you are going to be offered these choices every minute for eight hours, of course you take option A. It will just be a matter of time before you outperform option B. If you have enough trials to be fairly confident that you will actually win half the time and lose half the time – as opposed to a single trial where the outcome is binary: you will either win or lose – then eventually you will have I£1,000 for half of your trials and nothing for the other half. That, though, is clearly better than I£450 every time. You can even calculate how much better it is. And this applies just as much to the single trial. It is still worth I£500, so you should always take the risk.

One potential objection here relates to the fact that Kahneman and Tversky (1979) did not actually offer people these choices. They instead asked their subjects to imagine that they were in this position and ask them what choices they would make. As I argue in Short (2015), one possible problem here is that this is a Theory of Mind task in which there could be a strong difference between simulating the situation and actually being in it. There would be what I call an affective mismatch between simulating to make the prediction of behaviour and actually behaving in the situation. By affective mismatch I just mean that S has a different emotional state to O. S is sitting in a lab being asked theoretical questions and so has little emotional investment in the outcome. O, on the other hand, has a very strong emotional investment in the outcome, as we saw above. In fact, we seem to be able to predict that this will be the emotional situation faced by O. In Short (2015) I explain systematic errors in Theory of Mind by suggesting that they are caused by exactly these affective mismatches.

Now, I will suggest that this is an occasion where my account suggests we will get it right. There will be no Theory of Mind error because there is no affective mismatch. We are very well able to make a prediction of the behaviour of O because we can get a good grip on O's emotional state. Of course, this has not been proven experimentally. As Kahneman and Tversky (1979, p. 265) note, the "experimental studies typically involve contrived gambles for small stakes" for the very obvious reason that it would be very expensive to actually run such an experiment with a statistically significant number of participants for major sums like I£1,000. But I think I can still reasonably argue that on my account, S has a better chance of making an accurate prediction of O's behaviour if S is closer to O's emotional state than otherwise.

Kahneman and Tversky (1979, p. 266) note how one expression of the Certainty Effect relates to differential treatment of probability changes depending on how close they are to the probability endpoints. This should not happen. If you are offered a 10% increase in the probability of a defined gain, you should value it at 10% of that defined gain irrespective of where the starting point is. In numbers, the change from a 50% chance of $100 to a 60% chance of $100 should be worth $10. Similarly, the change from a 90% chance of $100 to a 100% chance of $100 should be $10. However, it transpires that people prefer the latter change to a great extent. They value the move to a certain payoff more than they should. I think part of this is due to some mild relief that they do not have to do much thinking or probability calculation. After all, a certain $100 is worth $100 and that is all there is to it. This reluctance to engage in probabilistic reasoning is perhaps well-founded. We are all rather bad at making these sorts of calculations and so there is value in avoiding them. Even people with good levels of mathematical ability – which is already fairly rare – and experience in making probability calculations can make serious errors when faced with new situations. So unless you have superb mathematical abilities, I do not recommend attempting to outperform on this parameter.

What you can attempt to do is look for situations where people will overvalue certainty. An alternative way to put that is to say that we are looking for situations where people overpay to avoid a risk change, when the risk change moves the risk value from very low to still quite low, or indeed from zero to some – but still very low.

In markets, it has been suggested that a variant of the Certainty Effect may be implicated in bubbles. Barberis (2013, p. 17) notes that "many people have a strong preference for lottery-like payoffs" as we know from the mere existence of lotteries. The type of Certainty Effect, whereby the "brain overweights low probabilities," could explain this (Barberis 2013, p. 17) because investors may overvalue tech stocks. These have lottery-like payoffs since they have a very low probability of providing a very high payoff. So as Barberis (2013, p. 17) notes, an account of this type "may be particularly suited to thinking about the high valuations of U.S. technology stocks in the late 1990s" and the subsequent crash, together with any similar tech bubbles. My advice here is to generally stay away from all tech stocks unless one is a specialist, because I think that understanding the likely future developments in technology and how to trade them is likely to be a full-time occupation on its own.

6.2 Reflection Effect

In this bias, people exhibit risk-related behaviour which is inverted by whether they are being offered choices between two gains or two losses. This adds another level of oddness. We have already seen that people make suboptimal choices when offered different gains at different probabilities. We would at least now expect them to make the same sorts of choices when faced with the possibilities of different losses at different probabilities, but this is not what is observed. In fact, people exhibit (excessive) risk aversion when faced with gains but then exhibit (excessive) risk-seeking behaviour when faced with losses. In other words, they are reluctant to take extra risk to make extra gains but happy to take extra risk to avoid larger losses.

Perhaps we can make a first approximation as to what is happening here by thinking of it in terms of loss aversion rather than risk aversion. Losses are experienced as so affectively negative that making a suboptimal decision to avoid them is preferred in the first case, when an adequately compensated risk of missing a gain is not accepted and taken in the second case, when a loss is so affectively negative that people even risk a larger one if there is thereby *any* chance of avoiding a loss altogether. So this is closely related to the Certainty Effect; people are overpaying to reduce risks to zero.

Kahneman and Tversky (1979, p. 268) define the Reflection Effect as being what is observed when "reflection of prospects around zero reverses the preference order," in accordance with the above description. They cite dramatic data, which is entirely consistent with their own extended data set, wherein "subjects were indifferent between (100, .65; −100, .35) and (0), indicating risk aversion. They were also indifferent between (−200, .80) and (−100), indicating risk seeking" (Kahneman and Tversky 1979, p. 268). What this means in the first example is that subjects were prepared to risk no more than a 35% chance of losing \$100[1] in order to obtain a 65% chance of winning \$100, whereas, of course, a 65% chance of winning \$100 is worth paying \$65 for, which is almost twice as much as the \$35 cost of risking a \$100 loss. So the subjects avoided risk more than they should have done here. On the other hand, in the other pair of choices, subjects were equally content with an 80% chance of losing \$200 and a certain loss of \$100. The 80% chance of losing \$200 is valued at a cost of − \$160 so here subjects accepted much more risk than they should have done in order to avoid the certain loss of \$100.

This data is inconsistent with axiom three, which claims that people prefer certainty. Rather, as Kahneman and Tversky (1979, p. 269) note, "certainty increases the aversiveness of losses as well as the desirability of gains." By the same token, the data causes problems for expected utility theory, which includes axiom three.

I think the explanation of this is that subjects are using their Theory of Mind on themselves and drawing the following conclusions in the different scenarios. They are deciding how they would feel in the different outcomes. In the first case, they think they are gambling and they feel guilty about it and think they will feel particularly bad if it does not come off, because they were not compelled to take the gamble. They could have walked away and not taken any risk. The only way to minimise the probability of this perceived negative affective outcome is to insist on a dramatic safety margin. If they lose, they have only lost \$35, or put another way, they have only 'paid' $35 in order to participate in this bet. So if they lose, they think they will be able to console themselves with the thought that the bet was 'worth it;' it was cheap in comparison to the prospects of winning. This is true, but the subjects have missed out on the true value in the bet. The results mean that fewer people would have paid $40 to join the bet and fewer still $50. Those people are missing out on value. Not only that, but I suspect you could explain this argument to them and it would make no difference to their behaviour. They are making an emotional decision, or more precisely, an affective forecast in relation to the negative scenario, and this is decisive.

In the second scenario, the same approach is taken. Here the subjects look at how they would feel in the two outcomes. Losing $100 is definitely bad. Losing $200 is much worse, and paying the extra $100 for a 20% chance of 'getting away with it' is not worth it. Taking the 20% option is, of course, a gamble, but the affective import seems to be reversed. The gamble does not look like a risky gamble which would be hard to explain to one's spouse in the negative outcome case. It looks like a last-ditch attempt to avoid a negative outcome. Taking the certain $100 looks harder to explain: it looks like a problem had been identified and one did nothing to avoid it. Losing the $200 is bad, but it can be spun to oneself as a desperate bid to avoid a certain loss which unfortunately has not worked. 'But at least I tried...' the unfortunate loser will say to himself.

Note the pattern of this explanation. We see that a bias (the Reflection Effect) causes a deviation from rational behaviour represented by the axioms of expected utility theory. If S works on the assumption that O is rational, then the axioms of expected utility theory look pretty plausible as an outline of how people may be expected to behave given the choices that were presented in this experiment. We might term this a Theory Theory approach to the Theory of Mind question here. The Theory Theory involved would be something like 'O is rational;' 'the axioms of expected utility theory are rational for persons seeking to maximise value;' 'if O is seeking to maximise value then O will follow the axioms of expected utility theory.'

Yet as we have seen, the data does not bear this out. As you might expect, since I favour Simulation Theory over Theory Theory, my initial position is that this is not a problem. It is just further confirmation that Theory Theory is not the correct account of Theory of Mind. How, though, does Simulation Theory fare with this data? My general position, which will crop up many times in this book, is that when S uses his Theory of Mind to predict the behaviour of O, S will fail to include the effects of bias in his simulation of O. This may be because S is not in the same affective situation as O. Here we seem to have the opposite scenario, so Simulation Theory also seems to have a problem. I will suggest that my account has a way out here.

I will discuss the Endowment Effect in §6.4, where I will argue that S was too affectively remote from O's situation to simulate correctly the way that O would ascribe more value to an item that O owned than to the same item when O did not own it. In this experiment I will then need to admit that we seem as Ss to be able to get the right answers. We can look at the choices between losing $100 definitely and taking an 80% chance of losing $200 and predict that O will in fact take the sub-optimal route of taking the additional risk. (Or more precisely, we can use our Theory of Mind to predict that O will be neutral between the two options as set out with these monetary values, because that was what was observed. Obviously if we were to shift the monetary values somewhat we could make O have a stronger preference in one direction or the other.) I suggest that this is because we are, in fact, in this experiment in the same affective situation as O. Remember that O was not asked to actually take the bets, because that would have been too expensive. O was merely asked to say what he would have done when faced with the bets. This is different to the situation in the Endowment Effect because there O *actually* owned the mug and S did not. That led to S making a Theory of Mind error about O to the extent that O was affected by a bias and S was not. In the pure monetary choices, we as Ss and O as an experimental subject are in a more similar position. Both S and O are facing choices between financial options but O is not the owner of anything.

We should expect the Reflection Effect to be widespread in market participants and ourselves. In order to be more specific about what this will mean in practice, we need to look for what actions in markets will be analogous to the types of behaviour seen in the experiment. Those were, broadly, that risk appetite inverts around zero. People are excessively risk-averse when there is an opportunity for gain and also excessively risk-seeking when there is an opportunity to lose. Now that, as it stands, is not sufficient to tell us what investors will do when considering a trade, because all investments exhibit the opportunity to gain and the risk of loss. But it is at least a guide to what to look for.

6.3 Isolation Effect

In this effect, people fail to consider the big picture when making choices involving risk. Kahneman and Tversky (1979, p. 263) define the Isolation Effect when they note that people often "discard components that are shared by all prospects under consideration." The idea is that if you are faced with two options where you receive A+B in one option and A+C in the other, you can forget about A because you are getting it either way. You are only interested in whether B is preferable to C in choosing between the two options. This seems eminently sensible, and we can readily use our Theory of Mind to predict that anyone presented with choices of this form will decide in this way.

The problem, though, with the Isolation Effect is that it "leads to inconsistent preferences when the same choice is presented in different forms" (Kahneman and Tversky 1979, p. 263). Kahneman and Tversky (1979, p. 271) provide a dramatic illustration of this when they rewrite one of their earlier problems. In

Problem 4, Kahneman and Tversky (1979, p. 268) had asked participants to choose between a 20% chance of obtaining $4,000 and a 25% chance of obtaining $3,000, observing a strong (65%) preference for the first option. We can assume that subjects saw both options presented as reasonable and similar chances of winning and thought that they might as well select the option which paid them more if they won. In other words, they were prepared to give up a 5% chance of winning – the differences between 20% and 25% for the additional value of $1,000 if they did win. This type of effect is seen more widely. As *The Economist* [2] reports, Matheson has found that in lotteries "sales of tickets are much more sensitive to the size of the jackpots than to the likelihood of winning." This must be true, given, as *The Economist* also notes, the chances of winning Powerball are 1 in 292m, which is four times the chance of being killed by an asteroid impact in a single year.

For the avoidance of doubt, my point here is that these odds are so slim that there is no financial value in purchasing a lottery ticket. This may look strange at first. After all, the value of a ticket should be calculated from the probability of winning multiplied by the prize, as in all of the other cases. If the prize is very large, as it may well be, then the ticket could still be valuable even if it confers only a microscopic chance of winning. If the prize is say $292m, then one ticket is worth $1 and should be purchased at that price or less if available. What this misses out is the probability of sharing the winning numbers with other tickets, a factor that is often missed by lottery ticket holders. Even so, we can still offset this if the prize gets bigger. Imagine that on average, each winning ticket is in a group of eight winning tickets. If the prize is 8 x $292m = $2.34bn then the ticket is still worth buying for $1 or less. Now while some major lotteries do boast prizes in the billion dollar range, I think this is not usually the case and people are not optimising their financial position if they buy a lottery ticket.

But I want to make a further point. I think the ticket is not worth buying for $1 even if the numbers stack up according to the above analysis. So now I need to explain why. My view is that the odds of 1 in 292m are effectively indistinguishable from zero. For the same reason that I do not advise anyone to seriously worry about being killed by an asteroid – randomly and under current circumstances, obviously we would be in a different position if we had information about a large asteroid heading for London in the near future – I do not advise anyone to buy a lottery ticket. It is just so improbable that you will win that the ticket is valueless. I have seen arguments that claim that what people buy when they buy a ticket is hope, even if only a vanishingly small sliver of it. While this may be true, that argument implicitly admits my point that the financial value of the ticket is not enough to explain why people buy them. If you are rich, then $1 does not matter. However, we know that very poor people – in the global context, earning less than maybe $2 a day – spend the bulk of that income on tobacco, gambling and religious observance. Almost any other choices would be better. Someone very poor who spends $1 a day on a lottery ticket will still almost certainly be very poor a year later. Someone who puts the $1 in a tin and receives no interest could buy a cow.

Returning to the examples in the experiment, we may note that the value of a 20% chance of obtaining $4,000 is $800. The value of a 25% chance of obtaining $3,000 is $750. So the subjects made the optimal choice in this statement of Problem 4. Now we come to the 'restatement.' (It is about to become clear why I have placed 'restatement' in inverted commas.)

Kahneman and Tversky (1979, p. 271) set out Problem 10 as involving two stages. In stage one, there is a 75% chance of immediate exit and a 25% chance of moving to stage two. In stage two, there is a choice between an 80% chance of obtaining $4,000 and a certain $3,000. We can immediately see what will happen. Stage one is ignored because it is common to both choices in an illustration of the Isolation Effect. Stage two alone is now seen as a choice between a certain valuable win and a larger but riskier win. Subjects overvalue the certainty and prefer option two by a large margin (78%).

The difficulty is that ignoring stage one has had a strange effect on the probability estimations. If the two stages are taken together, as seems optimal, then the combined outcome is found by multiplying the probabilities together. In other words, we just multiply by the 25% chance of getting through stage one. The combined options now represent a choice between option one, with a (25% x 80%) = 20% chance of obtaining $4,000 and option two, a 25% chance of obtaining $3,000. But this is just Problem 4 again. So subjects greatly prefer the second choice when Problem 4 is split into stages and greatly prefer the first choice when Problem 4 is not split into stages. This is the inconsistent choices of which Kahneman and Tversky (1979) complain.

What has happened here is that the Isolation Effect has had the effect of eliminating stage one from consideration of the options in Problem 10. This then allows the Certainty Effect to come to the fore. Having ignored the uncertainty in stage one, subjects overweighted the value of the certainty in stage two. It is important to bear in mind here that stage one does not present any choices. It just involves a specified percentage chance of going through to stage two. Since going on to stage two is randomly determined, subjects do not have any choices to make and so they feel they can ignore stage one: since there are no choices in stage one, they feel, they will not feel bad about having made a bad choice in stage one. This is consistent with them thinking it would be bad luck to exit in stage one. But that is very different to thinking that they brought that bad luck upon themselves by making a poor choice or taking excessive risk. Those outcomes would carry a negative affective component.

6.4 Endowment Effect

People tend to think that something they own is more valuable than something identical which they do not own. Kuehberger *et al.* (1995, p. 432) write that the "endowment effect [...] means that simply being endowed with a good gives it added value." It can be seen when students are asked to estimate the price of a visible item such as a mug with a university crest on it. They make an estimate and are then actually given the mug and asked what they would sell it for. It turns out that they demand a much higher price for the mug now that they own it than the figure they gave previously for its value. This is, of course, not rational. Who owns the mug should make no difference to how valuable one believes it is.

Similar results are obtained in a series of experiments involving lottery tickets. Nichols *et al.* (1996) run one version of a lottery experiment. Their subjects assigned a higher value to tickets they had chosen than to ones they were given, although the economic value of the tickets was identical irrespective of whether they had chosen them or not. It seems as though their sense of ownership was more awakened by having made a choice of tickets.

I think this has roots in an asymmetry in affective forecasting of the type I mentioned in §6.1. We have to predict how bad we will feel in the different scenarios. We predict that we will feel much worse if we sold back a winning ticket that we had chosen than if we sold one back which we were given. This is not rational, of course. It is an open question as to whether we will be right in this prediction. In general, we are terrible at affective forecasting (Gladwell 2013, p. 148). Later, in §8.3, I will discuss how the apparent disadvantage of 'lack of empathy with oneself' could be of assistance in scenarios like this, in making it affectively less aversive to make the economically optimal decision.

Taleb (2007, p. 240) discusses the Endowment Effect. He mentions a trader maxim to the effect that it is a problem if one has become married to one's position. He rightly points out that the correct question to ask yourself, if a stock has changed price, is whether you would acquire it at the current price. If it has gone up, and the answer to this question is no, then the stock is overvalued. Or at least, that is your opinion. So you should check using some metrics whether that opinion is correct. If you conclude that it is, you should sell the stock.

One can ask the same question if the stock has gone down. Asking the question under those circumstances may be even more valuable. It is quite possible that you would in fact buy the stock at these new, lower, levels. If so, you should have no difficulty in holding it. In real life, we know that few things are more painful than holding a losing position. So asking this question may help.

To return to the Deutsche Bank position that I am currently holding, and which I mentioned on a number of occasions in this book, it is currently showing heavy losses as a result of the unexpected Brexit referendum result. So this is an example of the sort of problem I am discussing here. It must be conceded to Soros that he appears to have called this correctly.[3] It is reported that he was short several million Deutsche Bank shares at around the time of the referendum. We do not know if this was the only position he was holding; he may have been long as well in a variant of the long volatility strategy which I have also discussed on a number of occasions. If that is so, then his profits on the short position would have been largely offset by losses on the long position. We cannot know, because the reporting may have been selective.

However, if Soros got this right, he has profited quite significantly from believing the polling data, which many of us discounted unreasonably. I see that error as a variant of the Curse of Knowledge (see §7.1) problem. My approach has been to sell the shares as they decline to each new level, but then buy them back. This makes sense in the context of strong gains in the rest of the portfolio, because it reduces the eventual tax liability. But it also means I am, at each point, asking the question as to whether I would buy the stock at this new price. Since I still believe that price to book ratio is a useful yardstick in judging the advisability or otherwise of buying bank stocks, I am still happy to own the stock. This will continue to be the case as the price declines, unless new information emerges which suggests that the price to book ratio is incorrect. And that could only occur if the book value is significantly different in reality to what is reported, which would be a serious event.

The Endowment Effect has one implication which, rarely, means that a bias sometimes works in our favour in markets. Garling *et al.* (2009, p. 10) note that the strength of the Endowment Effect "increases with the length of possession" meaning that we will tend to value even more highly than we ought to a share that we have held for a long time. This could work against the Disposition Effect, which is the tendency to sell winners too early and hold on to losers too long. The Endowment Effect could then overcome the Disposition Effect in relation to winning stocks that we have held a long time, and cause us to hold them longer since we value them more highly. In general, though, the Endowment Effect will not be helpful since it will tend to make us value stocks we own more highly than the market does, when the market is of course authoritative on the question of what a stock is worth; at least in terms of how much cash we could raise by selling the stock.

6.5 Conclusions

Considering all three of the effects that Kahneman and Tversky (1979) have noted, we can see that expected utility theory is in trouble. When we are attempting to predict what market participants are going to do, applying expected utility theory to them will not work. However, running a mental simulation of them seems more auspicious. After all, it was fairly clear what people would do once we had seen how Kahneman and Tversky (1979) phrased their problems. Note that this is a correct prediction of how people are likely to behave, rather than a correct decision of what is the best way to behave. That remains attempting to maximise your utility and running through the best probability analysis you can. So the conclusion here seems to be to apply expected utility yourself but do not expect others to do so.

A way to avoid the Isolation Effect is to consider all new propositions in the context of your overall net asset value. This should make it easier to accept risks that are, in fact, valuable and worth taking because even in the worst case, they will not move the needle much on your net asset value. If you work hard and save $5,000, then invest it in the stock market and lose it all, we can be sure that you are going to feel very bad about it. If it was the only $5,000 you will ever be able to obtain, then you probably should feel bad about it. But anyone who retains any kind of earning potential should try to remain stoical here. You can always come back with another $5,000 and, ideally, a better strategy next time.

Try turning the position around. Most people, whatever their wealth, will give up a 50% chance of $1000 for between $300 and $400 (Kahneman and Tversky 1979, p. 277). Would you not like to go around the streets offering people that bet all day?

There seem to be two practical objections here, neither of which, I think, quite work. Both of them are variants of the idea that it is better to take the certain $300 because the 50% chance of $1000 may not really be 50%. There are two ways this could be a concern, which underlie the two objections. The first way is that the probability only seems to be 50% from the current standpoint. Setting aside difficult philosophical issues about whether probabilities are fixed or not, it seems as though what appears to me now to be a 50% chance of winning could, in fact, be less because of external events. There is after all some probability that the person offering me the bet will become insolvent before I have a chance to collect my winnings, or that I could become involved in an accident between now and when I collect my winnings, or the bank transfer could fail for miscellaneous IT reasons. There are a myriad of improbable events that could intervene before I can actually collect my cash. It would then be plausible to think that what people are doing in taking the $300 is trying to allow for the known and unknown unknowns that could mean that the 50% is really less than 50%. I accept this point at some level, but deny that all of these factors add up to a $200 deduction. Saying that is being excessively risk averse.

The second variant of the objection looks similar but is more epistemological. This says that whatever the real nature of the 50%, whether it is fixed or not, we rarely have access to accurate measures of probability. In casinos and betting shops we do, and the probability analysis suggests that frequenting such places is not optimal. But we do not know what is the probability that GE shares will increase by 1% today. We, in fact, have in principle no access to that probability, assuming it exists now. All we can do is backtest and find out how many days in the last 10,000 trading days that happened. This is an interesting number, but does not fix the future. I think the answer is to go out as long as possible. What is the probability that GE shares go up 1% today? I have no idea. What is the probability that they have gone up 50% in the next 30 years? I still do not know, but I have at least removed the noise from the signal. I think there is a pretty good chance of that happening; if it does not and one has attempted to foresee what might be problematic then it will be because something unforeseeable occurred. And I choose not to blame myself for not having foreseen the unforeseeable.

Taleb (2007, p. 192) associates Prospect Theory with what he calls a trader heuristic: in particular, the maxim that one is only as good as one's last trade. It appears as though the aspect of Prospect Theory to which he is referring is the Isolation Effect. A trader who thinks that only his last trade is significant is ignoring all previous trades on the grounds that those are now fixed parts of the past. The problem, of course, with this way of looking at things is that it will lead to excess risk aversion. As always, one should consider one's entire net worth position when contemplating a trade. For what it is worth, when I have heard people say that they are only as good as their last trade, they have tended to say it with irony. They clearly want their ability as a trader to be assessed over a longer period, if not their entire career. Nevertheless, one hears this maxim frequently enough to mean that one can be confident that there is an underlying effect in our psychology which causes us to think that way. It does, indeed, look as though the Isolation Effect is the root cause here.

Taleb (2007, p. 197) also notes the research that suggests we have two systems of reasoning (Sloman 1996). The opposition between the two systems is basically between the use of heuristics in system one and the more drawn-out processes of reasoning under system two. Using system one, or applying heuristics in other words, is quick, dirty and effortless. Heuristics have to be like that in order for them to pay their way in our cognitive architecture. Using system two reasoning, by contrast, is expensive in terms of time and effort so we only use it when it appears as though the rewards will outweigh those costs. Taleb (2007, p. 197) makes the interesting observation that in his opinion what professional traders are doing when they are "practising their probabilistic game" is generating a probabilistic machine from experience within system two, which then is automated and integrated into system one. This seems plausible. As Taleb (2007, p. 197) notes, there is evidence that expert chess players play intuitively using system one while everyone who starts to learn chess does so with great effort using system two to begin with and non-experts never get past using system two. It might be the case that all processes of becoming an expert involve shifting skills and reasoning from the difficult and effortful system two, to the quick and easy system one.

Finally, we may note a very important point that the pioneers make as a consequence of their Prospect Theory. This is their improvement on expected utility theory. Kahneman and Tversky (1979, p. 287) note that "incomplete adaptation to recent losses increases risk seeking." This is seen in many contexts; for example, the gambler bets bigger in an attempt to recoup his losses. I think this is to be avoided at all costs. One should attempt to take the right amount of risk at all times, and what that right amount will be is not path-dependent; in other words, it does not depend on the past. One would obtain better results overall if one were able to forget one's losses. This is an example of the counterintuitive view of Nietzsche

(1998, p. 35) that "forgetting represents a force, a form of strong health" when we normally see it as a weakness, with remembering being a powerful force. How one can do this without being Nietzsche's Übermensch is another question. I recommend falling back on the net asset value point I have already raised above. Unless you have just lost your entire net worth, your losses are more stressful than they need to be and than they ought to be for your optimal participation in markets. But also bear in mind that you can sometimes choose to forget events which are simply not helpful for you to remember. Think about something else, for example. This looks trite as a piece of advice, but it works for me. I sometimes use a mental image of a speedboat. Things left behind in the water are not important any more. Find something that works for you and just move on.

By the same token, it is important to avoid having 'gain targets' which force you to take extra risk because you need to make a certain amount of profit in a month. Again, this will lead you away from optimal risk-taking. This means that you should not place yourself in a position whereby you need to pay your rent from the proceeds of your investments, for example. Looked at another way, it results in the old and wise adage that you should only invest money you can afford to lose. Obviously this applies more in some cases than others. You can probably invest your rent money in US Treasuries that mature next month, but you cannot rationally invest your rent money in a stock, no matter how safe it appears or how certain you are that it will appreciate.

Notes

1 The authors are still using I£, but I have switched to $ because it will not make any difference.
2 *The Economist*, vol. 418, no. 8972, 16 Jan 2016, p. 72
3 It is fascinating that Taleb (2007, p. 240) suggests in his discussion at this point that Soros may be genetically different to the rest of us in that he is a rational decision maker. That would explain a lot if it is true.

7
SOCIAL BIASES I

7.1 The 'Curse Of Knowledge'

People exhibit this bias when they assume that everyone else knows what they know. This bias has a name which strikes one as immediately paradoxical. Knowledge is power, and knowledge can only be a good thing, we are inclined to retort. There are, though, some situations, particularly in the Theory of Mind arena, where less knowledge results in better performance. The problem here is specified by Bernstein *et al.* (2007, p. 1376) as describing the way that "adults have trouble ignoring knowledge that they possess when trying to estimate what another, naive person knows." In other words, adults tend to hold on in some circumstances to the errors made by children too young to pass the False Belief Task, in that they think at some level that if S knows something then so does O.

A more moderated form of the Curse of Knowledge may involve failing to adjust sufficiently for the different abilities of others. S will start from S's own ability level which may be very high, suspect that O is less capable, and thus predict that O has reasonable abilities in X. This may be totally over-optimistic: O may have extremely low abilities in X.

Similar effects are visible in the wider population. Bertrand and Morse (2011, p. 1879) found that almost 40% of payday loan borrowers thought that the Annual Percentage Rate (APR) on a payday loan was 17% when the loan charged $17 per $100 borrowed until the next pay cheque. This is a dramatic understatement since people are generally paid every two weeks in the US, so the true APR is well over 400%. If you think that no-one who takes out a payday loan will be a stock market investor, bear in mind that Bertrand and Morse (2011, p. 1877) also report that 13% of their subjects earned more than $50,000 p.a. and

16% had a college degree. One might think that none of this more sophisticated group would have made the very low APR estimate, and that might be correct, but it still means that some relatively well-paid college graduates are using payday loans, when this is extremely financially irrational. The authors were able to reduce borrowing amounts by pointing out the dollar costs of repayment, but when they included a savings planner, borrowing amounts actually increased (Bertrand and Morse 2011, p. 1885). I suspect this was because it included a list of items that could be saved on – e.g. beauty treatments, auto detailing – which had the unfortunate side effect of making the enjoyable activities on which the money could be spent less abstract, and crucially less abstract than the desirable but entirely theoretical goal of living within a sustainable budget.

I find it difficult to place myself mentally in a situation in which I am desperately short of cash to the extent that I would consider a payday loan. My first question would be how it had become possible for such a situation to arise: there must have been some severe planning failure; or a series of extremely unfortunate and unpredictable developments. This is consistent with the observation of Bertrand and Morse (2011, p. 1889) that the "dollar information treatment is least effective at reducing borrowing among the most highly educated borrowers." That means, I think, that the highly educated borrowers already knew that what they were doing was expensive and irrational; they felt they had no choice. The less educated borrowers were gaining new and important data. The authors asked whether the loans would be for gratification or non-gratification purposes. Gratification purposes include, for example, gifts, apparel and vacations, while non-gratification purposes include, for example, rent, medical bills and personal emergencies. Bertrand and Morse (2011, p. 1888) report that only 9% of borrowers were going to use their loan for 'gratification' purposes (or, only 9% admitted to this, more precisely).

What all this suggests to me is that there can be scenarios so remote from our own that simulation of Os in them is difficult; this is an effect of the Curse of Knowledge. We can, perhaps, imagine a set of desperate circumstances but it is difficult to imagine not knowing that paying $17 to borrow $100 for a week is not an annual 17% interest rate, because we know that a week is less than a year. So we can expect some market participant behaviour to be outside the scope of prediction. This could be very significant since prices are set at the margin. There is a further bias mismatch explanation of the Theory of Mind error here; it is hinted at by the authors and I implied above that the shift from the abstract to the concrete could be involved. Bertrand and Morse (2011) imply that the reason their programme of dollar amount information works is that it encourages people to think about the future; they have made the repayment less abstract and more vivid to the borrower. Consideration of repayment should, of course, always be front and centre of any borrowing decision. How certain am I that the asset I acquire with this loan will pay me more than the costs of the loan?

I imagine there are some people reading this who have been in such a situation and for whom reading this book is part of a programme which they resolved to undertake when they said to themselves 'never again' in a payday lending store. If that is you, I commend you. Turn the setback to your benefit.

It is often surprising to specialists or even the averagely competent when people struggle with what appear to be basic tasks in an unfamiliar arena. City lawyers are invariably extremely intelligent and worldly people who are highly effective under most circumstances. Some of them have something of a blind spot when it comes to mathematics or, rather, simple arithmetic. I am not talking about the ability to solve quadratic equations – though even that is, in fact, fairly straightforward to anyone with a reasonable mathematics background. I mean the immediate ability to spot that 10% of 150 is less than 20 and that 22 × 32 is something like 600. Obviously, if someone knows that this is a weak point for them, they can use a calculator, but without the kind of mathematical intuition I describe above, it will be very hard to spot mistakes.

I was in my first six months in The City when, as inevitably happens, I ended up operating way beyond my level of seniority because the two people senior to me who had been scheduled to attend were called away to fight fires elsewhere. One choice here I suppose would have been to reschedule the meeting, but this did not occur to me. I walked into a meeting room which had about 12 lawyers working for my firm in it and a similar number representing the interests of others, which were not necessarily aligned with those of my firm. Now, my lawyers were very good at protecting me from various difficulties that arose in the course of the meeting, and I said little until a tax leakage point came up. There would be some tax payable even though there were no profits because of an obscure rule determining that some things that were countable on the way in were not deductible on the way out. This was a problem because we were discussing a pass-through vehicle that was expressly designed to do nothing much in particular apart from act as a conduit for cash and having a tax bill as a result of it was highly unwelcome. One expects to pay tax on profits but not otherwise.

Deciding exactly how unwelcome was clearly important. Doing so involved a calculation of about a dozen steps of a straightforward kind, somewhat like 'start with $x m, find 15%, deduct $y m, assume all the numbers go up with inflation for 30 years, add up the entire amount, compare this sum with the value of the transaction.' I did all this very roughly in my head in about ten seconds and concluded that the problem was in fact immaterial in the context of the transaction and could therefore safely be ignored. This changed the atmosphere in the room completely; the effect could scarcely have been more dramatic if I had levitated or reformulated quantum mechanics on the spot. This, amazingly enough, constituted a significant victory for my side on an issue with which the lawyers had been struggling for some time. When I got back to the office later, I was commended for solving a problem as opposed to creating a new one, which might have been expected from someone as junior as I was at that time. My point is not that I was particularly brilliant in doing this calculation: getting it approximately right should be within the grasp of anyone who studied the amount of maths that is compulsory in school. My point is that if I had fallen victim to the Curse of Knowledge in simulating the likely reaction of those around me, I might not have said anything. I could have assumed that everyone else in the room was as capable as I was of doing this calculation in real time without paper and missed the opportunity to solve a problem.

Sometimes, a lack of knowledge about what constitutes an advantage or a disadvantage can be helpful, because, in fact, we are often wrong about what will help us or hinder us. Sometimes apparent advantages can be disadvantages and the other way around. If we do not have any 'knowledge' about whether something is good or bad for us, we may be in a better position to let it work in our favour; or parts of it may be helpful and we avoid throwing the good out with the bad, if that is possible. If it is not possible, then we can nevertheless rest assured in some cases that certain aspects of our psychology may have hidden benefits. I will consider these hidden benefits of apparent disadvantages in the next subsection.

7.1.1 The Advantages Of Disadvantages

One apparent advantage of this sort could be termed 'psychological health.' Naturally, that is overall a good thing to have, but an excess of psychological health can lead people to be "too conventional, too obedient and too unimaginative" (Gladwell 2013, p. 142) to succeed where success requires non-conformist thinking. Financial markets are certainly one of those environments. The idea is that if one is psychologically healthy, then there is little drive to take charge of one's psychology and do something useful with it. So this would be an example of an apparent advantage of not being of any assistance in the financial arena.

Other apparent disadvantages can really be advantages. It is known that many denizens of the trading floor score at psychopathic levels on tests of empathy, and I am no exception. This does not mean I am a psychopath. If you are trying to spot a psychopath, find out whether the individual exhibited 'McDonald's Triad' as a child: bedwetting, arson and animal cruelty. I am not admitting to any of those in this book. While it is rather unclear what empathy actually is (Coplan 2011) – indeed, Batson (2009) offers eight plausible candidates – or whether it is ethically useful (Prinz 2011), it is generally and imprecisely agreed to be an ability that can approximately be described as 'feeling someone else's pain.' So I do not do that very much and this could well be regarded as a social disadvantage. However, I have also suggested here and elsewhere (Short 2015; Short and Riggs 2016) that Theory of Mind is closely tied up to affect. Much of the literature also agrees with me that Theory of Mind is used in relation to oneself in counterfactual situations and at future times. In the jargon I have adopted, S uses Theory of Mind to predict the behaviour of O using affective input and O can also be S.

If I have a great deal of empathy with my future self, then I will experience a great deal of negative affect now in relation to projected negative affect in the future. Recall how I suggested in Ch. 3 that the operation of our Theory of Mind is fast and mandatory even if we do not notice its work. So I do not suggest that you can solve the problem by switching off your Theory of Mind. Many clinical groups such as autistic subjects (Baron-Cohen, Leslie, and Frith 1985) and schizophrenic subjects (Abu-Akel and Abushua'leh 2004) struggle with Theory of Mind tasks. Moreover, otherwise healthy subjects who display a 'hostility bias,' tending to see others as harbouring aggressive tendencies, also exhibit Theory of Mind deficits (An *et al.* 2012). And chronic cannabis users display alterations in brain function in regions thought to be associated with Theory of Mind (Roser et al. 2012). So one fascinating prediction of my account is that such subjects will be better traders, providing of course that their conditions do not otherwise impede their abilities. Schizophrenic subjects in remission would be a good choice of study since they do not exhibit cognitive deficits. All of these studies could also illustrate further examples of the advantages of apparent disadvantages. The key conclusion that we already have is that psychopathic subjects or, at least, those of us who are low in empathy, will be better able to take risk now because we feel our own future pain less acutely.

Graver (2007, pp. 124–125) discusses the low empathy of psychopaths in the context of Stoic views on emotions and sees it as a disadvantage. She notes that they can have a lack of empathy "even with their past or future selves" and suggests that this will impair the development of behavioural inhibitions. Whether this is positive or negative, of course, depends on whether these behavioural inhibitions are useful or not. Graver (2007, pp. 124–125) takes a negative view on this, because she thinks the inhibitions are a necessary precursor to moral behaviour. Again, whether this is positive or negative depends on whether it is useful to behave morally. I would suggest that there are no moral inhibitions relevant to making a legal profit in markets; if so, then traders will not benefit from either morality or behavioural inhibitions. Of more concern would be the tendency Graver (2007, p. 125) notes for this lack of empathy to result in the bypassing of "even obvious considerations of self-interest." This, of course, would be extremely unhelpful to the trader. So we need to avoid that consequence, while retaining the beneficial aspects previously mentioned.

Taleb (2007, p. 240) suggests that "purely rational behaviour on the part of humans can come from a defect in the amygdala that blocks the emotions of attachment" in psychopaths. If so, they would be able to assess their beliefs more rationally than others. They would not be prone to the problem of becoming "married to one's position." If they decided that the original facts which caused them to purchase the stock had changed, they would immediately sell the stock. They might, in addition, be less prone to Confirmation Bias (§5.1) since they would experience less negative affect on being forced by new data to change their beliefs.

It has been noted that people who have had abusive childhoods outperform on Theory of Mind tasks because they had to practise (Gladwell 2006, p. 108). Will such people or others who have strong Theory of Mind abilities outperform in markets? I have been suggesting that poor abilities in Theory of Mind could be a disadvantage, but that seems counterintuitive. Surely if someone can better predict the behaviour of others, they will be able to trade more effectively, as we saw in Chapter 3. That has been the central message of this book, so I need to square this circle. I think a key distinction is the *target* of Theory of Mind. I am suggesting in this narrow section that good, affectively vivid performance on Theory of Mind *in relation to oneself* is a problem, because it makes the future pain of a potential loss apparent now. That will not apply to others, because I will not feel the pain of another investor who may lose money in the future – or at least, I will not feel it anything like as intensely as he will. So the optimal position is some combination of excellent Theory of Mind in relation to others and none in relation to oneself. This outcome may not be obtainable, or learnable if it is obtainable, but there are some artificial enhancements available to Theory of Mind. Intranasal oxytocin, for example, improves Theory of Mind in schizophrenic subjects (Pedersen *et al.* 2011).

The effects of running Theory of Mind on myself in a postulated adverse future scenario will be aversive and unhelpful. I could be terrified at the prospect of future losses because I can feel today the pain associated with them. If you feel this description applies to you, and you do not think you can do anything about it, because you have tried hard to do something about it and failed, it may be that the stock market is not for you. Life is too short to spend sleepless nights worrying about anything, and if the prospect of investment losses causes you that much concern, it is really not worth it. Similarly, while empathy is generally seen – in my view, mistakenly – as a virtue, it is undoubtedly a flaw in a wide range of circumstances. We would not want a surgeon to feel our fear when he is discussing how he is about to operate on us. It would be extremely unhelpful for him to have any strong negative affect. So here we see another example of a scenario in which an apparent disadvantage is really an advantage.

Similarly, as Taleb (2012, p. 45) writes, "additional quantities of motivation and willpower [...] stemming from setbacks can be also seen as extra capacity." This is the type of idea behind the venture capital sector of private equity. Here, one could imagine concluding ten investments. One would expect to have maybe five or six of them break even. One or two would be unmitigated disasters. Two would be extraordinary successes. In even more risky fields where one is financing startups, it could be that 99 of 100 are total failures while the other one makes so much money that it pays for all the rest ten times over. In either case, the mantra is simply to fail quicker; that is just a cost of doing business. This requires a certain amount of willpower. Gladwell (2009b, p. 74) writes of Taleb that he never thought he was invincible – and was prepared for the financial devastation of 2007–2008 – because he "had watched [his] homeland blow up and had been the one person in 100,000 who gets throat cancer."

It is important to remain realistic about what can be achieved. No one can start from scratch and trade their way to becoming a billionaire. Wilkin (2015) presents an extended and persuasive argument to the effect that the only people who become billionaires have one or both of two key characteristics: The first is significant seed capital in amounts up to perhaps $100m. The second is close political connections. Bill Gates is possibly an exception, but he was probably unique in the world in that he had 10,000 hours of coding experience on mainframes gained in the 1970s at a young age.

If you do not have these two characteristics, you should forget about becoming a billionaire. Any system which tells you you can do this is fraudulent. However, successful trading can pay significant dividends. It is possible to earn enough money in five years and then to trade that capital successfully over a further 10 years so that one need no longer work for money. I know that this is possible because I have done it, starting without capital. So one advantage of not starting with $100m and political connections is that you can aim for something more reasonably achievable and much less risky than starting your own business. I applaud entrepreneurs, but the risks that must be taken and pay off in order to start up a billion-dollar business are immensely dangerous and immensely unlikely to pay off.

Again, Pinker (2015, p. 409) notes that common sense "says that victory goes to the side with the most intelligence, self-interest, coolness, options, power [but this] is wrong [because each] of these assets can be a liability in contests of strategy [...] where behaviour is calculated by predicting what the other guy will do in response." This, I think, is true but is hard to explain other than on my account, which holds both that simulation is the basis of how we predict the behaviour of others, and that such simulation can be thrown off by the starting point. If S has power and options, his first approximation of how O will behave is based on the assumption that O also has the same level of power and options etc. This may lead to systematic errors in predicting the behaviour of O.

Pinker (2015, p. 138) uses the example of nuclear retaliation to support his line. The point of nuclear weapons is deterrence: the enemy must think that you will use them in order to be deterred from using them himself. The paradox, of course, is that once there has been enemy action which might cause you to retaliate, there is no longer any point in such retaliation since deterrence has failed. But thinking too much about this in advance may result in accidentally letting the enemy know that you are thinking too much and therefore may not, in fact, retaliate. This has some echoes in the 'Madman' strategy allegedly employed by Nixon: he considered that his best bet was to make the Russians think he was capable of anything. The Madman strategy works best when it is completely convincing and actually being the Madman is among the ways of being very convincing.

This does not, of course, mean that you are best off in markets when you lack power and options. Sure, there will be the usual benefits of disadvantages in that perhaps lacking some of these qualities means you have to develop alternatives which are rare and provide unique opportunities. But, in general, one is best off possessing these attributes. The point is to be aware that we are set up to assume them in others as well. Avoid this error.

And as a further example, Lewis (2010, p. 128) discusses a counterintuitive case in markets where arriving late – but not too late – to a market can be a positive. The investors he discusses wished to short subprime mortgage Collateralised Debt Obligations (CDO) just before the market collapsed. Since a handful of other market participants had had the idea already, there was a lot of relevant research available and they were able to move quickly.

In fact, many of the heroes of Lewis (2010) are rather odd characters who seem to succeed in markets exactly because they are not as other men. Lewis (2010, p. 52) writes of another investor who profited mightily from shorting subprime mortgages that "one of the fringe benefits of living for so many years essentially alienated from the world around him [was that he] could easily believe that he was right and the world was wrong." Another way of putting that is that outsiders can develop an immunity to Conformity Bias (§7.4) which in this case, enabled them to make the trade of the century.

One instructive scenario in which bad news is really good news, since it develops willpower or mental strength played out in my physics career as a young post-doctoral researcher in Hamburg. I was working on shift on a particle physics experiment named ZEUS (Short 1992). A major component of this experiment, contributed by the UK, was the Central Tracking Detector ("CTD") including a large number of wires. These could be broken by raising the wire voltage at inappropriate times. If so, a display would light up showing white for a broken wire. We had lost maybe 20 wires of the 4,608 at the time in question. On one night shift, I accidentally raised the volts when the proton beam was unstable. They tripped out, as they were designed to do, and I realised my mistake and shut down. Some time later, we had stable beams and I raised the volts again to check the display for any extra white wires. I was hoping that the number I had broken would be small or similar to the number lost so far.

The display came up all white. It was telling me I had broken all the wires. This was of course beyond extremely disappointing. I did a number of things which I thought people never really did. I went into the restroom and said to my reflection in the mirror, "this has not really happened." I consider whether I should say nothing, leave immediately for the airport and be seen by no-one ever again. Obviously my career was over. I spent two hours thinking through the ramifications. There was only the one CTD; it was too expensive for a backup to have been made. The experiment as a whole was useless without it. ZEUS had cost something like EUR 700m; you could probably make it up to EUR 1bn if you also added in the time of the perhaps 1,000 physicists and engineers who had worked on it and the overheads of providing them with laboratories and equipment. All of these people had wasted more than maybe five years because, solely, of my mistake.

I eventually decided that I had to confess. I called the Run Coordinator, a notoriously cheerful and resourceful chap who met all news of difficulties with an immediate helpful response. When I told him what I had done, his only response was 'ah ...' He told me he would come in to the experiment at once, which, since it was around 04:00, did nothing for my state of mind. However, when he arrived, we eventually found out that an interlock had been installed that day by another component to prevent CTD voltage being applied if their detector element was not ready. When we resolved this, it turned out that I had only broken two or three wires.

This was, I think, about the greatest moment of relief in my life. My point in retailing this anecdote is what it did for me afterwards. Quite simply, nothing that happened to me subsequently was anything like as bad. Not the time I found that I had made a $100m tax error against us in a spreadsheet I had been writing for the investment bank I worked at. Not even the time when I discovered that I had some time previously accidentally deleted the new multimillion-pound headquarters building for a social housing association in another exhilarating episode with spreadsheets. This, I think, is what Nietzsche (2005, p. 157) means when he famously writes "From life's school of war. – What doesn't kill me makes me stronger."

In a trading context, what this is likely to translate to is a heavy loss scenario. Providing it does not wipe you out, you can emerge much stronger. I have experienced a couple of total losses on individual stocks. These were minor positions, which helped, and also illustrated the value of diversification. On a portfolio basis, I do not think I have so far seen losses of worse than 30% at any one time. I think that the benefit of the horror of the apparent total loss of the CTD meant that I was able to weather this extremely unpleasant period, which was protracted, until eventually markets turned up again. If you have a similar negative experience, try to recall during it that the largest benefits only accrue from a really terrible experience. Whether you do or not, it is true all the same.

7.2 Dunning-Kruger Effect And Expertise

Part of a lack of expertise in a topic is the failure to recognise that same lack of expertise. After all, if you knew you were bad at an important activity, you would either avoid the activity, improve your abilities or get help. The effect applies in both intellectual and social domains.

In this effect, people who are poor performers at a particular task do not recognise their own poor performance and people who are good performers also fail to assess accurately their own performance level relative to others. I class this as a social bias because much of it is to do with comparisons between oneself and others. It can be seen to arise in a fairly intuitive way. After all, if S is bad at X, S may be so bad that S also does not know what counts as good at X. S cannot then recognise a high level of competence at X in O. If S could do that, S could take steps to emulate O or find out how he got to be good at X. So we may assume prima facie that S does not have that ability precisely because we have already stipulated that S is bad at X. Worse, in the Dunning-Kruger Effect, poorly performing Ss are unaware of their poor performance.

The canonical experiment here involved asking psychology students who had just taken an exam how well they thought they had done and how well they thought they had mastered the material. Both questions were asked on a percentile ranking basis, so that the students were asked to say where in the percentage ranking of students they had come. Dunning *et al.* (2003, p. 84) report of the lowest quartile students that while "their performance actually put them in the 12th percentile, they estimated their mastery of the course material to fall in the 60th percentile and their test performance to fall in the 57th." The 12th percentile means 12% up from the bottom here. So it is clear that the bottom quartile of students dramatically over-estimated their performance.

This, of course, makes sense from a number of perspectives. Firstly, the students probably thought they were in reasonable shape for the exam and so did less revision than needed. Secondly, there is a general tendency to think somewhat more positively of oneself than is strictly justified, in a self-esteem maintenance effect — see also §8.3. Our primary interest in this bias will be the extent to which it can cause investors to be over-confident in their own abilities and risk too much too soon in their investment career. I will be suggesting some metrics to help avoid this.

This mistake made in relation to oneself is, to some extent, a kind of Theory of Mind error, as are caused by the other biases I discuss in this book. The other side of the coin — making the error in relation to others — is more clearly a Theory of Mind error. It is a variant of the Curse of Knowledge problem (§7.1). This is because if S is a sophisticated and skilled investor, S starts from the assumption that O is also sophisticated and skilled. Plenty of Os are, but plenty are not. It is important to bear this in mind. When trying to assess whether a market reaction is rational and proportionate, an assumption that all investors are performing optimally with a high level of skill is not just implausible, but shuts down the option to decide that the market is over-reacting and removes important trading opportunities.

One problem resulting from this effect is that it could lure one into trading too much too soon when one is in the early stages of an investment career. The reason I discuss how much work is required to become a good trader here is that it is important to make that decision while avoiding the Dunning-Kruger Effect. It is important to do so because otherwise one might end up taking excessive risks based on an illusion of competence too early in one's investment career. As I will suggest in §8.1, it is more important to put the hours in than it is to be a certain sort of person. Indeed, I suggest that there is little value in the very idea of there existing a certain sort of person, unless one counts willingness to do a lot of work as a characteristic.

A facet of the Dunning-Kruger Effect is seen when Hirshleifer (2001, p. 1565) notes that an "investor who overestimates his ability to [acquire information] will underestimate his errors in forecasting value." The methods of acquiring information include meeting management, analysing financial statements and reading internet chat. The first method is not open to the average investor; the second can be difficult; the third can be deeply misleading, though also a source of crucial intelligence on popular misunderstandings that can be exploited. In all these scenarios, avoiding the Dunning-Kruger Effect means escaping the risk of placing undue reliance on the information obtained.

So, what can we say from data about how much work might be required? The short answer is probably much more than you think. Konnikova (2016, p. 51) notes disquieting evidence about retirees in Colorado who are reportedly highly alert to fraud, think "that they [are] very knowledgeable about investing," and of whom "over 60% were investors in stocks, bonds and other securities." Nevertheless, over 6% of them had been victims of investment fraud and 10% of those victims had lost over $100,000. Konnikova (2016, p. 54) also reports that the victim percentage is lower than the US national average, which is an extraordinarily concerning fact. Since avoiding fraud is probably the most basic and important decision in the investment arena, this suggests to me that investors do not, in general, spend sufficient time becoming acquainted with how markets work before they invest. It is an example of the Dunning-Kruger Effect since clearly the retirees believed that they had enough expertise to spot investment fraud and they did not, in fact, have that expertise.

I will make a couple of recommendations here, although it is slightly outside my remit; I hope you will forgive the brief digression since if it prevents even one fraud, it will have been worth our time. Recognised – in both senses, i.e. well-known and officially regulated – main boards of stock exchanges like the NYSE (New York Stock Exchange) and the LSE (London Stock Exchange) place onerous reporting requirements on all stocks listed on them. There can still be fraud at listed companies of course – such as at Enron – but in my view this is much less frequent. You will also be joining in your risk with a large community of investors, short sellers and analysts, who can generally be relied upon to spot problems or, at least, will in aggregate be able to spend a lot more time on the problem than any one individual investor. This is better protection than you will find offered on any investment in unlisted securities from local salesmen, however plausible. In the UK as well, anyone offering financial advice must be authorised by the Financial Conduct Authority which maintains a public register of such individuals together with disclosure of any disciplinary measures against them. There are *no circumstances at all* under which you should deal with an unauthorised individual.

Let us consider whether the amount of expertise can be reduced to a number of hours. Famously, and to my mind persuasively, Gladwell (2009a, ch. 2) argues for 10,000 hours of experience in an area as sufficient to produce true expertise in it. Pinker (2015, p. 361) suggests that even a genius "pays dues for at least ten years before contributing anything of lasting value" which is roughly consistent if we assume that the ten years are very intense and committed. However, it would be unreasonable to suggest that investors spend that amount of time practising trading before they even begin to do any trading; I guarantee, however, that if you do, you will be brilliant. If you are not doing it professionally, it would take you too many years. Moreover, one of the most important ways to learn to trade is to put some trades on. You can – and should – start with dummy trading accounts, but this will not prepare you for the adverse affective impact of losing actual money. The affective import of such losses must be handled. The importance of mastering one's own psychology in this way is a recurring theme of this book.

The Stoic account of emotion has much to commend it here. This account, contrary to popular belief, does not condemn affective responses out of hand. What it does do is to insist that emotions are intimately and indissolubly combined with judgments. These judgments can be appropriate or inappropriate; similarly the emotions can be appropriate or inappropriate in their nature or extent. As Graver (2007, p. 83) observes, on the Stoic account, it is "in our nature to respond affectively, but it is not in our nature to be overpowered by our own affective responses." She suggests that the appropriate response to market reversals is not to seek to remove the negative affective response thereto, but to seek to ensure that it is measured to the magnitude of the reversal. Since very few market developments will result in a material adverse change to our net wealth, our affective response should be minor and short lived. One way to assist yourself in this regard is to have a spreadsheet showing your entire net wealth broken down into sectors. If you are lucky, your house price will go up on some days when the stock market goes down, which will help. If not, you can at least see that even a terrible day for one stock in your diversified portfolio does not do too much damage to your total net wealth.

We might, in addition, ask questions as to which emotion is the appropriate one here. If anger is appropriate, then against whom it is to be directed? A target must be identified. It is presumably not useful to be angry with oneself, and being angry with the market also does not appear sensible as a way to proceed. Fear is also a possible response. On the Stoic account, fear is a judgment that a future evil will occur. This judgment can be questioned. But in our case, it appears as though fear is not provoked by an existing loss, but by the prospect of future losses. If that is the problem, then one can accept one's losses and withdraw from the market. Or one could overcome the fear: one can remain in the market. In either case the fear will disappear. All of this gets easier with practice.

It must be conceded that the Stoics do not attribute much value to material wealth or, indeed, anything in the external world. For this reason, one might think that they would have little time for the project in this book. It is worth bearing in mind, however, that anyone who was a Stoic philosopher or anyone likely at that time to have been reading Stoic philosophy would probably have been an aristocratic and wealthy slave-owner. They were already free to pursue philosophy, or other valuable projects, without needing to generate wealth. So although fondness for money is listed as a "sickness" (Graver 2007, p. 138), I think we should read this as fondness for money beyond the amount required to create freedom. The rest of us, by contrast, need to solve that problem before moving on to the more valuable areas of human flourishing described in Stoic and other philosophy, or any other area in which one is free to choose one's own work.

One problem with running dummy portfolios is that they do not fully replicate the affective import of trading, and that is important. Lo, Repin, and Steenbarger (2005, p. 357) note that "paper-trading provides some of the same emotional stimuli of live trading but is not a perfect simulacrum." The same authors also report their experiment which supported "the common wisdom that traders too emotionally affected by their daily profits-and-losses are, on average, less successful" (Lo, Repin, and Steenbarger 2005, p. 357). Learning to be relatively dispassionate in this way can perhaps only be done on the job, as it were. People who are less neurotic – which, as I will discuss later in §8.1, is one of the few stable personality traits on which behaviour predictions can be founded – will have a natural advantage here. One useful criterion has been introduced which relates to the ability to benefit from filtered or unfiltered market information. Filtered information means financial reportage prepared by financial journalists either in print or on CNBC, for example.

Unfiltered information means raw and difficult to understand data such as regulatory filings by corporates and surveys of national economic activity.[1] Nofsinger (2016, p. 18) notes that inexperienced investors gain more benefit from filtered information, while experienced ones gained more from unfiltered information. I think this means that new investors are enabled by the journalistic input to avoid crass mistakes of interpretation. An example: I was once asked to confirm that a large number of block trades in a stock was good news for that stock. A block trade is just a large number of shares being traded, presumably by an institution rather than an individual. Of course, the answer depends on whether the trades are purchases or sales, and is not that illuminating either way. Good journalists or guests on CNBC may state opinions with which you disagree – indeed there are few things more instructive and valuable than violently disagreeing with a pundit – but they are unlikely to allow you to fall into basic errors like that.

The problem is that dealing with the unfiltered information is extremely tedious and very hard work. It is worth doing, but I think there is actually a third level. I believe I can also benefit from CNBC discussions because I can see what the unfiltered data must have been, where journalists have added beneficial insights and where they have, perhaps forgivably, been compelled to over-simplify. An obvious corollary of this is that it is essential to rely only on impeccable journalistic sources. *The Economist*, for example, will always cite its sources and basically makes a living by giving you some primary data and then telling you what it might mean. This gives you the opportunity to decide whether you like the interpretation or not. So I think another initial test of whether you are ready to manage your own money is whether you are prepared to work with unfiltered data and whether you then benefit from it.[2] A further source of filtered data is internet chatrooms and other areas of the internet where retail investors gather. These commentaries are invariably poorly argued, partisan and scarcely literate and must be avoided at all costs by every serious investor, of whatever level of expertise.

Rusbridger (2013) gives us another estimate of how much effort is required to attain expertise. He is working in a different field, that of piano playing, but I think we can still learn from his estimate. Recall that Gladwell's estimate is field-independent. In both fields and, indeed, maybe in all of them, you get out what you put in and it is reasonable to ask how many hours are needed to reach a high level. Rusbridger is probably well described as an extremely good amateur who could, perhaps, have been professional if he had continued and specialised. Piano exams have eight grades and Rusbridger just managed to scrape through grade VI of VIII (or IX, if one also counts the performance diploma). This is about the level I think we could look to as a comparable level which anyone should have before they start trading serious money. Rusbridger (2013, p. 3) tells us that he gained only around 2,000 hours before the age of 18. This, I think, is a reasonable intermediate target; it is after all something like ten hours a week for four years.

If you are not prepared to commit that kind of time, I think you should probably either buy trackers or hire fund managers. Though even then, you will need to put in some serious hours to avoid being ripped off. It is reported by *The Economist*[3] that 7% of US financial advisers were disciplined for misconduct over a ten-year period. Moreover, 44% of those were subsequently rehired by a different firm. These advisers who have been disciplined "seem to congregate in relatively wealthy, elderly and less educated counties" such that in parts of Florida and California, "one in five advisers has a record of misconduct." Since you are reading this, you are not uneducated; and now you know where there are investors who are. And as we just saw, even the apparently better informed retirees in Colorado experienced difficulties.

Attaining the Rusbridger (2013) 2,000 hour number still represents a serious amount of effort. But it includes everything you do that could plausibly be described as time invested in becoming a better investor, which will include, for example, such activities as reading *The Economist*, considering geopolitical events, their likely future progression and what all of this would mean for the correct trades. It would also include trading dummy accounts and trading accounts with a relatively minor amount of cash invested. Beyond 2,000 hours, the amount of money at risk can be stepped up. If you get to 10,000 hours, you can risk your entire disposable net worth if you see a compelling opportunity.

What exactly you should do is open to question. Ryle (2009) investigated the distinction between knowing how and knowing that; he concluded that the two are separate. Most people can ride a bicycle without being able to specify how to do it; children are taught to do so basically by having a go with some backup in case of error. That is knowing how. It is, in a way, easier to transfer information in the 'knowing-that' format since it is just propositional knowledge that can be written down. Some mix of the two seems appropriate – finding the right mix is a question of trial and error. "Doing can be wiser than you are prone to believe – and more rational" (Taleb 2012, p. 261). I think this is right: a heavy component of the time should be spent operating practice trading accounts. You can learn a lot from your mistakes if you are honest about them. On the other hand, you will learn a lot more from your mistakes when they cost you serious money. So I suspect this mixture will be differently optimised for different people.

There is evidence that when you ask people whether they have learned something, they make erroneous self-assessments since actually, their positive reports of how much they learned are correlated not with that but with whether the learning experience made them happy (Armstrong and Fukami 2010). The same authors also suggest that, in fact, learning experiences are associated with pain. Nietzsche (1998, p. 37) goes even further and suggests that "only what does not cease *to give pain* remains in one's memory." So this might mean that your most powerful learning opportunities are the ones in which you lose the most money.

There might be other ways for you to decide when you are ready to risk serious money. Let us examine two characteristics of expertise that have been discussed in the literature. Gladwell (2006, p. 107) notes that "when experts make decisions, they do not logically and systematically compare all available options; " instead they draw on "experience and intuition and a kind of rough mental simulation." Also, Gladwell (2006, p. 123) notes that often "a sign of expertise is noticing what does not happen." I think that both of these observations are correct as signs of expertise and so you could try to notice them in your own behaviour. You can, of course, equally use these heuristics as a way of improving your own performance in the Theory of Mind task of assessing when other people are experts.

It has to be conceded though that on many occasions when it would be useful to assess expertise, you would have to already be an expert yourself to do so. Consider an example of the second type of case above when noticing absences is a sign of expertise. Experts notice when the usual consequences of an event are absent. A market observer may say something like: 'when I last saw a situation like this in Japan, it seemed to have been caused by rising interest rates in the US; but this time US rates are falling.' Obviously they will then have to produce some type of interesting analysis of why this has happened, but at a very basic level, their observation depends on being able to compare the current situation with their expectations based on relevantly similar past scenarios. They will also have had to make a good decision on what constitutes 'relevantly similar', a decision which on its own will often require significant expertise. In the real world, of course, you might demand something much more sophisticated; here I am just trying to illustrate the principle.

The first type of criterion, that of not needing to consider exhaustive lists of options, is, I think, also a key marker of expertise. A true expert simply does not spend an hour working out how to express in a trade the view that US rates are going to rise. He knows that there are several ways of doing that and one may suggest itself more strongly than others. Possibly the best option may be one that also works well in conjunction with other opinions that the expert holds. It may be that the expert comes to an effortless conclusion on this not by dispensing with consideration of the options but by having automated them so that the consideration now lacks phenomenology.

It might be objected that making important decisions this quickly cannot possibly be right. As Gladwell (2006, p. 13) notes, "we are innately suspicious of this kind of rapid cognition." We think that more information is always better, but I do not think this is the case, particularly if it leads to paralysis and overload. Gladwell (2006, p. 138) notes that sometimes "we can do better by ignoring what seems like perfectly valid information." It is a mistake to think that every relevant piece of data about stock X must be considered before making a decision in relation to stock X. For a start, every potentially relevant fact would have to be considered to see whether it is actually relevant. This is impossible, in a variant of what is known as the Frame Problem (Shanahan 2009), because the list of potentially relevant facts is not finite. Consider, also, when Gladwell (2006, p. 13) quotes the son of George Soros on his father: "the reason he changes his position on the market or whatever is because his back starts killing him." This does not, of course, mean that you should examine your phenomenology for back pain when considering whether to make an investment decision. What it means is that some of Soros's expertise is subconscious and manifests itself in pain symptoms.

This also does not mean that you should never carefully consider a decision. Often it will be very important to do so. For instance, forming some view on the likely future path of central bank interest rates in the US and elsewhere from the standpoint of early 2016 is both difficult and valuable. It will require constant monitoring and thought, and a great deal of gathering of data and opinion, all of which must be examined critically. However, let us say that you have at length reached a view or a set of views, and you now think you should buy a defensive stock in the pharma sector. You narrow it down to major pharmaceutical companies that are mega-caps, i.e. members of the Dow Jones Industrial Average. You check the P/E ratios and the dividend yields and they are both attractive. There are no obvious red flags raised by either stock. At this point, many people would do a great deal of extra work in making the final decision as to which stock is the best one to buy, but I think you can just make a call and get on with the trade quickly. It is likely that anything that could happen later was not foreseeable by you in your current information state or one you could reasonably have got to on a fair assessment of the cost/benefit of your use of your own time. So in some circumstances you will outperform by making a lot of decisions quickly. Similarities in rapid thinking styles have been noted between successful traders and US Marines (Gladwell 2006, p. 108). Both operate on limited data and, with both types of individual, results are extremely important and process, provided obvious errors have been avoided, less so.

I estimate that on the wider measures I outlined above including, for example, reading *The Economist*, I currently have around 35,000 hours of time spent relevant to trading. I have definitely not spent that amount of time actually trading; not least because executing a trade often takes less than half a second. That illustrates another reason why preparation time should be included in the relevant measure of 'time to expertise.' This, of course, also does not mean that I am three times more skilled than someone at the 10,000-hour 'true expertise' level. It does not mean I should risk more than my net disposable wealth by betting my apartment, for example. It does have some advantages, though, in that I have traded through a number of cycles. This means I have seen a number of catastrophic scenarios from the dot-com crash through the 2007–2008 crisis which is continuing to make its effects felt in 2016. That, I think, is valuable because it assists in risk management, as I will now discuss.

One variety of the Dunning-Kruger Effect can be seen when Marks (2011, p. 55) notes that investors "vastly overestimate their ability to recognise risk." This is one of the mechanisms which can lead to bubble situations developing. Investors take more risk than they are aware of taking. I think managing the downside is, in fact, the major aim of successful investment. The upside will look after itself; if one is invested in any asset class at all which is common in the market, then it must have some reasonable prospect of either paying some running yield or increasing its capital value. If not, it is not an investment vehicle but a scam or a fraud.

On the other hand, much more attention should be paid to the downside. Being able to recognise risk requires, at a minimum, making an assessment of how much a portfolio would decline if another 2007–2008 were to occur. As Marks (2011, p. 66) correctly points out, in the long term "most investors' results will be determined more by how many losers they have, and how bad they are, than by the greatness of their winners." One valuable discipline which I would recommend to everyone initially, even though I do not pursue it myself, would be to set automated stop losses such that no investment can decline more than 10%. This would represent terrific downside management and would take this entire issue off the table. Investors are, of course, reluctant to do it because there is always the hope that the asset might recover. Investors run a Theory of Mind simulation on themselves in the scenario in which the asset recovers and they have already sold it, thus missing out on the recovery. They conclude, probably inaccurately, that they would feel terrible and they thus favour bearing the ongoing pain of an underwater position to crystallising a final loss.

There are a couple of reasons why I do not do this myself, and I think it is a matter of the quality of one's own self-knowledge when deciding which approach to take. I sell losers frequently, taking advantage of the tax benefits. It does not upset me at all. I never ever look at what happens to the asset subsequently − or at least, I do not do so in order to find out whether I have made a mistake. You can drive yourself mad watching an asset appreciate after you have sold it at a loss. I might look again at the asset if I am considering entering the asset again at a different price point. Rationally, subsequent events cannot alter whether or not you made a mistake in selling the asset. If that was the best decision at the time based on your reasonable risk management requirement to avoid losses of greater than 10%, and it was not reasonably foreseeable that the asset would recover, then it remains the best decision you could have made. If you think you will be able to ignore the temptation to check the price of an asset you sold yesterday or will not care if you do, then you can insulate yourself from the worst effects of this bias. It remains the case, though, that placing a 10% stop loss on all your investments will automatically mean you have controlled excessive risk.

There is also an interesting corollary which we might see as the inverse of the Dunning-Kruger Effect. Dunning *et al.* (2003, p. 85) refer to it as the "undue modesty of top performers." This variant of the effect is a systematic Theory of Mind error I touched on above and is easily explained on my simulationist account of Theory of Mind. S's starting point for the capabilities of O is S's own high level of expertise which then causes a decline in S's ranking of S's abilities relative to those of O's in general. The problem here, of course, in market terms is that one may have made an accurate judgment of the right trade and one may know that one has made such an accurate judgment, but one may not back oneself to the appropriate extent. It is just as important to market performance to take big bets when they are right as to avoid bad ones altogether or make them smaller.

The solution to this is seen when Dunning *et al.* (2003, p. 85) note that "one can disabuse top performers of this misperception by showing them the responses of other people." I think this tracks through to markets in that one can consider the performance of other investors, making sure, of course, that one has accurate records of one's own performance. Statistics are available occasionally on how well on average a group of investors has performed in recent times; one will also need to consider risk-adjusted performance rather than merely absolute returns.

One can also examine the arguments of other investors. In the comment sections after investment articles on the CNBC website and the like, it is possible to see a wide range of exceptionally poor arguments. However, it is often so poor that it would give one a misleading idea of one's own performance by comparison. Similarly, it is reported of US persons who are no doubt representative that "three out of four respondents could not correctly identify the relationship between long-run interest rates and bond prices" (Wilcox 2008, pp. 47–48). This is somewhat unfortunate since this inverse relationship is in one sense rather obscure, but it is also so basic as to mean that 75% of Americans should never be allowed to make any financial decisions if competence is the only yardstick. It is, for example, an excellent reason not to buy UST's at the current (mid-2016) juncture since we are at the start of a Fed tightening cycle.

I suppose my demand of the reader would not be so much as to already know this, though that is optimal, but to understand it now and recall it later. This type of environment creates great difficulties for the top performer in finding adequate self-evaluation metrics. A better metric might be to look at the arguments of respected commentators and see how their quality stacks up against the sort of argument that one could make oneself. That is obviously also a useful exercise in terms of improving one's own arguments.

7.3 False Consensus Effect

The idea here is basically 'everyone agrees with me.' This may have some links to Self-Presentation Bias (cf. §8.3), since someone with healthy self-esteem will believe that his own reasoning powers are in excellent shape, and so, surely, everyone else must come to the same conclusion. If they do not, there must be something wrong with their data, or their intellect, or they are biased.

Ross, Greene, and House (1977, p. 279) define the False Consensus Effect when they write that "social observers tend to perceive a 'false consensus' with respect to the relative commonness of their own responses," where responses might be actions, choices or opinions. So, "raters estimated particular responses to be relatively common" (Ross, Greene, and House 1977, p. 279) – viz., the ones they had themselves made.

Ross, Greene, and House (1977, p. 279) conducted a number of experiments: one of them was called the 'supermarket story.' Subjects are asked to imagine that they are just leaving a supermarket, when they are asked whether they like shopping there. They reply that they do, since that is, in fact, the case. It is then revealed that the comments have been filmed, and the subject is requested to sign a release allowing the film to be used in a TV advertisement. The key question is then asked: the subject or 'rater' is asked to estimate the percentage of people who will sign the release.

The results were that raters overestimate the percentages of others who make the same choice they would. Ross, Greene, and House (1977, p. 294) conclude that "raters' perceptions of social consensus and their social inferences about actors reflect the raters' own behavioural choices."

The False Consensus Effect may exacerbate the type of herding behaviour seen in bubbles. As Marks (2011, p. 49) observes, in such scenarios investors "forget caution [and] obsess about the risk of missing opportunity." This will be worsened if investors also think that many other investors are also thinking the same way as they are. It will appear that only a minority of excessively cautious investors are still concerned about risk. The majority of investors, who surely cannot be wrong – goes the flawed thinking – are looking to buy and if I do not join them, I will miss out. In reality, there are no circumstances ever in which caution is inappropriate and, in fact, it is most valuable at times when no-one else is exhibiting it. The antidote to the False Consensus Effect is to assume that no-one else is thinking like you are. If you are doing a properly contrarian job, holding this assumption will be made easier by the fact that it will be true! But even when this is not the case, challenge everything and do not rely even implicitly on the idea that everyone else shares your views and so they must be right.

Psychological factors can change and cause prices swings in markets even in the absence of substantial changes in fundamentals. Frydman and Goldberg (2011, p. 167) report that "the up-trend in the inflation rate that began in 2004 was no larger than the downtrend that prevailed between 2001 and 2003. Nonetheless, *Bloomberg News* reported that the importance of inflation as a main driver of stock prices (measured by the average proportion of days each month that this factor was mentioned in Bloomberg's stories) changed dramatically, rising from below 5% during the earlier period to 45% by 2005." So, although there was only a minor directional change in inflation, its importance in explaining how investor views affected stock prices changed dramatically. What happened was less that investors changed their forecasts and more that they changed their forecasting strategy. They took the view that even if there was currently no reason to expect radical changes in inflation, what changes were reasonably to be expected should be accorded much greater weight in the forecasting of future stock price movements. Such changes in forecasting strategy can then lead to price swings in stock markets before the fundamental factor begins to move itself.

Again, the False Consensus Effect will only exacerbate this. Investors will simulate other investors from their own shifted viewpoints and will now assume that inflation is a much more significant input factor for all market participants. This is, in a way, a self-fulfilling prophecy in that investors will be reading the news stories and all moving in the same direction at once. Everyone starts worrying about the same possibilities, partly because they assume that everyone else is worrying about them. So, do not assume that all investors are using the same major inputs to forecasting as you are. Be aware that even if everyone shares the same view of a fundamental factor – say inflation – different investors could apply differing weights to its importance in driving future price developments.

Another malign interaction of the False Consensus Effect may be seen in the way that mutual fund investors exhibit a "barn door closing" mentality (Patel, Zeckhauser, and Hendricks 1991) whereby they invest today in what would have been profitable yesterday. This is a variant of momentum trading: funds which have gone up go up some more. The problem is that it leads to a classic error of buying funds when they are expensive and later, in panic, selling them when they are cheap. This behaviour is extremely widespread and extremely expensive. It is easy to understand, though, why investors engage in such value-destructive behaviour: it is psychologically very difficult to stand by while an investment loses money. One's ability to do this will be enhanced if one can avoid letting the False Consensus Effect cloud one's Theory of Mind such that it produces an automatic prediction that everyone else will be selling. Sometimes that will be true, and the rational response is to try to sell first. But otherwise, once that horse has bolted, you may as well leave the barn door open.

An obvious question here is how to distinguish inadvisable behaviour under adverse performance from an advisable sale of a deteriorating asset. The answer is that the former can be identified from the description I just gave: if you do not have anything other than 'I think there may be a problem and so everyone else does,' you should hold. That will involve ignoring a lot of ill-informed internet chatter. One of the best ways of ignoring it is to avoid it altogether. If, on the other hand, the investment case has significantly weakened, then selling becomes realistically considerable. For example, if the case for buying Deutsche Bank stock rests largely on its trading at distressed levels of price/book of around 0.30, then an accounting scandal or legitimate revaluation which resulted in a material adverse change to that ratio would be a legitimate sell signal, if you could get out in time. Falling prey to the False Consensus Effect will prevent one from even considering such a case appropriately, so this is a bias which is both bad for us directly and bad for our Theory of Mind – which is indirectly bad for us.

7.4 Conformity Bias

We all have a tendency to go with the flow or follow the herd. Often it is a useful shortcut. If you are standing at a pedestrian crossing in London waiting for the lights to change, you are much more likely to wait if others around you are doing so. Conversely, if one of the pedestrians breaks ranks and decides to cross anyway, there is a much greater likelihood that you will do, probably after checking that the breakaway pedestrian has got it right and there are indeed no cars coming. If this is correct, you cross earlier and save some time. This sort of behaviour also forms part of culture, widely defined. In Hamburg, as in most parts of Germany, it is very rare to cross without waiting for the lights to turn green and, indeed, if you do so, you will be publicly reprimanded for setting a bad example to children. Again, everyone tends to conform to general expectations, rather than employ extensive rational analysis to optimising their actions on some basis. We can see this as a bias in their behaviour. As Marks (2011, p. 154) puts it, the "power of herd psychology to compel conformity and capitulation is nearly irresistible, making it essential that investors resist them." I will term this particular bias Conformity Bias. It is sometimes referred to with different names in the literature. Often it is called the Asch Effect after the first researcher to discuss it (Asch 1952). In my usage I am following Plotkin (2011), who does not, however, give a brief definition of the term. Prentice (2007, p. 18) also uses the term in the way I do: "conformity bias strongly pushes people to conform their judgments to the judgments of their reference group."

Asch (1952, p. 467), summarises that he has observed "a great desire to be in agreement with the group;" the thwarting of this desire leads to fear, longing and uncertainty. The reference group might be those physically present or a group that the subject identifies with. The bias is often called "the Asch effect" after its pioneer in the literature, but I would prefer a more descriptive term.

The most significant chapter of Asch (1952) from the perspective of conformity is Chapter 16, on "Group Forces in the Modification and Distortion of Judgements." Asch describes experiments where small groups of individuals are asked to judge which of three test lines are identical in length to a given standard line. All participants call out their answers. A deception is involved, because all but one of the participants are, in fact, in confederation with the experimenter. They have been instructed to call out obviously false answers. The key question is what will the non-confederated participant – the 'critical subject' – say in the face of such a perplexingly obtuse majority.

The results are that the error rate of the critical subject is 33.2% if the majority is wrong but only 7.4% if the majority is correct. This means that the critical subject is induced to abandon his correct choice in favour of an obviously false group choice with a much higher frequency than can be explained by genuine error. This majority influence meant that "erroneous announcements contaminated one-third of the estimates of the critical subjects" (Asch 1952, p. 457). This observation forms a clear illustration of the Asch Effect or Conformity Bias. This bias is very strong; Prentice (2007, p. 18) notes that "[m]ore than 60 percent of the subjects gave an obviously incorrect answer at least once."

Conformity Bias is illustrated in two of the most famous experiments in social psychology. The first measures how people are apparently willing to dish out extremely strong electric shocks to more-or-less innocent strangers, and the second relates how subjects in a simulated prison environment act with high levels of apparently unnecessary brutality. In both cases, the behaviour of subjects is shocking and surprising which illustrates a total failure of our Theory of Mind to predict how the subjects will behave. This, then, also means that we need to be very careful to try to check whether we have adequately allowed for Conformity Bias when predicting the behaviour of market participants.

In the first experiment, on willingness to give electric shocks (Milgram 1963), there were originally three protagonists: the experimenter, the real subject and the 'fake subject.' The real subject is an innocent member of the public. The real subject believes that the fake subject is also a random stranger, but this is not the case. In fact, the fake subject is in cahoots with the experimenter. The ostensible purpose of the experiment is to find out whether giving someone electric shocks helps them learn word pairs.

A charade is performed whereby the real subject thinks there has been a random choice as to whether they or the other person will be giving the shocks or learning the word pairs. In fact, this is always rigged so that the fake subject is doing the learning. In the standard version of the experiment, the fake subject goes to a different room and communicates only via a panel with lights on it. They are asked to remember some word pairs and the real subject assesses how well they do. It is also arranged that the fake subject will make a lot of mistakes, and these will have to be punished by the administration of electric shocks of various strengths. Of course, no real shocks are given to the fake subject, but he behaves as if they have been.

The fake subjects make a lot of noise as the experiment proceeds, as one might expect. At high levels, they stop communicating altogether. Later, "[w]hen the 300-volt shock is administered, the learner pounds on the wall of the room in which he is bound to the electric chair" (Milgram 1963, p. 374). It is scarcely imaginable that people will continue to dish out the shocks. The real subjects believe from the panel in front of them that they have administered shocks ranging from 'Moderate' through 'Intense' to 'Danger: Severe Shock' and beyond to the mysterious 'XXX' category.

If the real subject does not wish to continue, the experimenter encourages them by saying "[p]lease continue, or [p]lease go on; [t]he experiment requires that you continue; [i]t is absolutely essential that you continue; [y]ou have no other choice, you must go on" (Milgram 1963, p. 374). Surely, we think, no-one will go ahead with this. The surprising results, though, were that: "[o]f the 40 [Os], 26 obeyed the orders of the experimenter to the end, proceeding to punish the victim until they reached the most potent shock available on the shock generator" (Milgram 1963, p. 376). This is a dramatic illustration of Conformity Bias, wherein the real subject does what he is told even though that seems unimaginable. He is persuaded to do so simply by being told to do this by the experimenter. He conforms with the experimenter's desires or, perhaps more precisely, he assumes that the experimenter is telling him to do what everyone else has done, and so he conforms with an imaginary reference group of subjects. It must be acceptable to behave like this because presumably everyone else who has done the experiment has behaved like this. Otherwise the experiment could not be run.

I turn now to the second experiment set in a mock prison. Subjects were randomly chosen to be either guards and prisoners. The guards were told to "maintain the reasonable degree of order" needed for the "effective functioning" (Haney, Banks, and Zimbardo 1973, p. 74) of the prison, without being told what to do to achieve this. We naturally expect here that the guards will do what is necessary to achieve the aim and may use strong methods of persuasion, but not beyond what is needed to maintain order. We do not expect the guards to forget that they are not, in fact, guards, not, in fact, in a real prison and not, in fact, protected by the power of the state if the 'prisoners' respond to violence with violence.

The results were that the guards were far more aggressive than expected. As Haney, Banks, and Zimbardo (1973, p. 69) write, "[a]t least a third of the guards were judged to have become far more aggressive and dehumanising toward the prisoners than would ordinarily be predicted in a simulation study." Despite the apparent normality of the subjects and the lack of guidance that would lead to this outcome, "the characteristic nature of their encounters tended to be negative, hostile, affrontive and dehumanising" (Haney, Banks, and Zimbardo 1973, p. 80).

A high proportion of the ten prisoners experienced extreme affect: "five prisoners […] had to be released early because of extreme emotional depression, crying, rage and acute anxiety" (Haney, Banks, and Zimbardo 1973, p. 81). One prisoner even developed a "psychosomatic rash" (Haney, Banks, and Zimbardo 1973, p. 81). The guards, on the other hand, "enjoyed the extreme control and power they exercised" (Haney, Banks, and Zimbardo 1973, p. 81) and "on several occasions [they] remained on duty voluntarily and uncomplaining for extra hours – without additional pay" (Haney, Banks, and Zimbardo 1973, p. 81).

The completeness of the failure of Theory of Mind here may be gauged from Haney, Banks, and Zimbardo (1973, p. 81) writing that these "differential reactions to the experience of imprisonment were not suggested by or predictable from the self-report measures of personality and attitude or the interviews taken before the experiment began." What has happened is that our Theory of Mind has failed to take account of Conformity Bias. The guards tend to conform with the other guards, and the prisoners tend to conform with the other prisoners. Positive feedback loops cause runaway intensification of the effects. The guards conform most with the most visible guards, who will be the most brutal. The prisoners will tend to conform most with the most notable prisoners, who will be the ones exhibiting most helplessness and negative affect. Both effects can then feed on each other as well as themselves.

In a more behavioural example of what, I think, is also an exemplification of Conformity Bias, Levitt and Dubner (2010, p. 121) ask perspicaciously whether "you are more likely to wash your hands in the office restroom if your boss is already washing hers." The answer to the question is very likely yes; this also does not, I think, depend on the superior status of the boss in the example. You are more likely to wash your hands if *anyone* else is doing so. Levitt and Dubner (2010, p. 206) also report on attempts to make doctors in a hospital wash their hands more often. Various methods were attempted until one was found that worked. While the successful method – introducing a displeasing screensaver of bacteria cultured from unwashed hands – undoubtedly had its strengths, I think part of the trick to moving the rate to "nearly 100%" was a positive feedback effect. Once hand-washing is perceived to be what everyone does all the time, then Conformity Bias can create a virtuous circle in that it is now what I do all the time as well.

There are obvious market effects of this bias, which are scarcely likely to be helpful. I mentioned early on in Chapter 3 that Conformity Bias can just be regarded as the technical term for thinking, likely to lead to herding behaviour. The argument from Keynes that sometimes investors are paying more attention to what other investors think is the value of an asset than to the actual value of the asset, can obviously lead to positive feedback effects and herding. In this way, as Baddeley (2010, p. 282) points out, "herding can propagate instability." Such a Theory of Mind judgment is tenuous and fragile, and can alter completely in an instant, whereas, normally, the intrinsic value of a stock should alter more slowly. Worse, that

Theory of Mind judgment is itself subject to herding behaviour so, in a bubble market, everyone can decide at the same time that it is over and that becomes a self-fulfilling prophecy.

The single most powerful argument against succumbing to Conformity Bias, to my mind, is that it prevents one from engaging in contrarian investments. In my view, contrarian strategies are most likely to pay off significantly over the longer term, and most investments should have a long-term horizon. Someone who does what everyone else is not doing is almost a definition of someone who has avoided Conformity Bias. In the Theory of Mind arena, Conformity Bias in S leads him to expect the same conformity in O. This will lead to a false prediction that there will be no or few contrarians active in the market, which, of course, is partly why it is sometimes possible to pick up absurdly cheap stocks that everyone is afraid of.

I suggest that one should trade against herding behaviour when one observes it, in ways which allow for patience. Baddeley (2010, p. 283) notes "evidence suggesting that individuals of lower cognitive ability are more risk averse and if herding is a response to risk" then cognitive factors may play a part in generating herding behaviour. In other words, on this account investors of lower cognitive ability are more likely to engage in herding behaviour because they think there is safety in numbers. This already constitutes a crude argument of a sort for avoiding joining the herd, because one would thereby be consorting with investors of lower cognitive ability. Moreover, "quick thinking is associated with contrarian behaviour" (Baddeley 2010, p. 283). But a more sophisticated argument has the same result by noting the instability of bubbles. Safety in numbers is quite likely valuable in the ancestral environment in which we evolved, but in financial markets it looks to me as though the environment is very different. I would not go as far as saying there is more safety in solitude, though if you are the only one to correctly identify the right trade or the right time then it will be extremely profitable. But it does seem as though staying in the market while avoiding the herd will pay off over the long term, since long-term results are more driven by the disasters you avoid than by the miracles in which you participate. The upside will look after itself if you stay invested long enough; focus entirely on avoiding the downside. Staying away from the herd is one way to do that. Of course, if large numbers of investors later join you in an investment, that is excellent news and to be welcomed, though you might then want to consider whether the trade is now crowded and should be exited.

Nofsinger (2016, p. 103) lists several examples of herding behaviour which damage investors, which would be amusing were they not tragic. The examples involve price sensitive information being released for companies which have a slightly different ticker than you would expect. A report on fraudulent investments being made by the Czech Value Fund caused the unrelated stock with ticker CVF to decline by 32% intraday. An announcement of a bid for MCI Communications caused a spike in the price of the unrelated stock MCI.

Nofsinger (2016, p. 103) counsels in this scenario that one should avoid making snap investment decisions and he is certainly right. However, another opportunity is also apparent. The price changes in the wrong stocks will reverse themselves in a day or two as investors understand the error. So one could trade against the initial move and profit from the herding behaviour of other investors. As Nofsinger (2016, p. 103) points out, CVF made back most of the 32% over the rest of the day, so there would have been an impressive opportunity available for the courageous during the day. Look at any moves in similar tickers to the one in the news, especially if the wrong one looks more like the right one than the actually correct ticker.

For what it is worth, Cipriani and Guarino (2009) find that financial market professionals almost never herd and, in fact, are more likely to go against the market than to follow it. It is equally fascinating and mysterious that Cipriani and Guarino (2009) also find that the actual traders greatly outperform the other subjects they studied, including, for example, investment bankers and equity analysts, despite apparently following the same strategy. This suggests to me that the skills required are non-declarative and can only be learned by exercising them.

Apparently against this, Garling et al. (2009, p. 37) note the claim of Soros that he "made his fortune by betting not on fundamental values (arbitrage) but on anticipated herding." One key distinction is that the claim includes the extremely important word *anticipated*. If you are highly confident that herding is about to take place, by all means go ahead and bet on it. Test your predictions a few times first, though. And, as usual, attempt to falsify your hypothesis. If you claim that all scenarios of type X will result in herding, you must attach far higher significance to one disconfirmatory result than three confirmatory ones. Perhaps Soros's gift is just this: he can spot herding behaviour before it happens. Conformity Bias will not assist one in making good predictions of this type: S's Theory of Mind will be predicting herding behaviour all the time and so the bell will not ring only when S should heed it. So Soros, perhaps, has developed mechanisms for reducing the influence of Conformity Bias in his own thinking but simulating it accurately in others. Perhaps he surrounds himself with iconoclasts.

Even if he has not done this, it would be a very useful mechanism. How might it be done? Garling et al. (2009, p. 20) suggest that "the tendency to follow others would be the strongest in times of excessive uncertainty (high volatility of stock prices)." This seems right to me: it would be a reflection of a natural human tendency to look more to what others are doing if one is unsure oneself. Thus the idea of trying to predict herding would become trying to predict volatility. While this is difficult, there are volatility instruments in existence, such as the CBOE VIX, and implied volatility in options prices, so the data is available. And, overall, I continue to maintain that joining a herd once it has been created is a bad idea: hence I can resolve the apparent tension between the suggestion that simulating herding will be useful when predictive, and the claim I made just previously that one should trade against the herd when one sees herding already happening.

Conformity Bias seems to be the effect underlying the genesis of one saying which I think has a great deal of truth in it: that markets panic first and think later. This is much in evidence at the time of writing (February 2016), where we are seeing US equity markets priced for a high risk of global recession when this is, in fact, highly unlikely. Note that this continues to be a mistake even if at the reader's later vantage point, such a global recession has occurred. The point is that the current risk appears small, and it is this probability that should drive markets. There seems to be a much higher probability of a slowdown in global growth, but that does not justify the savage falls in equity markets. Combining this bias with the False Consensus Effect (§7.3) could form a sort of positive feedback loop as well, exacerbating the initial tendency. It is extremely hard to take the advice which everyone admits in practice is the best way to handle equity market declines, which is not just to avoid selling but to actively buy stocks. Buying under such circumstances, of course, requires successfully making some difficult market timing decisions unless one is prepared to see further declines. I think the best way to steel one's own psychology for this admittedly very difficult task is to think very long term. It used to be the case that you could pick any five-year period and look at the FTSE-100 and see that you would have made money investing in the index. Unfortunately, this has been falsified many times in recent five-year periods. Before the Brexit referendum it seemed as though there was no force on earth that could make the FTSE-100 go north of 7000. Over long periods, it oscillates between 4000 and 7000, having done so about three times in the last 20 years. (The S&P 500 does not seem to suffer such a limitation – one major reason why I have been heavily invested in it recently.) Having said all this, I find it very hard to believe that if you hold equities for very long periods, such as 50 years, you will not make money. Even catastrophic falls look like blips when looked at over a multi-decade perspective. If you buy equities which pay dividends – another place I have been invested in recent times – you get paid to wait for the rest of the market to catch up with you. So avoiding Conformity Bias can pay off in the long run.

Notes

1 I will pause to note that while analysis of the speeches of Trump and Clinton suggested that understanding their speeches required reading ages of fourth and seventh grade respectively, understanding the Fed's Beige Book required the equivalent of several years of graduate school.
2 So you can decide to skip this if you get to 35,000 hours, for reasons I will explain shortly.
3 *The Economist*, vol. 418, no. 8979, 05 Mar 2016, p. 69

8
SOCIAL BIASES II

8.1 Fundamental Attribution Error

In this section, I am going to attempt the difficult task of persuading you that there is no such thing as character or 'personality.' Thinking otherwise in quite a strong way is the essence of this particular bias.

As a way into this, let us consider the useful discussion of Gladwell (2000, pp. 150–151) on the great power of context in driving behaviour. There is a well-known theory in criminology known as 'Broken Windows.' The idea is that if a neighbourhood has broken windows, the message is conveyed that no-one is in charge and no-one cares about what goes on there. Similarly, graffiti in subway trains sends the same message that this is a domain beyond the law. Gladwell (2000, pp. 150–151) mentions the Goetz case of a shooting in the subway following a demand for cash as an example.

The crime rates on the subway in New York and more widely in the subway declined dramatically when the graffiti and the broken windows were fixed. Counterintuitively, fixing the apparently minor issues first led to an environment in which the major issues fixed themselves. This is explained by the power of context. Gladwell (2000, p. 150) summarises: "the showdown on the subway [...] had very little to do [...] with the tangled psychological pathology of Goetz, and very little as well to do with the background and poverty of the four youths who accosted him, and everything to do with the message sent by the graffiti on the walls and the disorder at the turnstiles." I think this is the correct explanation. It has the great merit of explaining why the broken windows theory has had substantial results. Note what it says about the protagonists. They acted as they did not because they had a certain character or personality type, but because of where they were, what it was like and what behavioural options that made salient and seem appropriate.

Now I need to caveat this somewhat. You will be thinking: this cannot be true. There are activities that some people will do and some people will never do, and this is enough to give some depth to the notion of character. I will concede that some people behave in some ways, and others in others, but will draw the line there. This is, if you like, a 'thin' notion of character which does not have much, if any, predictive power. Just because your aunt never rides the subway is not enough to support a 'thick' notion of character in which someone's personality or 'who they are' is the dominant cause of their behaviour. Who knows; if we put your aunt on a dirty subway with a gun and terrified her, she might shoot someone. If we put her on a clean subway with no threats, she would not. The dominant causes of her behaviour lie around her in this sort of case, and looking to her personality is not a good way of predicting her behaviour. Recall the experiments on electric shocks we have just been discussing (§7.4). Clearly those subjects' personalities were not a good guide to their behaviour, while the context was enough to make most of them behave in extremely surprising ways. And it seems to be a very poor sort of explanation to say something like 'well of course he would do X, he just has the sort of character to do X' because it seems to be circular, i.e. A explains B and B explains A so we end up with no explanation of anything.

Committing the Fundamental Attribution Error means making this mistake of looking more to someone's putative personality to explain their behaviour than to what they think is going on around them. Some of the participants in the other experiment discussed in §7.4 subsequently gained insight into how they had committed the Fundamental Attribution Error themselves in relation to themselves. Gladwell (2000, p. 154) notes that one prisoner said afterwards that he now saw that his "prisoner behaviour was less under my control than I realised." In other words, the prisoner could now see that the context drove his behaviour more than any personality variables.

The Fundamental Attribution Error is formally defined by Ross, Amabile, and Steinmetz (1977, p. 491) as "the tendency to underestimate the role of situational determinants and overestimate the degree to which social actions and outcomes reflect the dispositions of relevant actors." Similarly, Andrews (2008, p. 13) argues that "folk psychology includes the notion that some behaviour is explained by personality traits," as is consistent with the Fundamental Attribution Error. The error reflects our false belief in stable personality: we ascribe the behaviour of others more to their 'characteristics' than to the situation they were in.

Central to a thick notion of personality is the suggestion that if people have a certain characteristic, they will exhibit that characteristic across different contexts. The leopard does not change his spots, if you like. However, this is also not borne out by the evidence. Kamtekar (2004, pp. 464–465) lists four areas in which experiments have failed to show stable character traits. The first example is the Milgram (1963) electric shock experiments discussed in §7.4. We saw it above as an example of Conformity Bias, but it can also be seem as evidence against stable behaviour. Presumably, the participants had a range of what observers might call personality types, but Milgram's (1963) whole point is that none of that mattered: everyone behaved in a similar and unexpected way in the experiment. There is no character trait we might understand as a tendency to brave resistance to malice in authority or, simply, courage.

The second example of failure to provide data supporting personality given by Kamtekar (2004, pp. 464–465) is labelled 'Good Samaritans.' In another famous experiment, seminary students were asked by Darley and Batson (1973) to give a talk on the topic of the Good Samaritan. Choosing seminary students was calculated to select a group of people who would have 'helpful' personalities, if anyone does. Moreover, the topic of the talk was selected to bring out that aspect of the students' personalities. The experimenters then had the students move to a different building under conditions where they were told there was plenty of time, where there was no hurry and where, in fact, time was very short. During the move to a different building, it was arranged that an actor would be collapsed in the corridor and obviously in need of help. The test was to find out whether the probability of the students helping was correlated with their personalities. Darley and Batson (1973, p. 108) found that "personality variables were not useful in predicting whether a person helped or not."

The helping or not was much more decided by whether or not the student was in a hurry; only 10% of those in a hurry helped whereas 63% of those not in a hurry helped (Gladwell 2000, p. 165). Thus again, context and not personality is much more decisive in terms of what people do. There is no character trait such as sympathy or helpfulness.

The third example of Kamtekar (2004, p. 465) is labelled 'Helping for a dime.' It looked at people who made calls from a payphone. Kamtekar (2004, p. 465) notes that some "subjects found a dime in the pay phone (planted there in advance by the experimenters), others did not." As the subject left the phone box, an experimenter dropped some papers in a way which gave the subject an opportunity to help. It turned out that finding the dime (this experiment was reported in 1972) was much more important than any supposed personality variable. Kamtekar (2004, p. 465) notes that 14 of 16 subjects who found the dime helped while only one of 25 subjects who did not find a dime offered help. These are, it must be admitted, fairly low statistics but they are so one-sided that they are still convincing. This gives us the same conclusion as the previous experiment did on the Good Samaritans. Kamtekar (2004, p. 465) notes that "Doris finds that this experiment falsifies the supposition that there is such a thing as behavioural reliability or cross-situational consistency that might need to be explained by character traits." It also tells us, interestingly, that "mood influences behaviour" (Kamtekar 2004, p. 465) in unobtrusive ways; the explanation given for the data was that finding a dime leads to a good mood, and good mood leads to helping. That, of course, offers nothing to support the idea of character traits but gives us a way of predicting behaviour, nevertheless.

The fourth example given by Kamtekar (2004, pp. 464–465) is on the topic of honesty. Asch (1946, p. 288) cites the pioneering work of Hartshorne and May "who studied in a variety of situations the tendencies in groups of children to act honestly in such widely varied matters as copying, returning of money, correcting one's school work," and found that correlations between the different types of dishonesty were "generally low." This was a very large study in which "8,000 schoolchildren aged eight to sixteen were placed in moderately tempting situations" (Kamtekar 2004, p. 465); and they simply did not exhibit the same sort of honest/dishonest behaviour in the different situations. So, once again, there simply is nothing measurable that grounds the common idea that 'honesty' is a trait.

Moreover, we think we have a good idea that we know the sort of person who would be susceptible to an online scam. They must be less intelligent, less educated, poorer, less logical and more impulsive and gullible (Konnikova 2016, p. 46). This is not the case, however. Konnikova (2016, p. 47) reports that "personality generalities tend to go out the window" when predicting who will fall for a scam. So there does not seem to be anything usefully action-predicting about the putative personality variables like intelligence, gullibility etc. in this context. Again, it is striking that we think we can predict this but we are dead wrong: our Theory of Mind does not seem to be set up to do it. That enables us to continue committing the Fundamental Attribution Error.

All of this amounts to a compelling picture that demolishes the ideas prevalent in our folk psychology that 'character' means something and can be used to make predictions. After all, when you make a decision, it seems to you as though you make it freely; you are not, as it were, a slave to your own personality. We nevertheless seem to expect this sort of slavery in others when we use our Theory of Mind on them. We think, wrongly, that there is a trait called, for example, honesty and that if someone is dishonest in one arena, they will be dishonest in another. This, as emphatically outlined above, is not what is found experimentally.

There are, though, some tendencies which could perhaps be referred to under the rubrics 'character' or 'personality.' They just tend to be deeper than people expect and much more of a set of tendencies rather than rigid rules of behaviour. As an example of the deeper elements of behaviour which do exhibit some regularities in behaviour, we may take the 'dark triad' (Konnikova 2016, pp. 23–29) of psychopathic tendencies, narcissism and 'high-Mach' or Machiavellian tendencies. This dark triad is heavily over-represented on Wall Street, in politics, law, marketing and in confidence tricksters (Konnikova 2016, p. 26). The psychopathic tendency I have in mind here is low levels of empathy, where I am understanding empathy as meaning something like 'S feels the emotion of O.' Narcissistic tendencies are self-explanatory and naturally to be expected in arenas which provide plenty of power, or money, or both. Persons with Machiavellian tendencies are more likely to behave as though the world needs to be manipulated to get it to do what you want and to act accordingly. 'High-Machs' also often believe that no-one will work hard unless they have to, or are well-paid. So there do seem to be some clusters of approaches to life that exhibit some empirical grounding, but notice that these sorts of tendencies are at a lower, different level than say 'honesty.' There must have been some High-Mach children, or even dark triad children, in the study of Hartshorne and May but they did not show up in the results as doing all of the different dishonest acts because no-one did: dishonest behaviour showed only low correlation across the different tests.

Lo, Repin, and Steenbarger (2005, p. 354) describe "the most widely accepted theory of personality traits" and list its five components: Extraversion, Openness, Neuroticism, Agreeableness and Conscientiousness. These are all fairly self-explanatory so I will not explain them further. The point is that if there are any stable elements to personality that can usefully predict behaviour, this is the level at which they are to be found. So, positing anything putatively stable like 'honest' which does not appear on this list is to make a Theory of Mind error and to commit the Fundamental Attribution Error. This is not inconsistent with the remarks above about the dark triad, which is the 'Wall Street personality type' if there is such a thing, since there could be a stable region in the five-parameter space which correlates with the dark triad.

Saxe (2009, p. 263) observes that "other people's actions are ascribed to stable traits, whereas one's own actions are generally seen as variable and situation-dependent" and this leads to Theory of Mind error. This should already be enough to make us suspicious of committing the Fundamental Attribution Error, unless we wish to take the surely unappealing line of saying that we do not have personalities but everyone else does. The way to avoid this particular Theory of Mind error is, then, to apply a more flexible simulation of market participants and, in particular, expect them to react to developments in variable ways rather than just be of a fixed character. They will not always exhibit the same behaviours in the same situations because they are flexible human beings, not monolithic personality machines. How might this approach be applied?

Let us now consider market applications. Hirshleifer (2001, p. 1553) gives one market example of application of the Fundamental Attribution Error when he notes that it may lead "observers of a repurchase to conclude that the CEO dislikes holding excess cash rather than that the CEO is responding to market undervaluation of the stock." This would lead to investors expecting, wrongly, that the CEO is going to execute more repurchases in the future whenever he is holding cash, rather than when he perceives the stock to be undervalued. Turning that around, some companies such as AAPL[1] are well-known for holding cash. We should not expect that this is because the CEO likes holding cash and will always do so. It is more likely that he is holding it as a flexible response to the environment because that, in his view, is the best approach in the current situation. Perhaps in the future AAPL will hold no cash at all at a point when the CEO judges that all-out investment in innovation is the best option. So we should be cautious of arguments like 'AAPL is a safe stock because they always hold a lot of cash.'

In the market, many tales are told of 'Mrs Watanabe.' In Japan, household finances are traditionally controlled by the woman. Mrs Watanabe is the name given to this collective body of market participants. Japan is a wealthy nation, and has quite a large population which saves heavily. These factors add up to mean that Mrs Watanabe is rather powerful. It is a fairly rare case of individuals – albeit in a large group – adding up to sufficient size to have significant influence on markets. One particular conundrum is why the Japanese Government can continue to issue debt at very low yields despite the fact that it is already highly indebted. The standard measure of this is the debt/GDP ratio. It is generally thought that going anywhere beyond 80% is ill-advised. Greece got into very serious trouble on this metric. Debt/GDP in Greece was on average 92% between 1980 and 2014, suggesting that the number was unsustainable at all points in the cycle. It peaked in the crisis at a totally unmanageable 177% in 2014.[2] Yet the debt/GDP ratio in Japan has been over 200% since 2010 and is continuing to climb strongly; it reached 230% in 2014. Many traders have bet that this cannot continue. The short JGB trade, however, is known in the markets as 'the widow-maker.' Many traders have gone bust waiting for a crash in JGBs. Mrs Watanabe seems to be more powerful than they are.

A number of explanations have been advanced for this unusual situation. One, often posited by UK Eurosceptics, is that Japan can get away with this because it prints its own currency. While that might explain why Greece had such a difficult time, in that once in the EUR it could no longer devalue and hope for the best, it does not really offer an explanation of the Japanese government's 'success' in issuing so much debt. I think the answer lies with Mrs Watanabe. She is, one might think, a very conservative investor. She will only buy Japanese investments and she will only buy them from institutions she knows well. She does not like risk. This is who she is; it is her fixed disposition or character and JGBs will be sellable at any debt/GDP ratio.

This, I think, is false, and is an illustration of the Fundamental Attribution Error as applied to all of the incarnations of Mrs Watanabe. It is the error of thinking that Mrs Watanabe is just, as it were, programmed to buy JGBs and she will never stop. A better analysis of what is happening is to note the occasions when Mrs Watanabe acts out of 'character.' She had a heavy flirtation with the Mexican Peso at one point, causing interesting moves in the cross rate between Mexican Pesos and Japanese Yen (MXNJPY). So, on that occasion, Mrs Watanabe appears to have been reacting to a novel opportunity rather than just doing what she always does. We, in any case, owe her more respect; I will argue below that women are better traders.

So why is she still buying JGBs? Because they have not defaulted. They do not produce much yield, but in a deflationary environment, yields do not need to be very positive. As I write, 10-year yields on JGBs have just gone negative for the first time, meaning that investors are paying for the privilege of lending to the Japanese Government. They do this by ignoring the possibility of higher interest rates elsewhere, because they believe that their capital is safe. Capital preservation is more important than return on capital in what is perceived as a dangerous environment.

When will this stop? When JGBs are no longer considered safe. There is no way to tell when that will be. It does not appear as though there is some magic number on debt/GDP which will cause a crash, because that number is already very high and has crossed through several psychologically-important thresholds without incident. International investors who are focussed more on debt/GDP than Mrs Watanabe do not appear to have the power to move the market.

What this adds up to, I think, is the idea that unless the Japanese Government is successful in managing the debt/GDP ratio down, as it plans, there will eventually be a JGB crash. This would have to happen, ironically, in relatively benign economic circumstances. They cannot be as dire as they are currently perceived to be, since investors will always look to safe haven assets in difficult periods. Note that this is not an element of their character so much as just a good idea. The problem, of course, is that we have no idea at all of how long it will be until the stars align in this way.

My general view, in fact, is that all market timing is extremely difficult. Gordon Gekko puts this well in *Wall Street: Money Never Sleeps* (2010) when he advises "ride the trends, don't try too hard for the turns." It is possible to spot what way the momentum is running, and to suspect that it will have to change, but there is no way of knowing when the turning point will arrive. So I think that 'the widow-maker' is the correct trade, but it is essential to find a way to play it which is not time limited, or not seriously time limited. There is no reason to suspect that JGBs will crash in three months from now, even if we are certain that they will eventually crash, so an instrument which only pays in three months and returns nothing if the expected event does not occur – as is a common pattern with options – is too risky here.

Market timing is also less important than one might think. Kramer (2008, p. 132) considers a hypothetical investor who puts $1,000 in the S&P 500 every year for 45 years under two scenarios. In the first scenario, she invests at the lowest point each year and in the second scenario she invests at the highest point each year. It looks as though the first scenario will be spectacular and the second catastrophic. In fact, she ends up with $380,000 in the first scenario and $475,000 in the second. This is an insignificant difference, especially over such a long time period when a lot of unknown factors will also have intervened. And most people will not buy at the very worst point in the year every year; it would be hard to do that if you tried. The conclusion is that market timing for long-term diversified investments does not matter.

A further, generally pernicious problem which arises as a result of the Fundamental Attribution Error is the idea that only very special and talented people can become great traders, or good piano players, or successful at anything. On this line, character is fixed and some types of character will be successful and others will not. All of this would imply that if you do not have whatever this special character is taken to be, then you are wasting your time trying to become a better trader, or indeed better at anything. I think this is a counsel of despair, and is wrong for several reasons. One of the most important is, of course, that it is just an illustration of the Fundamental Attribution Error.

One of the central and most important messages of existentialism (Sartre 1956) is that there is nothing to us beyond our actions. That seems highly plausible to me, taken together with the empirical support adduced above. However, I lack space in this book to discuss purely philosophical argument. I think that the key to everything is hard work. Perhaps there are some aptitudes that can be fostered and some people start with something of a head start in all fields. But I would much rather have a massive edge in hours of work than a minor one in initial talent. The key talent to have is to put in a ton of work in terms of preparation, study and research.

8.2 Halo Effect

The Halo Effect is seen whenever people make a judgment about the quality of something or someone, based just on one visible characteristic. Angels have halos; the idea is that one sees that and assumes that every other quality of a person is strongly positive. The basis for this snap judgment is that often we need to make quick assessments of others, and if we only know one aspect of their behaviour, then that single item of data will weigh heavily in our judgment. In sum, we tend to think that someone is all good or all bad based on one observable item. I have already suggested that this is an error since traits such as honesty do not, in fact, exist enough to allow predictions across situations (§8.1) – it is even worse to extrapolate to all other characteristics.

Analogous effects in markets can be seen when one piece of data about a stock causes investors to over-react. If there is likely to be a forthcoming rights issue, then actually everything about the stock is bad. It is not just in need of extra capital, but its revenues are under threat, its staff are leaving, and it faces severe regulatory and legal problems. Conversely, a company that announces a novel product which is well received by the markets is free of all regulatory and legal difficulties, experiences no difficulties in recruitment and will be returning capital to shareholders. There is, of course, no basis to extrapolate to these other factors from one observation in relation to capital. The Halo Effect can explain magnification of price movements beyond what is strictly justified by the incremental news-flow. This can also occur in relation to markets more widely, not just in relation to single stocks.

The Halo Effect is one of the most venerable cognitive biases in the literature, having been first described by Thorndike (1920). He noticed quite dramatic effects in USAAF surveys of officers by their superiors which stood out because the raters had been explicitly instructed to consider each of several independent categories separately. We may assume that USAAF officers are not unused to understanding and obeying clear instructions precisely as given, so this is further evidence for the extreme difficulty people have in making independent judgments of each element of another individual's performance – or, in other words, how hard it is to eliminate cognitive biases.

Nisbett and Wilson (1977, p. 244) write that their "experimental demonstration of the halo effect, showed that the manipulated warmth or coldness of an individual's personality had a large effect on ratings of the attractiveness of his appearance, speech, and mannerisms, yet many subjects actually insisted that cause and effect ran in the opposite direction." It seems once again, then, that we have limited insight into the workings of our Theory of Mind. We claim that we derive our view of an individual's warmth from a composite of the perceived attractiveness of his appearance, speech and mannerisms. That would be reasonable, since one could define warmth as a composite of those underlying elements. However, the way our Theory of Mind actually works is that we make a snap judgment of warmth and then apply it across the board. We will then use this to predict behaviour and we will often be wrong as a result.

Bramel (1962, p. 126) defines the Halo Effect as "a well known judgmental tendency which leads a person to perceive others as possessing traits consistent with his general evaluation of those others." For example, if you decide that someone is well-dressed, you are likely also to decide that they are a good speaker and, indeed, a good hire if you are interviewing them. This is why it is generally agreed that one should dress well when attending job interviews – though, of course, what 'well-dressed' means will differ in a conservative investment bank from what it means in a Valley startup. Similarly, if you decide that someone does not have a good vocabulary, you are likely to give a poor assessment of their other abilities, even when these seem unrelated to vocabulary. Someone you have initially given a poor assessment to will have extra work to do to persuade you of their qualities; they will also be contending with Confirmation Bias (§5.1).

There are clear links between the Halo Effect and the Fundamental Attribution Error. The latter bias is needed to explain the way our folk psychology judges falsely that helpfulness is a reliable trait in the behaviour of others. The former is needed as well to make the extrapolation from a single observation of someone helping, to the idea not just that they are a helpful person, but that they are now also a generous and honest person as well.

Mensh and Wishner (1947, p. 188), replicating Asch (1946), note that what is seen is that "[s]ome traits are always of a central quality, and these affect peripheral traits by making them consistent with the central trait." They mean that certain key traits are apt to generate the Halo Effect such that once S has made a judgment that O is a warm or cold personality, then everything else will follow from that. Mensh and Wishner (1947, p. 190), give the following lengthy list of attributions which they tested for dependence on 'warmth' and 'coldness.'

1. Generous
2. Wise
3. Happy
4. Good-natured
5. Humorous
6. Sociable
7. Popular
8. Reliable
9. Important
10. Humane
11. Good-looking
12. Persistent
13. Serious
14. Restrained
15. Altruistic
16. Imaginative
17. Strong
18. Honest

Mensh and Wishner (1947) obtained a number of interesting results. They found that all of the characteristics other than Reliable, Persistent, Serious and Restrained were heavily correlated with 'warmth,' while those four were correlated with 'cold.' This, I think, is another blow for the notion of 'personality;' the regularities we think we observe in the behaviour of others are, in fact, just our application of the Halo Effect on a regular basis. Some of the correlation strengths observed by Mensh and Wishner (1947, p. 190) were extremely strong. They found, for example, that 88% of their sample agreed that the 'warm' person was generous while only 27% said that of the 'cold' person. Note that the only difference between the personality input they were given was the change from 'warm' to 'cold.' This might be because warmth is seen as related to generosity but this need not be so. The groups also showed an 82% to 10% split on 'humorous' and it is harder to believe that humour, precisely, is really driven by warmth. This sort of defence – suggesting that we can allow a high correlation of 'generosity' with 'warmth' because generosity is part of warmth – can, in general, not succeed, because it entails that *all* of the above characteristics except the 'cold four' are part of warmth. If that is so, then 'warmth' is such a wide, washed-out category that it loses all meaning.

As usual, it is not a good objection to respond that one is not subject to such biases as the Halo Effect. Pronin, Gilovich, and Ross (2004, p. 784) list it among the experiments examining the influence people acknowledge from biases on their own thinking, which "have generally documented a failure to recognise such influence." So the answer is probably to be aware that it will be happening and to attempt to spot its effects and accord less weight to judgments made using it, rather than to try to eliminate it.

I think that the Halo Effect may lie behind the glorification of successful investors and fund managers. It is, I think, in general a poor idea to attempt to emulate star investors, at least in the simplistic way of investing in what they invest in. It may well be possible to learn something valuable from their methods of selecting investments. The Halo Effect is worsened in the case of fund managers, who generally add little value, do not continue to perform well over decades, and charge high fees. Some managers make one extremely successful trade and then the Halo Effect leads investors to think that they have magical talents and that everything they touch in future will be enormously successful. This is false and clearly an expensive mistake to make.

The literature on the Halo Effect often restricts itself to the social arena, viz. it refers to the tendency we have to make positive or negative ascriptions of people's abilities across the board based on information about one of their abilities, especially if that ability stands out in some way. It could be an unusual ability or it could be an extremely positive or an extremely negative exhibition of that ability. But I think we can also see analogous effects when people make assessments of items other than persons. For example, *The Economist*,[3] when discussing lotteries, notes "after a particularly big prize is won, there is a [H]alo [E]ffect, whereby ticket sales remain high even though the jackpot has reverted to the norm." While it is already irrational to take part in a lottery, it is even more so to assess the overall quality of a lottery based on a single factor which no longer applies.

A way has been identified in which the Halo Effect can influence stock prices in efficient markets. If they are not efficient, I have suggested that they are at least partially efficient, so the effect would be weakened but not eliminated. Hirshleifer (2001, p. 1542) notes that a "stock being good in terms of growth prospects says nothing about its prospects for future risk-adjusted returns" because those risk-adjusted returns are zero. In other words, the efficient market has already included those growth prospects in the stock price. This looks like an application of the Halo Effect. Although it is not a judgment about the personality of others, it is the unjustified extrapolation from one positive quality to a number of other qualities which will lead to poor decision making in markets. It may be that our frequent exhibition of the Halo Effect in judging personalities softens us up to make similarly unjustified extrapolations in others arenas. Thus, Hirshleifer (2001, p. 1542) continues to argue that if investors apply the Halo Effect, they may "mistakenly extend their favourable evaluation of a stock's earnings prospects to its return prospects [so] growth stocks will be overpriced." Once again, the key to successful investing is less understanding the stock and more understanding what others are thinking about the stock, and when biases will cause them to be wrong.

8.3 Self-Presentation Bias And Over-Confidence

Most of us want to feel good about ourselves. Exactly why this is may not need much explanation: it seems to be just part of human nature. If an evolutionary perspective were to be taken, it is possible to construct a story on which people who feel good about themselves are able to persuade others of their superiority – because nothing convinces like conviction – and this resulted in selection advantages. But it does not appear to be a question open to empirical investigation.

At least two aspects feed into this. We will try to make ourselves look good in the eyes of others, and we will also try to make ourselves look good in our own eyes. More generally, we may agree with Pronin, Gilovich, and Ross (2004, p. 788) who observe that there is "mounting evidence that people are motivated to view themselves, their assessments, and their outcomes in a positive light." There is not too much wrong with this from one perspective; it seems necessary to the maintenance of self-esteem. One term for this particular bias is Self-Presentation Bias (Igoe and Sullivan 1993; Kopcha and Sullivan 2006). Mineka and Sutton (1992, p. 65) found that depression "appears to be associated with a memory bias for negative mood-congruent material." This suggests that the absence of Self-Presentation Bias, which could reasonably expect to have depressive effects, will make subjects more likely to remember negative material. In the context of trading, that would be a systematic error which we would need to avoid. We need to examine *all* of the relevant data in as objective a manner as possible if we are to make an optimal decision.

Self-Presentation Bias is behind what Levitt and Dubner (2010) generously term a 'perception deficit' in different rates of hand-washing by doctors, reported by the doctors themselves, and by nurses covertly observing them. It is well-known that the failure of medical personnel to wash their hands between seeing patients spreads infection. Levitt and Dubner (2010, p. 205) note that doctors reported their own rate of hand-washing as 73% whereas the nurses reported that the actual number was 9%. Even allowing for some reasonable under-reporting by the nurses, who may have missed some of the hand-washing events, there is clearly a gulf between what the doctors actually do and what they say they do. The gap is explained by Self-Presentation Bias: the doctors wish to see themselves and be seen by others as complying with a protocol requirement which is known to save lives.

It seems as though Self-Presentation Bias is closely linked to self-esteem or, indeed, to vanity. Care is needed, however, in exploring this link. Nietzsche (1961) is relevant here as the philosopher of self-creation *par excellence*. Vanity is a motivating factor which is closely linked to Self-Presentation Bias. Sullivan (2011, p. 21) notes Nietzsche's view on vanity as a double-edged sword when he observes that vanity "falls within Nietzsche's purview as something which might be turned to good account" since the "vain person typically may be ingenious in the arts of self presentation, [and] will have the actor's ability to assume many guises." So this means that there could be ways of employing or exploiting Self-Presentation Bias to maintain a positive self-view without treating the relevant data non-objectively. There do not appear to be many limits to this in terms of its effectiveness; McKay and Dennett (2009) even describe how some false beliefs about the self may aid performance. For example, students who believe that they will do better on an exam actually do.

Taleb (2008, p. 151) mentions that "protection of self-esteem" explains why financial market experts continue to believe in their own predictions. It has been shown, as Taleb (2008) also points out, that assuming that all numbers will remain the same produces a lower error rate than expert predictors. It is also possible that all of these experts know that they are not adding much value when they make predictions, but also know that they will not be paid for admitting this. Similarly to the point I made earlier about newspapers, it is perhaps more important to pay attention to what expert commentators say, in terms of what it tells us about what market participants think, than to know what the GDP will be in two years from now.

All of this suggests to me a number of points. Firstly, we will not do well in any field without maintaining a positive self-image. This is consistent with the 'anti-bias' approach which I am outlining in this book, since we also know that depressed subjects exhibit marked Theory of Mind impairments (Zobel et al. 2010). You will not be able to trade well if you are depressed because, according to my account, you will have a memory bias for negative material and you will make Theory of Mind errors in forecasting the behaviour of other market participants. Finding ways to avoid these two factors of 'bias in self' and 'bias about others' is my primary message. Also, Kramer (2008, p. 129) notes that depressed subjects exhibit excess risk-aversion, which suggests that an even temperament is valuable for trading even if no Theory of Mind is involved. If you can avoid making any decisions while depressed, you will obtain a more optimal outcome. I can also confirm the opposite from personal experience; trading under the influence of euphoria is, if anything, more dangerous. Baddeley (2010, p. 283) notes evidence that "extreme moods impair trading performance."[4]

But secondly, a way to maintain this positive-self image is not to apply the reverse memory bias. It is not the right answer to focus only on positive memory items such as all of the successful trades one has conducted. That would result in a very unbalanced and inaccurate view of one's own trading performance. The way forward is to recognise that Self-Presentation Bias is an inevitable and beneficent feature of one's own psyche and that of others, but to use it beneficially. You can nurture your own self-image by being aware of the bias in yourself and others, and then trading accordingly. If that works, you will have a better portfolio performance and a better self-image, without having ignored any data.

This is not what is observed, in at least some markets. As discussed previously in §5.1, there is a question as to why some markets persist even though the individual participants mostly lose and 'the house' mostly wins. I am thinking again of betting shops and casinos. We know that the house mostly wins in these cases since the businesses persist and are profitable. But since gambling is a zero-sum game, this means that the individual punters mostly lose. So why do they continue? Lay observers who are asked this question, which is a Theory of Mind matter, respond with the idea that they persist because they forget their losses.

They pay them less attention. However, as mentioned previously, Gilovich (1993, p. 32) found that gamblers pay *more* attention to their losses than to their wins.

Wilcox (2008, p. 54) notes correctly that we "make efforts to construct our financial lives in ways that make us happier," which is obviously connected to Self-Presentation Bias. This is not the benign effect of striving to maximise our income and assets. It is unfortunately the malign effect seen when someone who pays $500 to an investment company which has made them $8000 is less happy than someone who receives a post-fee investment cheque for $7500. In other words, we do not care about fees if we do not know about them and so we tend to behave in ways that hide fees from ourselves. The whole topic of self-deception is fascinating and paradoxical – 'who is deceiving whom?' is a very deep question, for example, as is 'is self-deception rational?' (Michel and Newen 2010) – but I can say no more about it here other than it can lead us to behave sub-optimally, as in the example above. This may be one bias that is so deep-seated as to be ineradicable from human activity.

Nofsinger (2016, pp. 42–45) describes a number of phenomena under the rubric of Cognitive Dissonance which I think are better understood as aspects of Self-Presentation Bias. Cognitive Dissonance is often understood incorrectly, sometimes even in academic literature, as referring to any situation when an individual has two cognitions, or beliefs, which conflict. I think it is worth getting this right, since it will better enable us to understand some important phenomena.

This is too wide a definition. The pioneers of Cognitive Dissonance (Bramel 1962; Bem 1967; Bem 1972) and more careful modern literature use the term more restrictively. It is used to describe situations where an individual has acted in a way which contradicts some of his beliefs. The slightly surprising outcome is that the individual then modifies his beliefs so as to reduce the dissonance between them and the action. For example, if someone who is opposed to the death penalty reads out some arguments in favour of it, they will subsequently be less opposed to the death penalty. This is true even if they were paid five dollars to read the arguments out, and were in no way committed to the consequence of the argument.

Nofsinger (2016, p. 42) partly gets this right. When he discusses the increased certainty of a gambler who has just placed a bet on a horse in comparison to the same gambler who is just about to place the bet, it may well be an example of Cognitive Dissonance. However, the next example given looks to me much more like an example of Self-Presentation Bias. The example focusses on young people who do not save for their retirement to avoid conflict between their positive self image and a future self image of a "feeble person with low earning power." While this is quite possibly a plausible explanation of why some young people do not save for pensions, it does not look like a good example of Cognitive Dissonance. For that, we need a belief and an action which are in conflict. This looks more like two beliefs which are incoherent. If we try to rescue the situation on behalf of Nofsinger (2016, p. 42), we might say that the action is the decision not to save for a pension.

But then it looks difficult to say what is the belief which is in conflict with that action. It does not appear as though the person previously had the idea that saving for a pension was a good move, and then decided that it was, in fact, a less good move having not decided to do it. Again, while that line might have some points to commend it, it is not the one to which Nofsinger (2016, p. 42) appeals. He simply says they want to "avoid the conflict between their good self-image and the contradictory future self image." That, I submit, is a straightforward appeal to Self-Presentation Bias. Nevertheless, Nofsinger (2016, p. 42) is right to warn that these scenarios may cause people to fail to make important financial decisions because it is too uncomfortable for them to examine the situation. That is an important warning, even if Nofsinger (2016, p. 42) has misdiagnosed the aetiology.

Nofsinger (2016, p. 43) goes on to cite various important studies showing that investors have unrealistically positive views about their own prior trading performance. He asks the very pertinent question: if "investors ignore negative information, how are they going to realise that an adjustment in their portfolio is necessary?" Again, this does not seem to me to meet a very strict definition of Cognitive Dissonance. It is, rather, the recruitment of Confirmation Bias in the service of Self-Presentation Bias. The warning is no less valid, for all that. Worryingly, Nofsinger (2016, p. 45) cites data showing that online investors in Germany overestimate their past returns by more than 10%. That is an enormous error, and it occurs in investors with a reasonable amount of experience. I can, again, only point to the importance of correct record keeping. One trick to consider here is always buying shares in round numbers. If all your purchases are for $50,000, it will be obvious how much each position has gained or lost, and you just need to have some idea of how long you have held the stock. This latter point is secondary though; you should not worry too much about how long it has taken for a position to appreciate unless you are certain you have quicker and highly probable opportunities elsewhere. These are few.

Before leaving the topic of Cognitive Dissonance, as correctly understood, I should mention a couple of further areas where it could actually cause problems. Recall that the technical definition is that someone has adjusted their beliefs after having acted in a way which is inconsistent with those beliefs. In a way this makes sense; after all, they can now not change the action, so modifying the beliefs is the only way to reduce the dissonance.

How might this play out in markets? One example might occur when people make 'fat finger trades' and then retain them. A fat finger trade is the generic term for any trade which is made by accident. The idea is that you can press the wrong button by mistake if it is adjacent to the one that you intended to press. So you buy instead of selling. Alternatively, you might buy more stock than intended. Some of the most spectacular fat finger trades take place in Japan, because the Yen is a low denomination currency. This means that it is sometimes possible to confuse a high number which is the share price in Yen with another high number which is the number of shares to be purchased. Experienced investors will immediately cancel such trades, even if they suffer a loss. Sometimes, less experienced investors will retain the trade and attempt to persuade themselves that what they did actually was the best move. This looks like a good example of Cognitive Dissonance and is to be resisted.

Consider another circumstance in which you have broken one of your rules for investing. In my case, I do not invest in tech stocks. This is partly because of the value-destroying end of the dot.com bubble, but mostly because I do not consider that I can pick the winners adequately in such a fast-moving area. Imagine I broke this rule and bought a tech stock. Cognitive Dissonance now exists between my action in buying the stock and my belief according to the rule that tech stocks are to be avoided. The dissonance will be reduced by the weakening of my belief that it is good to avoid tech stocks despite the fact that I need have no new evidence that tech stocks are good buys. The dissonance reduction may even go far enough as to make me abandon my rule altogether. This is, I think, a poor strategy. Stick to your rules unless you can see a powerful argument not to; perhaps circumstances change, or you decide after lengthy analysis that MSFT is impregnable. (This is not my belief; I am merely illustrating the type of development that might cause me to abandon the rule rationally.)

I now return briefly to Confirmation Bias (§5.1). Soros has been praised for his ability to look for data which would falsify his position, thus avoiding Confirmation Bias. Taleb (2008, p. 59) suggests that this "is true self-confidence, the ability to look at the world without the need to find signs that stroke one's ego." This is similar to saying that Soros performs better because he has escaped at least part of the effects of Self-Presentation Bias. I suspect that this is because he has already had more than enough success to feel relaxed about some failures. This should remind us all to consider our whole record in the round, especially the successes, and to remember that a stock which is 10% up is still a success even if it was previously 20% up.

An interesting empirical prediction can be made here by considering the interaction with depression. I noted above that depressed subjects focus more on negative memory items. This would work against the outcome noted by Gilovich (1993) to the effect that gamblers focus on losses and recast them as 'near wins.' So, depressed gamblers might stop gambling more quickly because they are more aware of their own losses, or they might never stop gambling because they focus on their losses more and recast them more. Care would be needed to design an experimental setup that could control for the fact that losses could, themselves, cause depression.

I have argued above and in Short (2012), once again using arguments from Nietzsche, that control of active and passive memory types is a key feature of strong, successful individuals. It is widely agreed that there are various types of memory (Tulving 1993); I suggest that the active/passive type distinction should also be among them or mapped onto them. I also discuss in Short (2012) a couple of examples of active memory management, which I will recap here next.

Sheehan (1988, p. 342) discusses a Vietnam-era Marine Lt-General, who was originally over-confident about US progress in that conflict. This General seemed, subsequently, to have genuinely forgotten his original position. This forgetfulness is described as being characteristic of the busy and powerful. This means not simply that busy people do not have time for reminiscence: it is the much more interesting (and Nietzschean) claim that successful and effective people are so partly *because* they are not hobbled by unhelpful memories, especially those about themselves.

Lewis (2004) notes that sometimes, less athletic baseball players can be more successful than much more physically gifted ones due to certain mental characteristics. This is perhaps slightly surprising: one might have thought that physical athleticism was absolutely paramount in sport. What is more surprising and noteworthy is that the mental characteristics which make the difference would generally be regarded as negative. The physically gifted failure speaks of the physically less gifted success as follows: "[h]e was able to instantly forget any failure and draw strength from every success. He had no concept of failure. And he had no idea where he was. And I was the opposite" (Lewis 2004, p. 46). This suggests that people who are able to forget failures are also able, somehow, to ignore 'match-day pressure' or public performance anxiety. That is another extremely valuable trait. Note, also, that this seems to be an active type of memory management of the form that Nietzsche, as I claim in Short (2012), recognises.

The common link between these two examples is the subject of the memory, which is the individual himself. I suggest that there are no circumstances in which it is helpful to retain negative memories about oneself. This could look, prima facie, inconsistent with the line I took above, which was to say that negative outcomes should be examined just as much as positive ones, if not more, and examined dispassionately. Anything less is to fail to consider all of the data available. So the answer is to retain the memory of the outcome but not the memory of any putative entailment about oneself, or one could retain that memory but, so to speak, sterilise it. In a way, this is just a form of avoiding committing the Fundamental Attribution Error (§8.1) about oneself, in that it denies that one has a fixed self which is of the sort that always makes the same mistakes.

One can make a mistake and learn from it and then forget the actual mistake, retaining only the benefit of what was learned. Looked at like that, it seems more like a cost of doing business than a mistake. Lewis (2010, p. 137) cites a comment on one of his financial markets' heroes to the effect that because "his memory is so selective, he has no scars from prior experience." It is interesting, indeed compelling, to note that the same author (Lewis 2004; Lewis 2010) has picked up on this rarely observed aspect of mental strength through active memory in the two arenas of sport and finance.

Also, both of these examples of mental strengths could be characterised in the vein of the advantages of apparent disadvantages that I canvassed above in §7.4. A 'bad' memory is actually more malleable, avoiding the pernicious effects of neurotic consideration of failure, retaining the positive benefits of success but without the negative consequences of failure. Even if you take the line that memory is uncontrollable – which I dispute – you still have the possibility to choose which memory items deserve focus.

Nofsinger (2016, pp. 41–42) points out the effects of the interaction of pleasant and unpleasant memories on investment decisions. It is known in the psychological literature that sharp moves at the end of a process are much more memorable than longer moves, even if they are eventually more significant. Thus a stock which is stable for 10 weeks and then loses 20% in a day would be remembered much more easily and much more regretfully than one which loses 25% in equal 2.5% amounts each week. The converse is true for winners. Clearly we should not let our memories trick us into thinking that losing 20% is worse than losing 25%. It remains a possibility that one should rationally analyse the situation and decide that the sudden loss stock is, in fact, the one to sell, because it has exhibited more volatility. That is fine: my point is more that we should do the analysis rather than just work on the basis of the affect heuristic – which tells us that things which make us feel good are good decisions – and distorted memories.

Garling et al. (2009, p. 12) report on a study of MBA students and their portfolio management that found that "memory for past performance was optimistically biased." I suggest that this is a result of over-confidence or Self-Presentation Bias. The students falsely believe that their portfolios actually performed better than they did. There is no real excuse for this. As mentioned previously, the trick I use is to invest in large, round numbers in each stock, but I do not invest in too many of them. Diversification requires maybe 10 to 15 stocks; I think 10 is fine as long as, of course, there are not two names in any one sector. If you have 10 stocks for which you paid $50,000 or $100,000, there is no difficulty holding on to what the book cost was and comparing it with where the portfolio is currently valued. Naturally, this will slide a little as you buy and sell winners and losers, but since I also suggest infrequent trading, that effect should be muted. There are also tax reasons why the effects of selling winners and losers may be reduced. In any regime with Capital Gains Tax, one will often sell some losers at the same time as one realised profits from a winner in order to reduce the CGT liability in any one tax year. So one will often be able to continue to use the same approximate starting book value for a very long period, and only change it occasionally.

I will now end this book by discussing over-confidence, which is a problem I see as closely linked to Self-Presentation Bias for obvious reasons.

8.3.1 Over-Confidence, Or Why Females Are Better Traders

A further set of investment problems arises from over-confidence. One will perform optimally if one is neither under-confident nor over-confident since that means one's confidence in one's performance is well-calibrated to one's actual performance. Such persons are unlikely to 'bite off more than they can chew.' They are less 'mis-calibrated,' of which more later.

Over-confidence can arise when people struggle to recognise their own limitations. It could be a reflection of the Dunning-Kruger Effect (§7.2) but need not be. Over-confidence can lead investors to make poor financial decisions and then compound them with an exaggerated view of their own competence. This makes it difficult for them to revise their decisions or even update them for changing circumstances. As reported by *The Economist*,[5] "[o]ver half of American men aged 18–24 and nearly 70% of women of that age cannot correctly answer at least three of five basic financial questions." The type of question involved, for example, was whether it is riskier to invest in a single stock or in a mutual fund. The answer to this is obviously that a mutual fund is less risky, because it is more diverse. Since it has exposure to many stocks, it is less likely to decline severely since normally not all of the stocks will be correlated with each other and so will rarely all decline together. This is one of two reasons to consider owning funds; the other one is to gain exposure to unfamiliar foreign markets such as Japan or India, which are interesting investment prospects but in which owning individual stocks would require significant time and specialist expertise. The other questions were similarly straightforward, or at least would be to anyone legitimately informed enough to invest their own money. We can see the effects of this sort of problem in such statistics as those also reported by *The Economist*,[6] to the effect that in 2013, 42% of US borrowers paid mortgage interest above 5% when they could refinance at 4%.

The author of the study reported, John Campbell of Harvard, defined the inability to answer at least three of the questions as financial illiteracy. He found that more than half of both men and women who were financially illiterate according to this definition expressed a high degree of confidence in their financial knowledge. This is extraordinary given the very basic nature of the questions asked. They did not even require any calculation, which often exposes lack of mathematical ability in the general population. The ability of subjects to answer the questions improves with age, but they also exhibit even more over-confidence. Only around 20% of men and 34% of women aged over 75 fell into the category of financial illiteracy but most of the men in that category expressed high confidence in their financial knowledge. The female subjects, of whom more were financially illiterate, at least demonstrated better self-knowledge – only about 75% of the financially illiterate women said they were highly confident in their financial knowledge. This is important: Hirshleifer (2001, p. 1538) points to evidence that while 'moderate over-confidence' is good for market performance, extreme over-confidence is not.

The extent to which financially illiterate persons are active in the stock market is unclear; it is relatively low is the US (Korniotis and Kumar 2011). In developed markets, the retail investor is not a major participant in any case, though it is worth noting that the price of a stock is set by those who actually trade. The retail investor is very significant in, for example, the Chinese stock market and there is no reason to assume that Chinese persons will outperform Americans on the financial literacy tests. And even the American individuals will have some input into stock markets, even if they are not directly invested, because they may well have pensions and other forms of investment over which they will exercise some control. I suggest that this means that the bar is set relatively low for out-performance in terms of gaining better financial knowledge. As *The Economist* [7] also reports, it seems that "financial education [...] had no beneficial effect" in the classroom, suggesting that it is too remote from the concerns of school-age children to be absorbed by the majority of them at that time. This would be consistent with the pattern of decreasing financial illiteracy as people age; apart from anything else, older people have more money and have been required to make more financial decisions.

Nofsinger (2016, ch. 2) puts over-confidence down to people simply being mistaken about their abilities. This is correct on one reading of 'mistake,' but I prefer a different reading. The over-confident do not lack data on their own abilities. How could they, when they are faced with the outcomes of their abilities, good and bad, every day? This, I think, is more a case of motivated reasoning (Kunda 1990) combined with Self-Presentation Bias. Quite simply, people believe what they want to believe, and here they wish to believe that they have exceptional abilities. Everyone thinks that they are an above average driver because it will be inconsistent with their Self-Presentation Bias to say otherwise. Everyone thinks that they are an above average investor for similar reasons.

Evidence has been found showing that stock market analysts making earnings forecasts are also subject to over-confidence, which impairs their performance. Hilary and Menzly (2006, p. 490) report that if "analysts have made a series of good predictions, they become overconfident in their ability to predict future earnings."[8] This causes them to deviate more from consensus in future predictions and such deviation is bad for accuracy, it transpires.

Recognising one's own inability to predict need not lead to paralysis. For example, I have recently been realising some profits arising in my portfolio after the Brexit referendum in June 2016. My portfolio was mostly invested in US dollar assets, and so the strong Sterling depreciation after the referendum resulted in portfolio appreciation. I do not know whether Sterling will continue to depreciate. This is definitely possible. I understand from one of my brokers that other clients are positioning themselves on the expectation that Sterling may well continue to decline. Obviously they are somewhat late to that particular party, but this may still be a sensible move.

The scenario I have been considering, without predicting it, is that the UK government sets out an intelligent negotiating posture with the European Union, and this is regarded positively in Brussels. If, for example, the UK government were to ask for membership of the European Economic Area, together with some rational and reciprocal agreement on immigration, and passport rights for banks based in the City of London, that would form a basis for negotiations. If the UK government were to, in addition, offer budget contributions, it might start to look as though an agreement could be reached quickly. In those circumstances, there could be a snapback rally in Sterling. Moreover, there is the possibility of a Trump victory in the US presidential elections, which would have extremely unpredictable effects in financial markets in the US.

If I were certain that either or both of these scenarios was going to transpire, I would liquidate my entire US portfolio and return the proceeds to the UK. Since I know I cannot predict well enough to be sure of either of those events transpiring, I am not doing that. I am only liquidating around 33% to 50% of the portfolio. This means that I can partially continue to benefit if Sterling continues to depreciate, as it will do in any of the difficult negotiation scenarios which are also plausible, but I am somewhat protected if it does not. This is a way of protecting oneself from one's own over-confidence in one's own predictions: hedge.

Hilary and Menzly (2006) propose a mechanism for how over-confidence can feed prediction errors. Their account is consistent with an effect known as 'self-attribution' which can be seen as an aspect of Self-Presentation Bias. Self-attribution is the tendency to ascribe success to one's own skills and positive qualities, and failures to uncontrollable external circumstances. This particular bias has been termed 'self-attribution bias;' here I will just consider it a species of Self-Presentation Bias. This is really a question solely of nomenclature and will not affect the argument. Whatever we call this bias, it will tend to be of assistance in maintaining a positive self-image and so is at least consistent with, if not identical to, Self-Presentation Bias. The process proposed is that analysts over-attribute prior success to their own skills as opposed to randomness and luck, and consequently develop over-confidence. This over-confidence naturally limits itself cyclically because the errors it leads to then cause a reduction in over-confidence.

Somewhat counterintuitively, the remedy proposed by Hilary and Menzly (2006, p. 490) is that if "two analysts are believed to possess identical skills and experience but only one of them had a recent series of superior predictions, investors may want to rely more on the subsequent forecast of the less-accurate analyst." This analyst will be less likely to exhibit damaging over-confidence. In a way, this can be seen as a contrarian or value approach to analyst selection: look for low-rated analysts who have had a poor run because they will be working harder and also sticking closer to consensus. The results also suggest that there is some value in consensus earnings forecasts.

Trying to make an honest assessment of how good one's decisions are is very important when trying to avoid over-confidence. While it will be dispiriting to assume that one is wrong, one can assume one is right but test that assumption to its limits. The fact that fewer of the female subjects who were financially illiterate nevertheless had a high confidence in their financial knowledge may enable us to explain the evidence I will discuss next that suggests that females outperform male non-professional traders. This looks initially difficult to explain since we have just established that females are more likely to be financially illiterate in all age ranges. However, the improved self-knowledge in females – or alternatively, their relative immunity to the Self-Presentation Bias which seems to make the males more likely to be over-confident – will make them avoid many common trading errors.

Women do seem to be less susceptible to over-confidence. One study of non-professional traders found that females outperformed males because they did not over-trade – they would, instead, wait more patiently for their portfolio to perform. As Hirshleifer (2001, p. 1562) points out, males tend to "trade too aggressively, incurring higher transactions costs without higher returns." Trading too aggressively here just means doing too much trading, rather than giving strategies time to work. That may mean waiting for years. Interestingly, Korniotis and Kumar (2011) start from the other direction and use portfolio turnover as a proxy for lack of investor sophistication and investor tendency to exhibit behavioural biases, such as over-confidence. This must be accorded great weight, since they are able to explain empirically observable effects.

Other studies confirm that over-confidence and over-trading are prevalent among males and highly damaging. One study examined investors who switched to online trading in the early years of that being possible. The authors argue plausibly that over-confident investors were more likely to make the switch. Barber and Odean (2002, p. 475) report the extraordinary fact that "average annual turnover increases from 73.7% to 95.5%." I say this is extraordinary because of the wild over-trading this represents, even before the switch to online. I would suggest that a more appropriate level would be 10% on average with maybe a peak of 50% in a year of special circumstances, such as a cyclical rotation. Once a decade or so, it may be appropriate to exit one's entire portfolio and switch asset classes. Of course, the convenience of going online makes over-trading an easier trap to fall into as well.

The consequences of this are severe. Barber and Odean (2002, p. 478) report that their online sample, which was 85.7% male, underperform the offline sample by 4.3% every year. That is relative value destruction on a large scale. And recall that this is in comparison with a sample of very similar investors, so there is no skill or experience disadvantage involved. These relative losses are caused solely by going online, being over-confident and indulging in over-trading. Barber and Odean (2002, p. 479) also note that online investors are more likely to make speculative trades and more likely to hold small growth stocks. I advise against both of these approaches and the over-confidence that they embody.

One way to persuade yourself into inactivity, if not naturally gifted with laziness, is to consider an earlier result by the same authors. Barber and Odean (1999, p. 46) report that for "winners that were sold, the average excess return over the following year was a highly statistically significant 3.4 percent more." In other words, just holding on to a stock that has appreciated will gain you 3.4% more than selling it will. That is a huge effect. It may not persist indefinitely, however, Barber and Odean (1999, p. 46) also note evidence of "price momentum in security returns at horizons of up to 18 months." But this suggests waiting for two years on the first occasion that you think of selling a winner. At that point, of course, many developments will have occurred in financial markets generally, and in relation to the particular stock in question, so you will need to review the entire question again. And not only will you be likely to make a bad trade, you will have to pay the bid/offer spread to do so. This argument does not apply to first setting up your portfolio, but should make you pause at all points afterwards.

Females are also less likely to make the two other errors of failing to cut losers quickly enough and not letting winners run – the two together are known as the previously mentioned Disposition Effect. Both of those trading errors can be seen as consequences of over-confidence. In the first case, the over-confident trader insists to the bitter end that he was right in the beginning and this stock must recover. In the second case, the over-confident trader either wishes to bolster what may, in fact, be rather a fragile self-image by locking in early winnings rather than letting them increase, and he may also feel that he has an exceptional ability to identify outperforming stocks. There is, then, no need to wait patiently for performance since another great idea is just around the corner. I suggest again, in sum, that while improving one's financial knowledge is important, having better psychological insight into oneself and others is even more important.

There are particular market circumstances in which over-confidence is especially unhelpful. Daniel, Hirshleifer, and Subrahmanyam (1998, p. 1859) note that "individuals tend to be more overconfident in settings where feedback on their information or decisions is slow or inconclusive than where the feedback is clear and rapid." They derive, as a consequence, the result that "mis-pricing should be stronger in stocks that require more judgment to evaluate, and where the feedback on this judgment is ambiguous." They further note that such ambiguous feedback is more likely for growth stocks. The former claim is well-supported in the empirical psychological literature. The latter claim also looks highly plausible. This suggests that one should analyse growth stocks with extra care or, indeed, avoid them altogether so as to also avoid some of the more severe adverse effects of over-confidence. Daniel, Hirshleifer, and Subrahmanyam (1998, p. 1859) are also right in my view to highlight stocks with "high R&D expenditures or intangible assets" as likely to provide environments which are high risk for over-confidence. Another option to avoid over-confidence is to look for situations with rapid feedback. Female traders need, of course, take no advice from me – though maybe an ability to profit from advice is a reflection of lack of over-confidence – and arguably should *specialise* in growth stocks, and those which are research-driven or with high intangibles. Female traders ought to outperform here since they will be competing in an environment where over-confident male traders create profit opportunities. This may involve shorting stocks, of course.

It has been shown in experimental markets that a specific kind of over-confidence is the problem: mis-calibration. Biais, Hilton, *et al.* (2005, p. 288) state that "[m]is-calibrated people tend to overestimate the precision of their information." This means that poor traders are less likely to have problems in that they are wrong about what their trades will do, but that they are assuming a higher accuracy level than is justified by the quality of their information or the mere fact that the future is highly unpredictable. So if a mis-calibrated investor is considering the prospects for a stock, he may believe that it is highly probable that it will appreciate in the next year by 5% ± 1%. The reality is that even if the 5% central estimate is correct, the variance should be a lot higher: the estimate should be 5% ± 10%. That would accord with my experience; and even the 10% variance will probably only cover less than half of actual outcomes.

This should lead one to back one's ideas less aggressively in many cases, predominantly by reducing the size of individual trades relative to the total portfolio size. So in a way, it is another type of diversification argument. One should be diverse in terms of ideas and approaches as well as industry sectors. Taken to its extreme, the ideal would be to have a diverse set of income sources, allowing some hope that employment income will be relatively uncorrelated with stock market returns. A poor market year might also be a good year for employment income. This means one should avoid excess exposure to stock in one's employer – unless they are offering extremely attractive matching funds. In that case, you should take the money but obtain some insurance in the form of separate transactions which will offer a hedge against the stock.

Biais, Hilton, et al. (2005, p. 288) go on to note that a "specific kind of overconfidence in one's judgement, which we refer to as mis-calibration, can offer an explanation for the failure of some participants to realise that their trades suffer from winner's curse risk and are consequently loss making." The 'winner's curse' refers to any situation in which one has 'won' an auction but should not have done – in other words, over-paying for an asset. The second-placed bidder has been lucky, even if he does not currently realise that. Only the winner gets to find out whether winning was a mistake. This is remarkable. It is one thing to suggest, as above, that some poor traders are poor because they are mis-calibrated as to the precision of their future stock performance estimates. It is another to suggest that mis-calibration also prevents them from observing post hoc that their trades are bad.

I suspect that this is bound up with the central bias of this section – Self-Presentation Bias – and also the fabricated 'near wins' stories that we saw in §5.1 on a type of Confirmation Bias in gamblers. So we would see poor traders make up stories in which their 5% appreciation estimate would have been accurate in a world very close to the real world, where only some freak and unpredictable mischance was the reason that the stock actually declined 5%. This story is driven by the investor's Self-Presentation Bias and means that he is unable to accept that his story was wrong. He can therefore continue to be over-confident and fail to learn from his mistakes.

Being smart does not help. Biais, Hilton, et al. (2005, p. 289) note that the mis-calibration effect "is also robust to the inclusion of IQ in the regressors," which is technical language for the point that intelligent men are still mis-calibrated and over-confident. Indeed, it may even make it worse – after all, intelligent people know that they are intelligent and have seen frequent examples of their intelligence in action helping them make good decisions.

Being experienced does not help.[9] Biais, Hilton, et al. (2005, p. 290) point out that the mis-calibration effect was robust to "previous professional experience in investment and financial markets." In other words, some of their subjects had such experience and it did not make them less mis-calibrated. Biais, Hilton, et al. (2005, p. 296) also note evidence from a study that "found similarly pronounced over-confidence in judgement even in a domain where the participants (Frankfurt currency traders) should have high expertise," which incidentally re-confirms the point I made at the very outset (Chapter 2) that one can beat the market.

In general, as Garling et al. (2009, p. 36) note, "markets do not themselves correct biases, nor does incentivising rational behaviour." These two statements are closely related for, as we have seen throughout, biases impair market performance and that will generally be expensive, so people are already incentivised to avoid biases and yet do not. There is every reason to expect this to continue in the future, even if everyone in the market has eventually read this book and so at least knows about the biases. As mentioned several times before, it is very difficult to eradicate biases – partly because they are basically who we are. There is some recent evidence (Balzan et al. 2013) that schizophrenic subjects can benefit from training which reduces their biases and improves their Theory of Mind – but it remains to be seen whether similar approaches could function more widely and would be widely adopted if so.

Something of a paradox lurks in the data. As Biais, Hilton, et al. (2005, p. 289) confirm, "mis-calibration does not significantly affect performance in women [but] it does lead to worse performance in men." And yet the authors do not measure any differences in mis-calibration between men and women, consistent with "other studies of mis-calibration which similarly found little or no gender difference" (Biais, Hilton, et al. 2005, p. 296). So it seems that while men do not exhibit more mis-calibration than women, it impairs their performance much more.

I find the explanation of this puzzle concerning, and so should you, if you are male. What is happening is that while both sexes are mis-calibrated, the females do not trade on their mis-calibrated beliefs; "their propensity to act on their mis-calibrated beliefs is different" (Biais, Hilton, et al. 2005, p. 305) and specifically so in that they avoid the winner's curse. Specifically, the experiment gave traders highly imperfect price signals about the value of the assets traded – as we see in real life. The shares involved could have one of only three values: 50, 240 and 490. Each trader was only told which of the values it did not have, for example 'not 50' or 'not 240.' This theoretically should make one extremely reluctant to trade, because one simply does not have enough information to do so; one also knows that others have information which could allow them to take advantage of us if we do trade. What happens, though, is that given "transaction prices close to 240, [mis-calibrated traders] will over-confidently believe that the value is 240 if their own signal does not rule out this value" (Biais, Hilton, *et al.* 2005, p. 297). This means that even though there was in the setup a better than 50% chance that the value was much different to 240, a market price in that region gives participants excess confidence to trade in that region. I find this concerning because I accept that it is exactly what I would be likely to do.

A further possibility is that a relatively low level of testosterone or other factors make female traders more likely to avoid being caught up in bubbles. Dale, Johnson, and Tang (2005, p. 262) suggest that in the South Sea Bubble, investors "simply developed over-confidence in their own intuition that later subscription issues would outperform previous issues." This is exacerbated, they write, by face-to-face arenas in which excitement can be infectious. It is easy to picture the mad scenes in Exchange Alley during the summer of 1720; all of the traders would have been men at that time.

Indeed, they mostly still are. I never met a female trader in my time on the floor. This naturally raises an objection to the points I have been laying out above. If female traders are so good, why are there so few professionals? I believe that this will change in the future. Shull (2011, p. 67) points out that the same senior, male trader told her both that she had the best trading instincts he had ever seen and that he thought a woman could not trade. When society not only ceases telling women that they cannot do things, but actively tells them that they can, much is possible that currently looks implausible.

It is not all bad news for men. One personality trait that seems to have *some* predictive power and stability is known as 'self-monitoring.' Biais, Hilton, *et al.* (2005, p. 288) explain that "[s]elf-monitoring is a disposition to attend to social cues and to adjust one's behaviour to one's social environment." Slightly surprisingly, "men are higher self-monitors than women" (Biais, Hilton, *et al.* 2005, p. 299) and "[H]igh self-monitors tend to earn greater profits" (Biais, Hilton, *et al.* 2005, p. 300). However, this does not lead to any proposed changes, since mis-calibration seems to be stable for individuals (Biais, Hilton, *et al.* 2005, p. 296) as well as self-monitoring (Biais, Hilton, *et al.* 2005, p. 296). While this just shows that it does not tend to change rather than that it cannot change, it also does not afford any confidence that these parameters can be altered. For that, though, we can appeal to the Fundamental Attribution Error (§8.1) and recall that we do not have fixed personalities.

Slightly more speculatively, it has been suggested that humans are well adapted to solve social problems. Such problems include "making inferences about the differently constituted minds of the opposite sex;" within these domains "emotions may be rational and cognitive biases functional" (Buss 2001, p. 223). If this is true, then it suggests that biases may assist in the Theory of Mind of males when simulating females. If so, then there is some hope that males can simulate females which would then allow them to at least have insight into superior, slower, trading styles, though knowing what they are and enacting them are two different things. And everyday experience does not allow us to regard the prospects of superior performance in cross-sex Theory of Mind with a high degree of optimism.

We must also take note of a possible systematic selection bias in the data. The trading data in Barber and Odean (2002), for example, derives from online brokerage accounts held by a group of which 85.7% were male. It is possible that the smaller female sample was drawn from a higher performing, self-selecting group of females. In other words, the effect we are seeing of apparent female outperformance would be due to a contest between male club swimmers and female Olympic swimmers, to exaggerate somewhat for clarity. However, while this is worth investigating, I suspect the outperformance is more fundamental and would survive a wider data selection. And it would still be true that majority of male traders would do well to imitate a lower turnover female trading style.

So in view of all this, I can only propose coming out on the other side of overconfidence. Call it 'uber-confidence' if you like, in homage to the Übermensch of Nietzsche (1961), who sets his own values rather than allowing them to be imposed on him by society. This is being so confident that you can admit your mistakes and learn from them. Try to avoid the winner's curse at all costs. You do not need to trade every time. You do not need to win every time – which is good, because you will not. Good luck.

Notes

1 It will be very interesting if the recent EU tax ruling on AAPL and Ireland causes some of the vast stock of cash held abroad by US corporations to be repatriated.
2 The Japanese Government also holds a lot of liquid assets which reduces the number quite significantly.
3 *The Economist*, vol. 418, no. 8972, 16 Jan 2016, p. 72
4 Cf. also Nofsinger (2016, ch. 10).
5 *The Economist*, vol. 418, no. 8972, 16 Jan 2016, p. 74
6 *The Economist*, vol. 418, no. 8972, 16 Jan 2016, p. 74
7 *The Economist*, vol. 418, no. 8972, 16 Jan 2016, p. 74
8 Cf. also Marks (2011, pp. 120–121)
9 At least to some level, being experienced does not help. I am naturally going to claim that 35,000 hours of experience is good enough!

BIBLIOGRAPHY

Abbink, K. and B. Rockenbach (2006). "Option Pricing By Students And Professional Traders: A Behavioural Investigation". In: *Managerial and Decision Economics* 27. 6, pp. 497–510. doi:10.1002/mde.1284.

Abu-Akel, A. and K. Abushua'leh (2004). "'Theory Of Mind' In Violent And Nonviolent Patients With Paranoid Schizophrenia". In: *Schizophrenia Research* 69. 1, pp. 45–53. doi:10.1016/S0920-9964(03)00049-00045.

Ackert, L. F. et al. (2009). "Probability Judgment Error And Speculation In Laboratory Asset Market Bubbles". In: *Journal of Financial and Quantitative Analysis* 44. 3, pp. 719–744. doi:10.1017/S0022109009990019.

An, S. K. et al. (2012). "Poster #134 Hostility Bias In Healthy Persons: Its Association With 'Theory Of Mind' Skills". In: *Schizophrenia Research* 136. S1, S139–S140. doi:10.1016/S0920-9964(12)70448-70446.

Andrews, K. (2008). "It's In Your Nature: A Pluralistic Folk Psychology". In: *Synthese* 165. 1, pp. 13–29. doi:10.1007/S11229-11007-9230-9235.

Aristotle (1998). *The Nicomachean Ethics*. Ed. by W. D. Ross, J. L. Ackrill, and J. O. Urmson. Oxford University Press. ISBN: 9780192834072. url: http://www.worldcat.org/title/nicomachean-ethics/oclc/47008570.

Armstrong, S. J. and C. V. Fukami (2010). "Self-Assessment Of Knowledge: A Cognitive Learning Or Affective Measure? Perspectives From The Management Learning And Education Community". In: *Academy of Management Learning & Education* 9. 2, pp. 335–341. doi:10.5465/AMLE.2010.51428556.

Asch, S. E. (1946). "Forming Impressions Of Personality". In: *Journal Of Abnormal Psychology* 41. 3, pp. 258–290. doi:10.1037/h0060423.

Asch, S. E. (1952). *Social Psychology*. Prentice-Hall. url: http://www.worldcat.org/title/social-psychology/oclc/254969.

Baddeley, M. (2010). "Herding, Social Influence And Economic Decision-making: Sociopsychological And Neuroscientific Analyses". In: *Philosophical Transactions of the Royal Society B: Biological Sciences* 365. 1538, pp. 281–290. doi:10.1098/rstb.2009.0169.

Balzan, R. P. et al. (2013). "Metacognitive Training For Patients With Schizophrenia: Preliminary Evidence For A Targeted, Single-Module Programme". In: *The Australian And New Zealand Journal Of Psychiatry* 48. 12, pp. 1126–1136. doi:10.1177/0004867413508451.

Barber, B. M. and T. Odean (1999). "The Courage Of Misguided Convictions". In: *Financial Analysts Journal* 55. 6, pp. 41–55. doi:10.2469/faj.v55.n6.2313.

Barber, B. M. and T. Odean (2002). "Online Investors: Do The Slow Die First?" In: *SSRN Electronic Journal* 15. 2, pp. 455–487. doi:10.2139/ssrn.219242.

Barberis, N. (2013). "Psychology And The Financial Crisis Of 2007–2008". In: *Financial Innovation*. Ed. by M. Haliassos. MIT Press, pp. 15–28. doi:10.2139/ssrn.1742463.

Baron-Cohen, S., A. M. Leslie, and U. Frith (1985). "Does The Autistic Child Have A 'Theory Of Mind'?" In: *Cognition* 21. 1, pp. 37–46. doi:10.1016/0010-0277(85)90022-90028.

Batson, C. D. (2009). "These Things Called Empathy: Eight Related But Distinct Phenomena". In: *The Social Neuroscience of Empathy*. Ed. by J. Decety and W. Ickes. MIT Press, pp. 3–15.

Bem, D. J. (1967). "Self-Perception: An Alternative Interpretation Of Cognitive Dissonance Phenomena". In: *Psychological Review* 74. 3, pp. 183–200. url: http://www.ncbi.nlm.nih.gov/pubmed/5342882.

Bem, D. J. (1972). "Self-Perception Theory". In: *Advances In Experimental Social Psychology*. Ed. by L. Berkowitz. Vol. 6. Academic Press, pp. 1–62. doi:10.1016/S0065-2601(08)60024-60026.

Bernstein, D. M. et al. (2007). "Hindsight Bias And Developing Theories Of Mind". In: *Child Development* 78. 4, pp. 1374–1394. doi:10.1111/j.1467-8624.2007.01071.x.

Bertrand, M. and A. Morse (2011). "Information Disclosure, Cognitive Biases, And Payday Borrowing". In: *The Journal of Finance* 66. 6, pp. 1865–1893. doi:10.1111/j.1540-6261.2011.01698.x.

Besharov, G. (2004). "Second-Best Considerations In Correcting Cognitive Biases". In: *Southern Economic Journal* 71. 1, pp. 12–20. doi:10.2307/4135307.

Biais, B., D. Hilton, et al. (2005). "Judgemental Overconfidence, Self-Monitoring, And Trading Performance In An Experimental Financial Market". In: *The Review of Economic Studies* 72. 2, pp. 287–312. doi:10.1111/j.1467-1937X.2005.00333.x.

Biais, B. and M. Weber (2009). "Hindsight Bias, Risk Perception, And Investment Performance". In: *Management Science* 55. 6, pp. 1018–1029. doi:10.1287/mnsc.1090.1000.

Bogle, J. C. (2008). "Black Monday And Black Swans". In: *Financial Analysts Journal* 64. 2, pp. 30–40. doi:10.2469/faj.v64.n2.9.

Bramel, D. (1962). "A Dissonance Theory Approach To Defensive Projection". In: *J Abnorm Soc Psychol* 64, pp. 121–129. url: http://www.ncbi.nlm.nih.gov/pubmed/13872441.

Bruguier, A. J., S. R. Quartz, and P. Bossaerts (2010). "Exploring The Nature Of 'Trader Intuition'". In: *The Journal of Finance* 65. 5, pp. 1703–1723. doi:10.1111/j.1540-6261.2010.01591.x.

Buss, D. M. (2001). "Cognitive Biases And Emotional Wisdom In The Evolution Of Conflict Between The Sexes". In: *Current Directions in Psychological Science* 10. 6, pp. 219–223. doi:10.1111/1467-8721.00153.

Butterfill, S. A. and I. A. Apperly (2013). "How To Construct A Minimal Theory Of Mind". In: *Mind And Language* 28. 5, pp. 606–637. doi:10.1111/Mila.12036.

Cherlin, A. (1990). "A Review: The Strange Career Of The 'Harvard-Yale Study'". In: *The Public Opinion Quarterly* 54. 1, pp. 117–124. url: http://www.jstor.org/stable/2749395.

Cipriani, M. and A. Guarino (2009). "Herd Behavior In Financial Markets: An Experiment With Financial Market Professionals". In: *Journal Of The European Economic Association* 7. 1, pp. 206–233. doi:10.1162/JEEA.2009.7.1.206.

Clotfelter, C. T. and P. J. Cook (1993). "Notes: The 'Gambler's Fallacy' in Lottery Play". In: *Management Science* 39. 12, pp. 1521–1525. doi:10.1287/mnsc.39.12.1521.

Coplan, A. (2011). "Understanding Empathy: Its Features And Effects". In: *Empathy: Philosophical And Psychological Perspectives*. Ed. by A. Coplan and P. Goldie. Oxford University Press. ISBN: 9780198706427. url: http://www.worldcat.org/title/empathy-philosophical-and-psychological-perspectives/oclc/767842620.

Corcos, A. and F. Pannequin (2006). "Conservatisme, Representativite Et Ancrage Dans Un Contexte Dynamique: Une Approche Experimentale". In: *Recherches Economiques De Louvain* 74. 1, pp. 77–110. doi:10.3917/rel.741.0077.

Cowan, J. L. (1969). "The Gambler's Fallacy". In: *Philosophy and Phenomenological Research* 30. 2, pp. 238–251. doi:10.2307/2106040.

Dale, R. S., J. E. V. Johnson, and L. Tang (2005). "Financial Markets Can Go Mad: Evidence Of Irrational Behaviour During The South Sea Bubble". In: *The Economic History Review* 58. 2, pp. 233–271. doi:10.1111/j.1468–0289.2005.00304.x.

Daniel, K. D., D. Hirshleifer, and A. Subrahmanyam (1998). "Investor Psychology And Security Market Under- And Overreactions". In: *Journal of Finance* 53. 6, pp. 1839–1886. doi:10.2307/117455.

Darley, J. M. and C. D. Batson (1973). "'From Jerusalem To Jericho': A Study Of Situational And Dispositional Variables In Helping Behavior". In: *Journal Of Personality And Social Psychology* 27. 1, pp. 100–108. doi:10.1037/H0034449.

Dawkins, R. (1976). *The Selfish Gene*. Oxford University Press. url: http://www.worldcat.org/title/selfish-gene/oclc/2681149.

Dennett, D. C. (1978). "Beliefs About Beliefs". In: *Behavioral And Brain Sciences* 1(04), pp. 568–570. doi:10.1017/S0140525X00076664.

Dennett, D. C. (2007). *Breaking The Spell: Religion As A Natural Phenomenon*. Penguin Adult. ISBN: 9780141017778. url: http://www.worldcat.org/title/breaking-the-spell-religion-as-a-natural-phenomenon/oclc/470564789.

Dunning, D. et al. (2003). "Why People Fail To Recognize Their Own Incompetence". In: *Current Directions in Psychological Science* 12. 3, pp. 83–87. doi:10.1111/1467-8721.01235.

Evans, J. S. B. T. (1990). *Bias In Human Reasoning: Causes And Consequences*. Lawrence Erlbaum Associates, Incorporated. ISBN: 9780863771569. url: http://www.worldcat.org/title/bias-in-human-reasoning-causes-and-consequences/oclc/35142289.

Fama, E. F. (1970). "Efficient Capital Markets: A Review Of Theory And Empirical Work". In: *The Journal of Finance* 25. 2, pp. 383–417. doi:10.1111/j.1540–6261.1970.tb00518.x.

Frydman, R. and M. D. Goldberg (2011). "Fundamentals And Psychology In Price Swings". In: *Beyond Mechanical Markets*. Princeton University Press, pp. 163–174.

Garling, T. et al. (2009). "Psychology, Financial Decision Making, And Financial Crises". In: *Psychological Science in the Public Interest* 10. 1, pp. 1–47. doi:10.1177/1529100610378437.

Gilovich, T. (1993). *How We Know What Isn't So*. Free Press. ISBN: 9780029117064. url: http://www.worldcat.org/title/how-we-know-what-isnt-so-the-fallibility-of-human-reason-in-everyday-life/oclc/832440458.

Gladwell, M. (2000). *The Tipping Point: How Little Things Can Make A Big Difference*. Abacus. ISBN: 9780349113463. url: http://www.worldcat.org/title/tipping-point-how-little-things-can-make-a-big-difference/oclc/224387573.

Gladwell, M. (2006). *Blink: The Power Of Thinking Without Thinking*. Penguin Books Limited. ISBN: 9780141014593. url: http://www.worldcat.org/title/blink-the-power-of-thinking-without-thinking/oclc/301647272.

Gladwell, M. (2009a). *Outliers: The Story of Success*. Penguin Books Limited. ISBN: 9780141036250. url: http://www.worldcat.org/title/outliers-the-story-of-success/oclc/501705589.

Gladwell, M. (2009b). *What The Dog Saw: And Other Adventures*. Penguin Books Limited. ISBN: 9780141044804. url: http://www.worldcat.org/title/what-the-dog-saw-and-other-adventures/oclc/501394900.

Gladwell, M. (2013). *David And Goliath: Underdogs, Misfits And The Art Of Battling Giants*. Penguin Books Limited. ISBN: 9780241959602. url: http://www.worldcat.org/title/david-and-goliath-underdogs-misfits-and-the-art-of-battling-giants/oclc/900730980.

Glaeser, E. L. (2004). "Psychology And The Market". In: *The American Economic Review* 94. 2, pp. 408–413. doi:10.1.1.160.1649.

Goldman, A. I. (1989). "Interpretation Psychologized". In: *Mind And Language* 4. 3, pp. 161–185. doi:10.1111/J.1468–0017.1989.Tb00249.X.

Gopnik, A. and H. M. Wellman (1992). "Why The Child's Theory Of Mind Really Is A Theory". In: *Mind And Language* 7. 1–2, pp. 145–171. doi:10.1111/J.1468–0017.1992.Tb00202.X.

Graver, M. (2007). *Stoicism And Emotion*. University Of Chicago Press. ISBN: 9780226305578. url: http://www.worldcat.org/title/stoicism-emotion/oclc/263708979.

Guttentag, J. and R. Herring (1984). "Credit Rationing And Financial Disorder". In: *The Journal of Finance* 39. doi:5, pp. 1359–1382. doi: 10.1111/j.1540–6261.1984.tb04912.x.

Haney, C., C. Banks, and P. Zimbardo (1973). "Interpersonal Dynamics In A Simulated Prison". In: *International Journal Of Criminology And Penology* 1. 1, pp. 69–97. url: http://www.prisonexp.org/pdf/ijcp1973.pdf.

Harris, P. L. (1992). "From Simulation To Folk Psychology: The Case For Development". In: *Mind And Language* 7. 1–2, pp. 120–144. doi:10.1111/J.1468–0017.1992.Tb00201.X.

Hasson-Ohayon, I. et al. (2009). "Metacognitive And Interpersonal Interventions For Persons With Severe Mental Illness: Theory And Practice". In: *The Israel Journal Of Psychiatry And Related Sciences* 46. 2, pp. 141–148. url: http://www.Ncbi.Nlm.Nih.Gov/Pubmed/19827697.

Hempel, C. G. (1945). "Studies In The Logic Of Confirmation (I)". In: *Mind* 54. 213, pp. 1–26. doi:10.2307/2265252.

Hilary, G. and L. Menzly (2006). "Does Past Success Lead Analysts To Become Overconfident?" In: *Management Science* 52. 4, pp. 489–500. doi:10.1287/mnsc.1050.0485.

Hirshleifer, D. (2001). "Investor Psychology And Asset Pricing". In: *Journal of Finance* 56. 4, pp. 1533–1597. doi:10.1111/0022–1082.00379.

Hume, D. (1739). *An Enquiry Concerning Human Understanding: With A Letter From A Gentleman To His Friend In Edinburgh; And An Abstract Of A Treatise Of Human Nature*. John Noon, London. url: http://www.worldcat.org/title/treatise-of-human-nature/oclc/938177823.

Igoe, A. R. and H. Sullivan (1993). "Self-Presentation Bias And Continuing Motivation Among Adolescents". In: *The Journal Of Educational Research* 87. 1, pp. 18–22. doi:10.1080/00220671.1993.9941161.

Johansson, P. et al. (2006). "How Something Can Be Said About Telling More Than We Can Know: On Choice Blindness And Introspection". In: *Consciousness And Cognition* 15. 4, pp. 673–692. doi:10.1016/J.Concog.2006.09.004.

Jonsson, S. (2009). "Refraining From Imitation: Professional Resistance And Limited Diffusion In A Financial Market". In: *Organization Science* 20. 1, pp. 172–186. doi:10.1287/orsc.1080.0370.

Jordan, J. (2003). "Repraesentativitaetsheuristik Und Werbewirkung: Die Bedeutung von Ratings Und Performance-Charts In Der Werbung Fuer Investmentfonds". In: *Marketing: Zeitschrift fuer Forschung und Praxis* 25. 4, pp. 273–288. url: http://www.jstor.org/stable/42746175.

Kahneman, D. and A. Tversky (1979). "Prospect Theory: An Analysis Of Decision Under Risk". In: Econometrica 47. 2, pp. 263–292. url: http://www.jstor.org/stable/1914185.

Kamtekar, R. (2004). "Situationism And Virtue Ethics On The Content Of Our Character". In: *Ethics* 114. 3, pp. 458–491. doi:10.1086/381696.

Keynes, J. M. (2016). *The General Theory of Employment, Interest and Money*. Atlantic Publishers and Distributors.

Konnikova, M. (2016). *The Confidence Game: Why We Fall for It … Every Time*. Penguin Publishing Group. ISBN: 9780698170995. url: http://www.worldcat.org/title/confidence-game/oclc/920739964.

Kopcha, T. J. and H. Sullivan (2006). "Self-Presentation Bias In Surveys Of Teachers' Educational Technology Practices". In: *Educational Technology Research And Development* 55. 6, pp. 627–646. doi:10.1007/S11423–11006–9011–9018.

Korniotis, G. M. and A. Kumar (2011). "Do Behavioral Biases Adversely Affect The Macro-economy?" In: *The Review of Financial Studies* 24. 5, pp. 1513–1559. doi:10.1093/rfs/hhql.

Kramer, L. (2008). "Psychology And The Financial Crisis Of 2007–2008". In: *The Finance Crisis And Rescue*. University of Toronto Press, pp. 123–135. url: http://www.jstor.org/stable/10.3138/j.ctt1287rzk.12.

Kuehberger, A. et al. (1995). "Choice Or No Choice: Is The Langer Effect Evidence Against Simulation?" In: *Mind And Language* 10. 4, pp. 423–436. doi:10.1111/J.1468–0017.1995.Tb00022.X.

Kunda, Z. (1990). "The Case For Motivated Reasoning". In: *Psychological Bulletin* 108. 3, pp. 480–498. doi:10.1037/0033–2909.108.3.480.

Labroo, A. A., S. Lambotte, and Y. Zhang (2009). "The 'Name-Ease' Effect And Its Dual Impact On Importance Judgments". In: *Psychological Science* 20. 12, pp. 1516–1522. doi:10.1111/j.1467–9280.2009.02477.x.

Leeson, N. and S. Fearn (2000). *Rogue Trader*. Pearson Education. ISBN: 9780582430501. url: http://www.worldcat.org/title/rogue-trader/oclc/44837075.

Leslie, A. M., O. Friedman, and T. P. German (2004). "Core Mechanisms In 'Theory Of Mind'". In: Trends In Cognitive Sciences 8. 12, pp. 528–533. doi:10.1016/J.Tics.2004.10.001.

Leslie, A. M., T. P. German, and F. G. Happe (1993). "Even A Theory-Theory Needs Information Processing: ToMM, An Alternative Theory-Theory Of The Child's Theory Of Mind". In: *Behavioral And Brain Sciences* 16. 1, pp. 56–57. doi:10.1017/S0140525X00028934.

Levitt, S. D. and S. J. Dubner (2010). *Superfreakonomics: Global Cooling, Patriotic Prostitutes And Why Suicide Bombers Should Buy Life Insurance*. Penguin Books Limited. ISBN: 9780141030708. url: http://www.worldcat.org/title/superfreakonomics/oclc/940714458.

Lewis, M. M. (2004). *Moneyball: The Art Of Winning An Unfair Game*. W. W. Norton. ISBN: 9780393324815. url: http://www.worldcat.org/title/moneyball/oclc/77897 4649.

Lewis, M. M. (2010). *The Big Short: Inside The Doomsday Machine*. Allen Lane. ISBN: 9781846142574. url: http://www.worldcat.org/title/big-short-inside-the-doomsday-machine/oclc/429603799.

Lewis, M. M. (2014). *Flash Boys*. Penguin Books Limited. ISBN: 9780141978154. url: http://www.worldcat.org/title/flash-boys-cracking-the-money-code.

Lo, A. W., D. V. Repin, and B. N. Steenbarger (2005). "Fear And Greed In Financial Markets: A Clinical Study Of Day-Traders". In: *American Economic Review* 95. 2, pp. 352–359. doi:10.1257/000282805774670095.

Malmendier, U. and T. Taylor (2015). "On The Verges Of Overconfidence". In: *Journal of Economic Perspectives* 29. 4, pp. 3–8. doi:10.1257/jep.29.4.3.

Marks, H. (2011). *The Most Important Thing: Uncommon Sense for the Thoughtful Investor*. Columbia Business School Publishing Series. Columbia University Press. ISBN: 9780231527095. url: http://www.worldcat.org/title/most-important-thing-uncomm on-sense-for-the-thoughtful-investor/oclc/726824487.

Mauboussin, M. J. (2008). "Right From The Gut: Investing With Naturalistic Decision Making". In: *More Than You Know*. Columbia University Press, pp. 104–109.

McGlone, M. S. and J. Tofighbakhsh (2000). "Birds Of A Feather Flock Conjointly (?): Rhyme As Reason In Aphorisms". In: *Psychological Science* 11. 5, pp. 424–428. doi:10.1111/1467-9280.00282.

McKay, R. T. and D. C. Dennett (2009). "The Evolution Of Misbelief". In: *Behavioral And Brain Sciences* 32. 6, pp. 493–510. doi:10.1017/S0140525X09990975.

Mensh, I. N. and J. Wishner (1947). "Asch On 'Forming Impressions Of Personality': Further Evidence". In: *Journal Of Personality* 16. 2, pp. 188–191. doi:10.1111/J.1467-6494.1947.Tb01080.X.

Michel, C. and A. Newen (2010). "Self-deception As Pseudo-rational Regulation Of Belief". In: *Consciousness And Cognition* 19. 3, pp. 731–744. doi:10.1016/j.concog.2010.06.019.

Midgley, M. (1979). "Gene-juggling". In: *Philosophy* 54. 210, pp. 439–458. doi:10.1017/S0031819100063488.

Milgram, S. (1963). "Behavioral Study Of Obedience". In: *The Journal Of Abnormal And Social Psychology* 67. 4, pp. 371–378. doi:10.1037/H0040525.

Mineka, S. and S. K. Sutton (1992). "Cognitive Biases And The Emotional Disorders". In: *Psychological Science* 3. 1, pp. 65–69. doi:10.1111/J.1467-9280.1992.Tb00260.X.

Mitchell, D. (2003). *Cloud Atlas*. Sceptre. ISBN: 9780340833209. url: http://www.worldcat.org/title/cloud-atlas/oclc/447571417.

Nagel, J. (2011). "The Psychological Basis Of The Harman-Vogel Paradox". In: *Philosophers' Imprint* 11. 5, pp. 1–28. url: http://hdl.handle.net/2027/spo.3521354.0011.005.

Nestler, S. (2010). "Belief Perseverance". In: *Social Psychology* 41. 1, pp. 35–41. doi:10.1027/1864-9335/A000006.

Nichols, S. et al. (1996). "Varieties Of Off-Line Simulation". In: *Theories Of Theories Of Mind*. Ed. by P. Carruthers and P. K. Smith. Cambridge University Press, pp. 39–74. ISBN: 9780521559164. url: http://www.worldcat.org/title/theories-of-theories-of-m ind/oclc/32311136.

Nietzsche, F. W. (1961). *Thus Spoke Zarathustra... Translated with an Introduction by RJ Hollingdale*. Penguin Books. url: http://www.worldcat.org/title/thus-spoke-zarathustra.

Nietzsche, F. W. (1998). *On The Genealogy Of Morality: A Polemic*. Hackett Pub. Co. ISBN: 9780872202832. url: http://www.worldcat.org/title/on-the-genealogy-of-morality-a-polemic.

Nietzsche, F. W. (2005). *The Anti-Christ, Ecce Homo, Twilight Of The Idols, And Other Writings*. Ed. by A. Ridley and J. Norman. Cambridge University Press. ISBN: 9780521816595. url: http://www.worldcat.org/title/anti-christ-ecce-homo-twilight-of-the-idols-and-other-writings/oclc/58386503.

Nisbett, R. E. and L. Ross (1980). *Human Inference: Strategies and Shortcomings of Social Judgment*. Prentice Hall. ISBN 9780134451305.

Nisbett, R. E. and T. D. Wilson (1977). "Telling More Than We Can Know: Verbal Reports On Mental Processes". In: *Psychological Review* 84. 3, pp. 231–259. doi:10.1037//0033–0295X.84.3.231.

Nofsinger, J. (2016). *The Psychology Of Investing*. Taylor & Francis. ISBN: 9781315506555. url: http://www.worldcat.org/title/psychology-of-investing/oclc/900238139.

Onishi, K. H. and R. Baillargeon (2005). "Do 15-Month-Old Infants Understand False Beliefs?" In: *Science* 308. 5719, pp. 255–258. doi:10.1126/Science.1107621.

Patel, J., R. Zeckhauser, and D. Hendricks (1991). "The Rationality Struggle: Illustrations From Financial Markets". In: *The American Economic Review* 81. 2, pp. 232–236.

Pedersen, C. A. *et al.* (2011). "Intranasal Oxytocin Reduces Psychotic Symptoms And Improves Theory Of Mind And Social Perception In Schizophrenia". In: *Schizophrenia Research* 132. 1, pp. 50–53. doi:10.1016/j.schres.2011.07.027.

Pinker, S. (2015). *How The Mind Works*. Penguin Books. ISBN: 9780141980782. url: http://www.worldcat.org/title/how-the-mind-works/oclc/909298633.

Plotkin, H. (2011). "Human Nature, Cultural Diversity And Evolutionary Theory". In: *Philosophical Transactions of the Royal Society B: Biological Sciences* 366. 1563, pp. 454–463. doi:10.1098/rstb.2010.0160.

Poole, R. (2008). "Memory, Responsibility, And Identity". In: *Social Research* 75. 1, pp. 263–286. url: http://www.jstor.org/stable/40972060.

Premack, D. and G. Woodruff (1978). "Does The Chimpanzee Have A Theory Of Mind?" In: *Behavioral And Brain Sciences* 1. 4, pp. 515–526. doi:10.1017/S0140525X00076512.

Prentice, R. A. (2007). "Ethical Decision Making: More Needed Than Good Intentions". In: *Financial Analysts Journal* 63. 6, pp. 17–30. doi:10.2469/Faj.V63.N6.4923.

Prinz, J. J. (2011). "Is Empathy Necessary For Morality". In: *Empathy: Philosophical And Psychological Perspectives*. Ed. by A. Coplan and P. Goldie. Oxford University Press, pp. 211–229. ISBN: 9780199539956. url: http://www.worldcat.org/title/empathy-philosophical-and-psychological-perspectives/oclc/767842620.

Pronin, E., T. Gilovich, and L. Ross (2004). "Objectivity In The Eye Of The Beholder: Divergent Perceptions Of Bias In Self Versus Others". In: *Psychological Review* 111. 3, pp. 781–799. doi:10.1037/0033–295X.111.3.781.

Quine, W. V. O. (1951). "Main Trends In Recent Philosophy: Two Dogmas Of Empiricism". In: *The Philosophical Review* 60. 1, pp. 20–43. url: http://www.jstor.org/stable/2181906.

Rey, G. (2013). "We Are Not All 'Self-Blind': A Defense Of A Modest Introspectionism". In: *Mind And Language* 28. 3, pp. 259–285. doi:10.1111/Mila.12018.

Riggs, K. J. and D. M. Peterson (2000). "Counterfactual Thinking In Preschool Children: Mental State And Causal Inferences". In: *Children's Reasoning And The Mind*. Ed. by P. Mitchell and K. J. Riggs. Psychology Press. ISBN: 9780863778551. url: http://www.worldcat.org/title/childrens-reasoning-and-the-mind/oclc/41958990.

Roser, P. et al. (2012). "Alterations Of Theory Of Mind Network Activation In Chronic Cannabis Users". In: *Schizophrenia Research* 139. 1–3, pp. 19–26. doi:10.1016/J.Schres.2012.05.020.

Ross, L., T. M. Amabile, and J. L. Steinmetz (1977). "Social Roles, Social Control, And Biases In Social-Perception Processes". In: *Journal Of Personality And Social Psychology* 35. 7, pp. 485–494. doi:10.1037//0022–003514.35.7.485.

Ross, L., D. Greene, and P. House (1977). "The 'False Consensus Effect': An Egocentric Bias In Social Perception And Attribution Processes". In: *Journal Of Experimental Social Psychology* 13. 3, pp. 279–301. doi:10.1016/0022–1031(77)90049-X.

Ross, L., M. R. Lepper, and M. Hubbard (1975). "Perseverance In Self Perception And Social Perception: Biased Attributional Processes In The Debeliefing Paradigm". In: *Journal Of Personality And Social Psychology* 32. 5, pp. 880–892. doi:10.1037//0022–003514.32.5.880.

Rusbridger, A. (2013). *Play It Again: An Amateur Against The Impossible*. Random House. ISBN: 9781448138692. url: http://www.worldcat.org/title/play-it-again-an-amateur-against-the-impossible/oclc/900353335.

Ryle, G. (2009). *The Concept Of Mind*. Routledge. ISBN:9780415485470. url: http://www.worldcat.org/title/concept-of-mind/oclc/297405035.

Rystrom, D. S. and E. D. Benson (1989). "Investor Psychology And The Day-of-the-Week Effect". In: *Financial Analysts Journal* 45. 5, pp. 75–78. doi:10.2307/4479263.

Samson, D. et al. (2010). "Seeing It Their Way: Evidence For Rapid And Involuntary Computation Of What Other People See". In: *Journal of Experimental Psychology: Human Perception and Performance* 36. 5, pp. 1255–1266. doi:10.1037/a0018729.

Sandroni, A. (2005). "Efficient Markets And Bayes's Rule". In: *Economic Theory* 26. 4, pp. 741–764. doi:10.1007/s00199–00004–0567–0564.

Sartre, J. P. (1956). *Being And Nothingness: An Essay On Phenomenological Ontology*. Philosophical Library. ISBN: 9780671867805. url: http://www.worldcat.org/title/being-and-nothingness-an-essay-on-phenomenological-ontology/oclc/261250.

Savina, I. and R. J. Beninger (2007). "Schizophrenic Patients Treated With Clozapine Or Olanzapine Perform Better On Theory Of Mind Tasks Than Those Treated With Risperidone Or Typical Antipsychotic Medications". In: *Schizophrenia Research* 94. 1–3, pp. 128–138. doi:10.1016/J.Schres.2007.04.010.

Saxe, R. (2009). "The Happiness Of The Fish: Evidence For A Common Theory Of One's Own And Others' Actions". In: *Handbook Of Imagination And Mental Simulation*. Ed. by K. D. Markman, W. M. P. Klein, and J. A. Suhr. Psychology Press. ISBN: 9781841698878. url: http://www.worldcat.org/title/handbook-of-imagination-and-mental-simulation/oclc/222134918.

Seybert, N. and R. Bloomfield (2009). "Contagion Of Wishful Thinking In Markets". In: *Management Science* 55. 5, pp. 738–751. doi:10.1287/mnsc.1080.0973.

Shanahan, M (2009). "The Frame Problem". In: *Stanford Encyclopedia of Philosophy*. The Metaphysics Research Lab, Center for the Study of Language and Information (CSLI), Stanford University. url: http://plato.stanford.edu/archives/win2009/entries/frame-problem/.

Sheehan, N. (1988). *A Bright Shining Lie: John Paul Vann And America In Vietnam*. Random House. ISBN: 9780394484471. url: http://www.worldcat.org/title/bright-shining-lie-john-paul-vann- and-america-in-vietnam/oclc/17301230.

Shiller, R. J. (2003a). "From Efficient Markets Theory To Behavioral Finance". In: *Journal of Economic Perspectives* 17. 1, pp. 83–104. doi:10.1257/089533003321164967.

Shiller, R. J. (2003b). "The Science Of Psychology Applied To Risk Management". In: *The New Financial Order*. Princeton University Press, pp. 82–98.

Shiller, R. J., S. Fischer, and B. M. Friedman (1984). "Stock Prices And Social Dynamics". In: *Brookings Papers on Economic Activity* 1984. 2, p. 457. doi:10.2307/2534436.

Short, T. L. (1992). "The Design Of The ZEUS Regional First Level Trigger Box And Associated Trigger Studies". PhD Thesis. University of Bristol. url: http://discovery.ucl.ac.uk/1354624/.

Short, T. L. (2012). "Nietzsche On Memory". MPhilStud Thesis. UCL. url: http://discovery.ucl.ac.uk/1421265/.

Short, T. L. (2014). "How Can We Reconcile The Following Apparent Truths: 'Sherlock Holmes Doesn't Exist' And 'Sherlock Holmes Was Created By Conan Doyle'?" In: *Opticon1826* 16. 8, pp. 1–9. doi:10.5334/Opt.Bs.

Short, T. L. (2015). *Simulation Theory: A Psychological And Philosophical Consideration*. Taylor and Francis. ISBN: 9781138816053. url: http://www.routledge.com/books/details/9781138816053/.

Short, T. L. and K. J. Riggs (2016). "Defending Simulation Theory Against The Argument From Error". In: *Mind & Language* 31. 2, pp. 248–262. doi:10.1111/mila.12103.

Shull, D. (2011). *Market Mind Games: A Radical Psychology Of Investing, Trading And Risk*. McGraw-Hill Education. ISBN: 9780071761529. url: http://www.worldcat.org/title/market-mind-games-a-radical-psychology-of-investing-trading-and-risk.

Sloman, S. A. (1996). "The Empirical Case For Two Systems Of Reasoning". In: *Psychological Bulletin* 119, pp. 3–22. doi:10.1037//0033–2909.119.1.3.

Soros, G. (1994). *The Alchemy Of Finance: Reading The Mind Of The Market*. Wiley. ISBN: 9780471043133. url: http://www.worldcat.org/title/alchemy-of-finance-reading-the-mind-of-the-market.

Sullivan, L. O. (2011). "Nietzsche And Pain". In: *Journal of Nietzsche Studies* 11, pp. 13–22.

Sutton, J (2010). *Memory*. url: http://plato.stanford.edu/archives/sum2016/entries/memory/.

Svetlova, E. (2009). "'Do I See What The Market Does Not See?': Counterfactual Thinking In Financial Markets". In: *Historical Social Research* 34. 2, pp. 147–157.

Taleb, N. N. (2007). *Fooled By Randomness: The Hidden Role Of Chance In Life And In The Markets*. Penguin Books Limited. ISBN: 9780141930237. url: http://www.worldcat.org/title/fooled-by-randomness-the-hidden-role-of-chance-in-life-and-in-the-markets/oclc/827950242.

Taleb, N. N. (2008). *The Black Swan: The Impact Of The Highly Improbable*. Penguin Books Limited. ISBN: 9780141034591. url: http://www.worldcat.org/title/black-swan-the-impact-of-the-highly-improbable/oclc/175283761.

Taleb, N. N. (2012). *Antifragile: Things That Gain From Disorder*. Penguin Books Limited. ISBN: 9780718197902. url: http://www.worldcat.org/title/antifragile-things-that-gain-from-disorder/oclc/818715766.

Thorndike, E.L. (1920). "A Constant Error In Psychological Ratings". In: *Journal of Applied Psychology* 4. 1, pp. 25–29. doi:10.1037/h0071663.

Tulving, E. (1993). "What Is Episodic Memory?" In: *Current Directions In Psychological Science* 2. 3, pp. 67–70. url: http://www.jstor.org/stable/20182204.

Tversky, A. and D. Kahneman (1973). "Availability: A Heuristic For Judging Frequency And Probability". In: *Cognitive Psychology* 5. 2, pp. 207–232. doi:10.1016/0010–0285(73)90033–90039.

Tversky, A. and D. Kahneman (1974). "Judgment Under Uncertainty: Heuristics And Biases". In: *Science (New York, N.Y.)* 185. 4157, pp. 1124–1131. doi:10.1126/science.185.4157.1124.

Tversky, A. and D. Kahneman (1983). "Extensional Versus Intuitive Reasoning: The Conjunction Fallacy In Probability Judgment". In: *Psychological Review* 90. 4, pp. 293–315. doi:10.1037/0033–295X.90.4.293.

Wall Street: Money Never Sleeps. (2010). Dir. Stone, O. Twentieth Century Fox Film Corporation.

Wang, Y. (1993). "Near-Rational Behaviour And Financial Market Fluctuations". In: *The Economic Journal* 103. 421, pp. 1462–1478. url: http://www.jstor.org/stable/2234477.

Wilcox, R. T. (2008). "The Psychology Of Money". In: *Whatever Happened To Thrift?* Yale University Press, pp. 46–69.

Wilkin, S. (2015). *Wealth Secrets of the 1%: The Truth About Money, Markets and Multi-Millionaires*. Hodder & Stoughton. ISBN: 9781473604858. url: http://www.worldcat.org/title/wealth-secrets-of-the-1-how-the-super-rich-made-their-way-to-the-top/oclc/918894671.

Williams, B. (1998). *New Trading Dimensions: How To Profit From Chaos In Stocks, Bonds, And Commodities*. Wiley. ISBN: 9780471295419. url: http://www.worldcat.org/title/new-trading-dimensions-how-to-profit-from-chaos-in-stocks-bonds-and-commodities.

Williams, B. A. O. (2004). *Truth and Truthfulness: An Essay In Genealogy*. Princeton University Press. ISBN: 9780691117911. url: http://www.worldcat.org/title/truth-truthfulness-an-essay-in-genealogy/oclc/748362424.

Wimmer, H. and J. Perner (1983). "Beliefs About Beliefs: Representation And Constraining Function Of Wrong Beliefs In Young Children's Understanding Of Deception". In: *Cognition* 13. 1, pp. 103–128. doi:10.1016/0010–0277(83)90004–90005.

Wittgenstein, L. (2001). *Philosophical Investigations: The German Text, With A Revised English Translation*. Wiley. ISBN: 9780631231271. url: http://www.worldcat.org/title/philosophical-investigations/oclc/496575871.

Wright, S. et al. (2012). "Construal-level Mind-sets And The Perceived Validity Of Marketing Claims". In: *Marketing Letters* 23. 1, pp. 253–261. url: http://www.jstor.org/stable/41488779.

Zobel, I. et al. (2010). "Theory Of Mind Deficits In Chronically Depressed Patients". In: *Depression And Anxiety* 27. 9, pp. 821–828. doi:10.1002/Da.20713.

INDEX

Abbink and Rockenbach 14–16
Abu-Akel and Abushua'leh 126
Ackert *et al.* 59–61, 72
An *et al.* 126
Andrews 150
Aristotle 97
Armstrong and Fukami 136
Asch 10, 142, 143, 152, 157
Availability Heuristic 53–55, 57–59, 61–65, 67, 73, 90

Baddeley 22, 24, 145, 146, 161
Balzan *et al.* 173
Barber and Odean 4, 63, 170, 175
Barberis 3, 43, 111
Baron-Cohen 126
Batson 125
Bayes's Rule 87–88
Belief Perseverance Bias 37–40
Bem 162
Bernstein *et al.* 31, 32, 91, 92, 95, 122
Bertrand and Morse 122–123
Besharov 7
Biais and Weber 94, 95
Biais *et al.* 171–174
Bloomberg 141
Bogle 78
Bramel 157, 162
Bruguier, Quartz and Bossaerts 24–26
Buffett 66, 67
Buss 174
Butterfill and Apperly 33

Campbell 167
Certainty Effect 107, 111, 112, 116
Cherlin 56
Cipriani and Guarino 147
Clotfelter and Cook 70
Clustering Illusion 69, 83–85
CNBC 134, 139
Cognitive Dissonance 162–164
Confirmation Bias 4, 9, 17, 32, 37, 74, 75, 78–79, 81–83, 94, 126, 157, 163, 164, 172
Conformity Bias 4, 7, 10, 28, 79, 129, 150, 237
Conjunction Fallacy 89, 90
Coplan 125
Corcos and Pannequin 78, 105
Cowan 70–72
Credit Default Swap 102
Curse of Knowledge 94, 99, 118, 122, 123, 125, 131

Dale *et al.* 4, 43, 44, 174
Daniel *et al.* 5, 171
Darley and Batson 151
Dawkins 51
Dennett 30, 51
Deutsche Bank 63, 117, 142
Disposition Effect 94, 118, 171
Doris 151
Dunning *et al.* 35, 131, 139
Dunning-Kruger Effect 35, 130–132, 138, 139, 167

Efficient Markets Theory 11–13, 72
Empirica 103–105
Endowment Effect 10, 113, 114, 116–118
Enron 98, 106, 132
Evans 57, 74
Expected Utility 107–109

False Belief Task 30, 31, 95, 122
False Consensus Effect 140–142, 148
Fama 11, 77, 105
Fischer 4
Frame Problem 137
Frydman and Goldberg 141
Fundamental Attribution Error 149, 150, 152, 153–154, 157, 165, 174

Gambler's Fallacy 68–74–84
Garling et al. 118, 147, 166, 173
Gauss 65, 77
Gilovich 83, 84, 162, 164
Gladwell 30, 33, 49, 50, 77, 98, 103–105, 125–127, 132, 135–138, 149–151
Glaeser 10
Goetz 149
Goldman 70, 71
Gopnik and Wellman 30
Graver 126, 133, 134
Guttentag and Herring 61

Halo Effect 45, 73, 156–159
Haney et al. 144, 145
Harris 86
Hartshorne and May 152, 153
Hasson-Ohayon et al. 27
Hempel 76
herding behaviour 4, 28, 140, 145–147
High Frequency Trading 14, 62
Hilary and Menzly 168, 169
Hindsight Bias 32, 64, 91–101
Hirshleifer 1, 12, 16, 22, 44, 47, 54, 55, 59, 75, 84, 131, 153, 159, 167, 170, 171
Hume 47

Igoe and Sullivan, H. 160
Inhibitory Control 31
Isolation Effect 107, 114, 116, 119, 120

Johannson et al. 85, 86
Jonsson 17
Jordan 42, 43

Kahneman and Tversky 107–112, 114–116, 118–120
Kamtekar 150, 151
Keynes 2, 3, 25, 145
Kodak 78
Konnikova 84, 85, 89, 132, 152
Kopcha and Sullivan, H. 160
Korniotis and Kumar, 7, 8, 167, 170
Kramer 6, 47, 93, 155, 161
Kuehberger et al. 117
Kunda 168

Labroo et al. 53, 57, 73
Langer 84
Leeson 65
Lehman 64, 64
Leslie, Friedman and German 31
Leslie, German and Happe, 31
Levitt and Dubner 55, 145, 160
Lewis 14, 32, 62, 63, 69, 79–81, 99, 103, 129, 165
Linda 90
Lo et al. 134, 153

Malmendier and Taylor 97
Marks 1, 3, 11, 14, 17, 22, 23, 46, 49, 67, 79, 92, 97 99, 106, 138, 140, 142, 153, 175
Matheson 115
Mauboussin 8
McGlone and Tofighbakhsh 50, 53
McKay and Dennett 96, 160
Mensh and Wishner 157, 158
Metzger 70
Michel and Newen 162
Midgley, 51
Milgram 143, 150
Mineka and Sutton 160
Mitchell 29

Nagel 68
Nestler 38
Nichols, Stich, Leslie and Klein 117
Nietzsche 120, 121, 130, 136, 160 164, 165, 175
Nisbett and Ross 57, 58
Nisbett and Wilson 85, 86, 157
Nofsinger 2, 4, 10, 33, 44, 61, 73, 84, 94, 134, 146, 147, 162, 163, 166, 168, 175

Onishi and Baillargeon 31, 95
over-confidence 7, 8, 25, 97, 159, 166–174

P/E ratio 1, 44, 137
Pareto 103
Patel *et al.* 97, 141
Pedersen C. A. *et al.* 27, 127
Pinker 6, 41, 56, 72, 82, 91, 128, 132
Plotkin 142
Poole 51
Position Effect 85–87, 89
Powerball 115
Premack and Woodruff 30
Prentice 142, 143
Prinz 125
Pronin, Gilovich and Ross 5, 158, 160

Quine 38

Reflection Effect 107, 111–114
Regression to the Mean 44, 69
Representativeness Heuristic 40–46, 67, 88, 105
Rey 5
Rhyme as Reason Effect 41, 49, 50, 53
Riggs and Peterson 35
Roser *et al.* 126
Ross, Amabile and Steinmetz 150
Ross, Greene and House 140
Ross, Lepper and Hubbard 38
Rusbridger 135
Ryle 135
Rystrom and Benson 22

Samson *et al.* 28
Sandroni 87, 88
Sartre 156
Savina and Beninger 27
Saxe 153
Self-Presentation Bias 5, 65, 96, 140, 159–164, 166, 168–170, 172
Seybert and Bloomfield 34, 35
Shanahan 137

Sheehan 165
Shiller 4, 10–13, 17, 42, 56, 61, 62
Shiller *et al.* 4, 10
Short 3, 6, 9, 12, 20, 22, 27, 29, 32, 33, 43, 70, 100, 110, 125, 129, 164
Short and Riggs 3, 125
Shull 2, 10, 73, 105, 174,
Simulation Theory 2, 3, 8, 28, 29, 30–32, 70, 113
Sloman 33, 120
Soros 4, 5, 44–46, 73, 117, 118, 121, 137, 147, 164
South Sea Bubble 4, 43, 174
Sullivan, L. O. 160
Sutton 50
Svetlova 35, 36

Taleb 20, 39, 40, 47, 55, 57, 58, 64, 65, 67, 68, 73, 74–78, 90, 92, 93, 99, 99–105, 117, 120, 120, 121, 127, 136, 161, 164
The Economist 16, 23, 115, 121,134, 135, 138, 148, 159, 167, 168
The Stoics 126, 133, 134
Theory Theory 2, 3, 30, 32, 113
Thorndike 156
Tulving 164
Tversky and Kahneman 32, 35, 41, 54, 90, 106

Wang 12, 35, 86
Wason 75, 76, 82
Wilcox 84, 139, 162
Wilkin 106, 127
Williams B. 19, 20, 78
Williams, B. A. O. 100
Wimmer and Perner 30
Wittgenstein 81, 82
Wright *et al.* 50, 54

Zobel *et al.* 161